FARTHER AFIELD
See pp92–101

**SOCIETY HILL AND
PENN'S LANDING**
*See pp56–67
Street Finder maps 3 & 4*

OLD CITY
*See pp38–55
Street Finder maps 3 & 4*

Old City

Delaware River

*Society Hill and
Penn's Landing*

0 met

0 yard

EYEWITNESS TRAVEL

PHILADELPHIA
AND THE PENNSYLVANIA
DUTCH COUNTRY

EYEWITNESS TRAVEL

PHILADELPHIA

AND THE PENNSYLVANIA DUTCH COUNTRY

MAIN CONTRIBUTOR: RICHARD VARR

LONDON, NEW YORK,
MELBOURNE, MUNICH AND DELHI
www.dk.com

MANAGING EDITOR Aruna Ghose
ART EDITOR Benu Joshi
EDITORS Ankita Awasthi, Bhavna Seth Ranjan
DESIGNERS Mathew Kurien, Divya Saxena, Shruti Singhi
SENIOR CARTOGRAPHER Uma Bhattacharya
CARTOGRAPHIC RESEARCHER Suresh Kumar
PICTURE RESEARCHER Taiyaba Khatoon
DTP COORDINATOR Shailesh Sharma
DTP DESIGNER Vinod Harish

MAIN CONTRIBUTOR Richard Varr

PHOTOGRAPHER Demetrio Carrasco

ILLUSTRATORS
Arun Pottirayil, T. Gautam Trivedi, Mark Warner

Reproduced by Colourscan (Singapore)
Printed and bound by South China Printing Co. Ltd., China

First American Edition 2005
09 10 9 8 7 6 5 4 3 2 1

Published in the United States by
DK Publishing, 375 Hudson Street,
New York, New York 10014

Reprinted with revisions 2007, 2009
Copyright © 2005, 2009 Dorling Kindersley Limited, London
A Penguin Company

Published in Great Britain by Dorling Kindersely Limited.
A CATALOGING IN PUBLICATION RECORD IS AVAILABLE FROM THE
LIBRARY OF CONGRESS.
ISSN: 1542-1554
ISBN: 978-0-75666-157-1

Front cover main image: Philadelphia skyline at night

We're trying to be cleaner and greener:

- we recycle waste and switch things off
- we use paper from responsibly managed forests whenever possible
- we ask our printers to actively reduce water and energy consumption
- we check out our suppliers' working conditions – they never use child labour

Find out more about our values and best practices at www.dk.com

**The information in this
Dorling Kindersley Travel Guide is checked regularly.**
Every effort has been made to ensure that this book is as up-to-date as
possible at the time of going to press. Some details, however, such as
telephone numbers, opening hours, prices, gallery hanging
arrangements and travel information are liable to change. The
publishers cannot accept responsibility for any consequences arising
from the use of this book, nor for any material on third party websites,
and cannot guarantee that any website address in this book will be a
suitable source of travel information. We value the views and
suggestions of our readers very highly. Please write to:
Publisher, DK Eyewitness Travel Guides,
Dorling Kindersley, 80 Strand, London WC2R 0RL, Great Britain.

◁ Philadelphia's skyscrapers towering over the Schuylkill River

CONTENTS

The Liberty Bell, one of the world's
greatest symbols of freedom

INTRODUCING PHILADELPHIA AND THE PENNSYLVANIA DUTCH COUNTRY

The relaxing environs of tree-
shaded Rittenhouse Square

A panoramic view of the Camden waterfront at dusk

Delicate bloom at the Magnolia Garden in Society Hill

The 18th-century Independence Hall

Trademark horse and buggy in the Pennsylvania Dutch Country

HOW TO USE THIS GUIDE

This Dorling Kindersley travel guide helps you get the most from your visit to Philadelphia. It provides detailed practical information and expert recommendations. *Introducing Philadelphia* maps the city and the region, sets it in its historical and cultural context, and describes events through the entire year. *Philadelphia at a Glance* is an overview of the city's main attractions. The main sightseeing section of the book is *Philadelphia Area by Area*, which covers all the important sights, with photographs, maps, and illustrations. *Farther Afield* suggests sights just outside the city core, while *Beyond Philadelphia* describes Dutch Country and historic Gettysburg among other areas. Information about hotels, restaurants, shopping, entertainment, and sports is found in *Travelers' Needs*. The *Survival Guide* has practical advice on everything from using Philadelphia's medical services and transport system to public telephones and post offices.

FINDING YOUR WAY AROUND THE SIGHTSEEING SECTION

Each of the four sightseeing areas in Philadelphia is color-coded for easy reference. Every chapter opens with an introduction to the area of the city it covers, describing its history and character, and has a Street-by-Street map illustrating an interesting part of that area. Finding your way around the chapter is made simple by the numbering system used throughout. Sights outside Philadelphia have a regional map.

Each area has color-coded thumb tabs.

1 Introduction to the Area
For easy reference, the sights in each area are numbered and plotted on an area map. This map also shows SEPTA subway stops and regional rail stations, as well as indicating the area covered by the Street-by-Street map. The area's key sights are listed by category.

Locator map

A locator map shows where you are in relation to other areas in the city.

A suggested route takes in some of the most interesting and attractive streets in the area.

2 Street-by-Street Map
This gives a bird's-eye view of the most interesting and important parts of each sightseeing area. The numbering of the sights ties in with the preceding area map and with the fuller descriptions of the entries on the pages that follow.

The list of star sights indicates the places that no visitor should miss.

PHILADELPHIA AREA MAP

The colored areas shown on this map *(see inside front cover)* are the four main sightseeing districts used in this guide. Each area is covered in detail in *Philadelphia Area by Area (see pp36–109)*, as are sights located outside the city center and the walks. These areas are also highlighted on other maps throughout the book. In *Philadelphia at a Glance (see pp24–31)*, for example, they help locate the top sights.

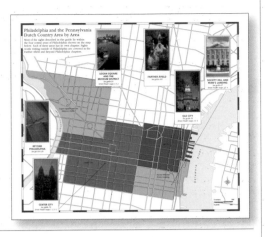

Numbers refer to each sight's position on the area map and its place in the chapter.

Practical information provides everything you need to know to visit each sight. Map references pinpoint the sight's location on the *Street Finder* maps *(see pp190–97)*.

3 Detailed Information

All the important sights in Philadelphia are described individually. They are listed in order, following the numbering on the area map at the start of the section. Practical information includes telephone numbers, opening hours, and map reference. The key to the symbols used is on the back flap.

The visitors' checklist provides all the practical information needed to plan your visit.

Story boxes provide information about historical or cultural topics relating to the sights.

4 Philadelphia's Major Sights

These are given two or more full pages in the sightseeing area where they are found. Historic buildings are dissected to reveal their interiors; color-coded floor plans in museums and galleries help you find important exhibits.

Stars recommend the features that no visitor should miss.

INTRODUCING
PHILADELPHIA
AND THE PENNSYLVANIA DUTCH COUNTRY

FOUR GREAT DAYS IN PHILADELPHIA

You could easily spend a few weeks enjoying all the historic sights and attractions in Philadelphia, not to mention separate excursions to the Pennsylvania Dutch Country and Gettysburg. Most visitors, however, only have a few days and will want to make the most of their time. Outlined here are ideas for four separate days of sightseeing and

Grave, Christ Church Burial Ground

enjoyment – three of them in Philadelphia and one in the Pennsylvania Dutch Country. They include suggestions on what to see, where to eat, and what to do for entertainment. Of course, the suggestions are just that, and can be modified to suit your requirements. The prices are indicative of the cost of transport and admission (if any) for two adults or a family of four.

Interior of Congress Hall, adjacent to Independence Hall

spectacular images flashed onto historic buildings. Reservations are needed for this one-hour show.

A SHOPPING DAY

- Browse boutiques along Rittenhouse Row
- Lunch at Rittenhouse Square
- Visit King of Prussia Mall

TWO ADULTS allow at least $60

Morning
Start by browsing through the elegant boutiques on **Rittenhouse Row** (see p156), which has such high-fashion names as Jones New York and Ann Taylor. Also visit the nearby **Shops at Liberty Place** (see p156). As noon approaches, check out the specialty shops at the **Bellevue Building** (see p156)

HISTORIC PHILADELPHIA

- Tour Independence Hall and National Constitution Center
- Lunch at Bourse Building
- Tour historic Old City
- Watch the Lights of Liberty Show

TWO ADULTS allow at least $60

Morning
It is best to arrive at the **Independence Visitor Center** (see p45) when it opens at 8:30am to pick up your free, timed tickets to **Independence Hall** (see pp42–3). The earlier you arrive, the better the chances of being admitted quickly. Note that tickets are usually gone by noon. Once you have your tickets the day can be planned accordingly. Visitors are first guided through the **Liberty Bell Center** (see p44), and

should spend the remainder of the morning visiting the **National Constitution Center** (see pp48–9). Stop for lunch at the satisfying food court in **The Bourse** (see p145) in Independence Mall East.

Afternoon
Start off by visiting the **Christ Church Burial Ground** (see p46) where Benjamin Franklin is buried. Allow 15 to 30 minutes here, and then go on to take a half-hour tour of the **Betsy Ross House** (see p52). Visit the Colonial portrait gallery at the **Second Bank of the US** (see p47) and pass by the imposing façades of the **First Bank of the US** (see p53) and the **Philadelphia Merchants' Exchange** (see p54). The **City Tavern** (see p55) is a good place to stop for some refreshment.

In the evening, take in the **Lights of Liberty Show** (see p175), which features

Mural at Italian Market, famous for specialty foods and eateries

◁ **Artist's impression of street life near the former State House (now known as Independence Hall) c.1800** and then have a quick bite at the building's upbeat food court. For restaurants with outdoor seating, head toward **Rittenhouse Square** *(see p78)*. **Pietro's Coal Oven Pizzeria**, **Devon Seafood Grill**, and **Parc** are good choices *(see p149)*.

Afternoon
Visit **The Gallery at Market East** mall *(see p156)* for some more shopping. Do not miss the nearby **Reading Terminal Market** *(see p73)*, and if you have time left over, head to the **Italian Market** *(see p97)* for coffee and Italian pastries. End your spree with a visit to the colossal **King of Prussia Mall** *(see p156)*.

The Franklin, at Fairmount Park, features hands-on exhibits

A FAMILY DAY

• **Visit museums around Logan Square**
• **Walk along Penn's Landing**
• **Take the RiverLink Ferry**
• **Visit the Adventure Aquarium**

FAMILY OF FOUR allow at least $175

Morning
Depending on time and budget, you may choose to visit one or more of the three museums on Logan Square – **The Franklin** *(see p85)*, **Academy of Natural Sciences** *(see p85)*, or the **Philadelphia Museum of Art** *(see p88–91)*. Break for lunch at one of the museum-

cafeterias before heading to the interactive **Please Touch Museum** *(see p170)* for children up to the age of seven.

Afternoon
Head over to **Penn's Landing** *(see p66)* and visit the **Independence Seaport Museum** *(see pp64–5)*. Later, take the RiverLink Ferry to the **Camden Waterfront** *(see p101)*. The ferry runs from April through mid-November. Make it a point to head to the **Adventure Aquarium** *(see p171)*, as the kids will love the aquatic life there. In the warmer months, the **Ghost Tour of Philadelphia** *(see p175)* is a great option for an evening activity. In winter, ice skate on one of the city's many rinks such as the **Blue Cross RiverRink** *(see pp168–9)*.

PENNSYLVANIA DUTCH COUNTRY

• **Tour Landis Valley Museum**
• **Have an Amish-style lunch**
• **Visit the Amish Experience**
• **Hop on board the Strasburg Railroad**

FAMILY OF FOUR allow at least $130

Morning
Arrive at **Lancaster Central Market** *(see p114)* by 8am to eat a hearty country breakfast. Only steps away are the **Lancaster Heritage Center Museum** and the **Lancaster**

The Blacksmith Shop at the Landis Valley Museum

Quilt & Textile Museum *(see p114)*. Go on to the **Landis Valley Museum** *(see pp116–17)* off Route 272 and spend some time exploring this living history village that provides an insight into the region's early farming communities. Head east on Route 340 through Bird-in-Hand and stop for a family-style lunch at the **Plain and Fancy Farm Restaurant** *(see p153)* next to the **Amish Experience** *(see p118)*.

Afternoon
Visit the Amish Experience and wander through the Country Homestead, a typical Amish home. Then watch the multimedia cultural presentation, *Jacob's Choice*, at the Amish Experience Theater. Spend the second part of the afternoon at Kitchen Kettle Village in **Intercourse** *(see p118)*, shopping for crafts and jarred foods. During the summer months, you can extend the day by hopping onto the 7pm train on the **Strasburg Railroad** *(see p119)* for the last ride through miles of farmland.

Tourists shopping for art and antiques in Lancaster

Putting Philadelphia on the Map

Located in the northeast region of the United States, Philadelphia sits on the southeastern edge of Pennsylvania along the Delaware River, which separates Pennsylvania from New Jersey. Founded by William Penn in the late 17th century, Philadelphia is now the nation's fifth largest city and the second largest on the East Coast. Close to 1.5 million people live within the city's 135 sq mile (350 sq km) area.

CANADA

Lake Ontario

TORONTO
Lester B. Pearson

Watertown

81

Hamilton

St. Catharines
Niagara Falls

Buffalo

Rochester

Syracuse

90

90

90

NEW YORK

Lake Erie

88

NORTH AMERICA

CANADA

UNITED STATES OF AMERICA

Philadelphia

ATLANTIC OCEAN

MEXICO

Gulf of Mexico

Caribbean Sea

PACIFIC OCEAN

SOUTH AMERICA

Elmira

Binghamton

17

81

PENNSYLVANIA

Scranton

84

Milton 80

Delaware

78

Susquehanna

Allentown

81

Reading

New Hope

Harrisburg

Hershey

Doylestown

Trenton

76

Lititz

Ephrata

Lancaster

Paradise

PHILADELPHIA

Strasburg

Philadelphia

Camden

Gettysburg

York

Wilmington

95

NEW JERSEY

MARYLAND

270

83

Baltimore

Baltimore-Washington

Dover

Delaware Bay

Washington-Dulles

WASHINGTON DC

Annapolis

Cape May

66

DELAWARE

VIRGINIA

13

KEY

▢	Greater Philadelphia
✈	Airport
═	Highway
▬	Major road
—	Railroad
–∙–	International border
⋯	Shipping route
– –	State border

0 kilometers	100
0 miles	50

Satellite view of Philadelphia with the Schuylkill River *(left)* and the Delaware River *(right)*

Central Philadelphia

Flanked by the Delaware and Schuylkill Rivers, central Philadelphia comprises several distinct neighborhoods, which together span more than three centuries of development. Much of the modern-day layout is based on city founder William Penn's original grid pattern – a crisscross of streets with five green squares. Four of these squares remain as pleasant, shaded parks today. The fifth, Penn's original Center Square, contains City Hall. The oldest districts are Old City and Society Hill.

Central Philadelphia
Center City (see pp68–79) skyscrapers can be seen along the Schuylkill River.

Statue of George Washington at Eakins Oval
A prominent equestrian statue pays tribute to America's founding father and first president against the backdrop of the imposing temple-like façade of the Philadelphia Museum of Art (see pp88–91).

Rittenhouse Square
One of William Penn's original five squares, this Center City park (see p78) is popular with downtown workers and residents. Extravagant high-rise buildings and upscale restaurants surround the square.

FAIRMOUNT PARK
KELLY DR
PENNSYLVANIA AVENUE
26TH ST
25TH ST
24TH STREET
BROWN STREET
20TH STREET
FAIRMOUNT AVENUE
22ND STREET
21ST STREET
WALLACE STREET
GREEN
Philadelphia Museum of Art
EAKINS OVAL
SPRING GARDEN STREET
THE MUSEUM DISTRICT
BENJAMIN FRANKLIN PKWY
22TH STREET
PARK TOWNE PL
19TH STREET
VINE STREET EWY
23RD STREET
22ND STREET
RACE STREET
CHERRY ST
LOGAN CIRCLE
LOGAN SQUARE
ARCH STREET
JOHN F. KENNEDY BLVD
22nd Street
MARKET ST
LUDLOW STREET
19th Street
CHESTNUT STREET
19TH STREET
WALNUT STREET
18TH STREET
LOCUST STREET
RITTENHOUSE SQUARE
SPRUCE STREET
20TH STREET
22ND STREET
RITTENHOUSE SQUARE
21ST STREET
PINE STREET
LOMBARD STREET
SOUTH STREET
BAINBRIDGE STREET

| 0 meters | 500 |
| 0 yards | 500 |

KEY

■	Star sight
S	SEPTA subway stop
R	SEPTA regional rail station
▭	Greyhound bus terminal
🚔	Police station
P	Parking
✚	Hospital
i	Visitor information
✝	Church
✡	Synagogue

Old City Hall
Located next to Independence Hall (see pp42–3) in the heart of Old City, where a new nation was born in 1776, Philadelphia's Old City Hall was home to the US Supreme Court from 1791 to 1800.

Penn's Landing
This waterfront area hosts summer festivals and is home to the city's tall ships, the submarine Becuna *and the USS* Olympia. *Also located here is the Independence Seaport Museum (see pp64–5).*

THE HISTORY OF PHILADELPHIA

W*illiam Penn first landed in the New World in 1682. Armed with a land charter, he founded a colony based on religious freedom that just a century later, would give birth to a new nation. Penn named the new city Philadelphia, derived from Greek words meaning "City of Brotherly Love."*

Before William Penn's arrival, the Delaware River basin and the Schuylkill River watershed were inhabited by Algonquian-speaking Native Americans known as Lenni-Lenape. They were mostly peaceful hunters and gatherers, and many lived along the Delaware River and its tributaries. They were named "Delawares" for that reason by the first European settlers.

Chief Tammany,
Delaware Indian chief

The first settlement in what is now Pennsylvania, however, did not occur until 1643, when Swedish Lutheran settlers – who had first settled in Wilmington, Delaware, in 1638 – established their capital of New Sweden on Tinicum Island, near present-day Philadelphia. Eight years later, the Dutch, whose previous colonial efforts had been directed elsewhere, seized control and annexed the region as part of the Dutch Colony. From 1655 to 1664, the Dutch controlled the area until the English captured the Dutch colonies, calling them New York, after the Duke of York.

FIRST EUROPEAN EXPLORERS AND SETTLERS

Chartered by the Dutch East India Company, Englishman Henry Hudson's ship, the *Half Moon*, sailed into Delaware Bay in 1609 and claimed it for Holland. Dutch navigators followed shortly after: Captain Cornelius Hendricksen sailed up the Delaware in 1616 to where it meets the Schuylkill River; and in 1623, Cornelius Jacobsen explored the region further, leading to the establishment of a number of trading posts, including one on the Schuylkill in 1633.

THE FOUNDING OF PENNSYLVANIA AND PHILADELPHIA

The son of a wealthy British admiral, William Penn was born in 1644. While attending Oxford University, Penn joined the Religious Society of Friends, the Quakers, a group who worshipped, without dogma or clergy, silently in unadorned meetinghouses. The faith was based on

TIMELINE

1609 Explorer Henry Hudson sails into Delaware Bay

Henry Hudson, English navigator

1638 Swedish Lutheran settlers arrive in Wilmington, Delaware

1644 Birth of William Penn

1664 England takes control of the Dutch colonies

1600	1615	1630	1645	1660	1675

1616 Dutch Captain Cornelius Hendricksen sails up the Delaware to the Schuylkill River

1623 Dutchman Cornelius Jacobsen explores the region further

1643 Swedes establish capital on Tinicum Island near present-day Philadelphia

1655 Dutch seize control of New Sweden

◁ Detail from *Penn's Treaty with the Indians* by Edward Hicks, 1830–1840

William Penn receiving the Charter for Pennsylvania from King Charles II of England

pacifism and equality. Expelled from university, Penn was later harassed and even imprisoned for his devotion to Quakerism. However, his wealth and social position allowed him to retain influence in the King's court.

The Charter for Pennsylvania was founded in 1681 as a result of a debt owed by King Charles II to Penn's father. The king repaid the £16,000 debt by granting the younger Penn land between Maryland and New York. In October 1682, Penn's ship, the *Welcome*, landed at New Castle in Delaware with many Quaker passengers. A few days later, Penn sailed up the Delaware to the capital of his new colony: Philadelphia.

As a Quaker, Penn espoused non-violence, and one of his first initiatives was to reach an agreement with the Delawares, thus forming treaties and enduring friendships with the Native Americans. The new colony also promised religious freedom, and was seen as a "Holy Experiment." More settlers followed, including both English and Dutch Quakers, German Mennonites, and the Amish, who settled in what is now called Pennsylvania Dutch Country.

Penn and surveyor Thomas Holmes designed Philadelphia in a grid pattern between the Delaware and Schuylkill Rivers. Their plan included five public spaces, as Penn and Holmes wanted to create a "green countrie towne." These tree-lined areas – Washington, Rittenhouse, Logan, and Franklin Squares – still remain today. City Hall now occupies the original "Center Square" at the junction of Market and Broad Streets.

Detail from *Peaceable Kingdom* by Edward Hicks (1780–1849), painted in 1826

TIMELINE

1683 Penn signs treaty with Delawares	**1684** Penn leaves Philadelphia and returns to England	**1699** Penn returns to Philadelphia	**1701** Penn grants charter to City of Philadelphia	**1718** Death of Penn in England
1680	**1690**		**1700**	**1710**
	1682 Penn arrives in Pennsylvania and establishes Philadelphia		**1701** Penn leaves America for good and returns to England	**1710** Christ Church built at 2nd Street
Gloria Dei Church **1677** Swedes establish Gloria Dei church				

COLONIAL EXPANSION

At the beginning of the 18th century, Philadelphia was already witnessing rapid growth. Penn had left Philadelphia in 1684 but returned in 1699 to find the population at more than 7,000. In October 1701, he granted a charter to the City of Philadelphia and left for England, never to return. As a port city, Philadelphia soon became an important center of commerce, with imports of sugar, rum, and molasses from the Caribbean. As trade flourished, so did manufacturing and shipbuilding. An increase in the number of homes led to a burgeoning community of craftsmen. The city also boasted a paper mill, furnaces, distilleries, tanneries, and a glass factory. One of its most famous residents, Benjamin Franklin *(see p53)*, arrived from Boston in 1723. His achievements as a scientist, inventor, printer, publisher, and statesman turned Philadelphia into a cultural center. In 1751, along with physician Thomas Bond, Franklin founded Pennsylvania Hospital, America's first public hospital.

The mid-1700s saw a clash between pacifist Quaker beliefs and the need to establish defenses for the colony. Pennsylvania was part of the British Empire and was involved in skirmishes against the French over land in North America. The conflicts climaxed with the French and Indian War, fought between the French and the British from 1754 to 1763, where a 21-year-old native of Virginia named George Washington received his first command. Britain was eventually victorious, but the war's end signaled a turning point for colonists, who now craved independence from Britain.

Franklin, famous Philadelphia resident

NEW NATION TAKES SHAPE

On July 4, 1776, independence from Britain was declared in Philadelphia, and in 1789, George Washington was elected the first president of the fledgling nation. The city remained the political heart of the country for a decade, serving as the capital from 1790 until 1800. During this time, America's first bank was chartered in 1791 to unify the nation's currency and to pay off war debts. The US Mint was established the following year.

In 1793, Philadelphia suffered a yellow fever epidemic, resulting in a large loss of life. Despite this, immigrants continued to flock to the city, increasing its population to nearly 70,000 by 1800, making it America's largest city at the time.

Yellow fever epidemic in Philadelphia, 1793

| 1720 | 1730 | 1740 | 1750 | 1760 |

1723 Benjamin Franklin arrives from Boston

1743 Franklin founds American Philosophical Society

1754 Start of the French and Indian War

1763 French and Indian War ends

1724 Carpenters' Company founded

Journal published by Franklin in 1741

1751 Pennsylvania Hospital founded

Pennsylvania Hospital

Colonial Philadelphia and the American Revolution

The years leading up to, including, and after the American Revolutionary War are arguably the most important years of the history of Philadelphia. Rebellion against British rule began as early as 1765 with opposition to taxation without representation in Parliament. A decade later, the colonists

Gunpowder casket, 1800s elected Washington to lead their army – the Continental Army – in the war for independence. In 1776, the Declaration of Independence was signed in Philadelphia, though by 1777 the city was again occupied by British forces. Freedom was gained in 1781, and Britain at last recognized the colonies' independence with the 1783 Treaty of Paris. Five years later, the US Constitution *(see pp48–9)* was ratified at Independence Hall, Philadelphia.

George Washington
The Second Continental Congress elected Washington to lead the Continental Army against the British in 1775.

Drafting the Declaration
Thomas Jefferson wrote the first draft of the Declaration of Independence. Leaders of 13 North American colonies later ratified it at Independence Hall.

DECLARATION OF INDEPENDENCE (1776)

Delegates of the Continental Congress ratified the Declaration of Independence on July 4, 1776. This 1817 John Trumbull painting shows the presentation of the Declaration by the drafting committee. The signing of the Declaration was completed that August.

TIMELINE

1774 First Continental Congress held

1775 Second Continental Congress in Philadelphia

1776 Signing of the Declaration of Independence

1781 British surrender at Yorktown, Virginia

Postcard depicting George Washington

1789 George Washington elected nation's first president

1775   1780   1785

1777 Continental Army retreats after losing battles at Brandywine and Germantown

1776 Washington's army crosses Delaware River and defeats hired Hessian soldiers at Trenton

1783 Signing of the Treaty of Paris

1788 US Constitution ratified

Crossing the Delaware River
Washington's army crossed the Delaware River on Christmas Day in 1776, as depicted in this 1851 Emmanuel Leutze painting. They later defeated British troops at Princeton.

The Battle of Germantown (1777)
British troops barricaded themselves behind the stone walls of Cliveden, a Germantown mansion, forcing the Continental army to retreat.

Valley Forge, 1777–78
After losing the battles of Brandywine and Germantown in 1777, Washington's army lost over 2,500 men to exposure and disease during the winter encampment here.

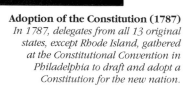

Adoption of the Constitution (1787)
In 1787, delegates from all 13 original states, except Rhode Island, gathered at the Constitutional Convention in Philadelphia to draft and adopt a Constitution for the new nation.

1790 Death of Benjamin Franklin	**1793** Yellow fever epidemic kills 4,000	**1800** Capital moves to Washington DC

White House, Washington DC

1790	1795	1800

1791 First Bank of the US chartered

1790 Philadelphia becomes the nation's capital

The First Bank of the United States

1799 Death of George Washington

The City & Port of Philadelphia (1800), engraving with watercolor by William Russell Birch

INDUSTRIALIZATION

By the 1830s, the city's financial and political prominence had begun to wane, as Washington DC, due to its location midway between the north and the south, became the nation's capital. Commercial activity and trade also diminished, as it could not compete with the more accessible port of New York City. Instead, Philadelphia turned to industry and manufacturing, becoming a regional center for textiles, iron and steel, and the shipping of coal. Shipbuilding continued along the Delaware. The city kept growing, with row houses built within the city limits and in surrounding boroughs and districts, including Germantown and Chestnut Hill. These areas soon became new neighborhoods by way of the city consolidation bill of 1854, under which they were incorporated within the city limits.

Growth also brought social clashes. For instance, there were rebellions against anti-slavery movements, and Pennsylvania Hall, the meeting place of the abolitionists, was set on fire in 1838. The 1840s saw violence against Catholics and immigrants, especially the Irish, with angry mobs burning down St. Augustine's Church, across from St. George's Church, in 1844.

POST CIVIL WAR PHILADELPHIA

The need for weapons, munitions, uniforms, and warships for the Union forces bolstered Philadelphia's economy during the Civil War years (1861–65). During the nation's centennial celebrations in 1876, the city held one of the first World Fairs and dedicated grand new buildings, some of which can be seen even today. These include Memorial Hall, a Beaux-Arts structure in Fairmount

Centennial Exhibition in 1876 at Fairmount Park, one of the oldest municipal parks in America

TIMELINE

	1844 Anti-Catholic rioters burn churches	**1856** Completion of Pennsylvania Railroad to Pittsburgh	**1876** City celebrates centennial with nation's first World Fair	**1907** First underground rail line commences	**1920s** Broad Street Subway completed
Burning of St. Augustine					

1840	1860	1880	1900	1920

1838 Anti-abolitionists burn Pennsylvania Hall	**1854** Surrounding boroughs incorporated	**1861** Civil War begins	*Wagons from the Civil War era*	**1890s** Electric trolleys introduced	**1914** World War I begins

Park, and the Victorian-style Pennsylvania Academy of the Fine Arts. Politically, however, this was a time of corruption as Republican leaders controlled city contracts and thousands of jobs. Their influence only waned in the 1930s and 40s when voter support was lost due to allegations of corruption and financial mismanagement in city government.

Streetcar on 9th Street, Philadelphia, 1921

THE EARLY 20TH CENTURY

The city's infrastructure was well-established by the end of the 19th century. For instance, its streetcar system was run by electric power as early as the 1890s. There were further improvements in mass transit with the completion of its first underground rail line, the Market Street Subway, in 1907. Economic and industrial activity in Philadelphia remained brisk during World War I (1914–18), though it registered a dip during the Great Depression of the 1920s and 30s. World War II (1939–45) revived steel, chemical, and petroleum production, but Philadelphia gradually lost most of its manufacturing sector to other regions of the US.

MODERN PHILADELPHIA

After World War II, the city lost jobs and population to the suburbs, and then underwent political restructuring in 1951, with a new city charter that called for a stronger mayor and new city departments. It was also a time of urban preservation efforts downtown, but some neighborhoods in the city's north and west deteriorated. Racial tensions mounted in the 1960s and through the mayoral terms of Frank Rizzo and W. Wilson Goode, the city's first African-American mayor, before stabilizing in the late 1980s. In 1985, during Goode's term as mayor, the controversial bombing of the headquarters of the black radical group MOVE took place, resulting in the deaths of 11 persons.

Today, Philadelphia's economy is diversified. While some manufacturing units remain, corporate business has gained ground. Companies here specialize in technology, banking, pharmaceuticals, and insurance. Tourism is also key to the local economy. The city has more than 80 universities, colleges, medical schools, and world-class hospitals. In 2000, it hosted the Republican National Convention, which nominated George W. Bush for president, and in 2008 the city bolstered its global presence by hosting two Olympic trials ahead of the Beijing games.

Celebrations at the Republican National Convention in 2000 in Philadelphia

	1941 World War II	1976 Bicentennial celebrations in Philadelphia	1985 Bombing of MOVE head-quarters	2000 City hosts Republican National Convention	2005 Philadelphia is the only US city to host a Live 8 concert, a global campaign to end poverty
1940		1960	1980	2000	2020
1929 Great Depression begins	1951 New city charter provides strong mayoral leadership	*Wilson Goode, Philadelphia's first African-American mayor*	1990s Philadelphia becomes a model for urban renewal despite a declining population	2008 Philadelphia is host two Olympic trial events – table tennis and gymnastics

PHILADELPHIA AT A GLANCE

Many of Philadelphia's most popular sights are to be found in Old City, within what's called "America's most historic square mile." They include Independence Hall *(see pp42–3)* and the iconic Liberty Bell *(see p44)*. Outstanding museums, including the Pennsylvania Academy of the Fine Arts *(see pp74–5)* and the Philadelphia Museum of Art *(see pp88–91)*, are in the city center, while the Barnes Foundation *(see pp98–9)* is just beyond city limits. More than 100 places of interest are described in the *Area by Area* and *Beyond Philadelphia* sections of this book. To help you make the most of your stay, the following six pages are a guide to the best of Philadelphia, with a selection featured below.

PHILADELPHIA'S TOP TEN SIGHTS

Independence Hall
(see pp42–3)

Liberty Bell Center
(see p44)

Barnes Foundation
(see pp98–9)

Fairmount Park
(see p95)

Philadelphia Museum of Art
(see pp88–91)

National Constitution Center
(see pp48–9)

Pennsylvania Academy of the Fine Arts
(see pp74–5)

Reading Terminal Market *(see p73)*

Penn's Landing
(see p66)

Liberty Place
(see p79)

◁ Staircase and Grand Foyer of the Pennsylvania Academy of the Fine Arts *(see pp74-5)*

Philadelphia's Best: Museums

Philadelphia has several world-famous museums that reflect its cultural diversity, as well as its maritime and colonial past. Many are sited along the Benjamin Franklin Parkway, including The Franklin, Academy of Natural Sciences, and the Philadelphia Museum of Art, which is the third-largest fine arts museum in the country. The Rodin Museum near Logan Square houses the largest collection of sculptor Auguste Rodin's works outside Paris, while the University of Pennsylvania Museum of Archaeology and Anthropology, just across the Schuylkill River, has an excellent collection of remnants from civilizations past and present. A few miles northwest of the city, the Barnes Foundation has an extraordinary collection of early French-modern and Postimpressionist art.

Philadelphia Museum of Art
This museum houses over 300,000 objects, including a 12th-century stone portal from a French Augustinian abbey (see pp88–91).

Rodin Museum
The Shade *is just one of nearly 130 plaster, bronze, and marble sculptures housed in an impressive temple-like structure along the Benjamin Franklin Parkway (see p86).*

Logan Square and the Museum District

Center City

The Franklin
The Giant Walk-Through Heart *is a key exhibit of this children-friendly science museum named after statesman and inventor Benjamin Franklin (see p85).*

Academy of Natural Sciences
A favorite exhibit at Philadelphia's natural history museum is Dinosaur Hall, *home to fossil constructions of the largest carnivores to ever walk the earth (see p85).*

The African American Museum in Philadelphia
This museum celebrates important aspects of African-American history through permanent and changing exhibitions (see p51).

Pennsylvania Academy of the Fine Arts
An ornate, arched foyer is the entrance to the country's oldest fine art school and museum. It was founded in 1805 with a collection of American paintings by artists such as Benjamin West and Impressionist Mary Cassatt (see pp74–5).

Atwater Kent Museum
Philadelphia's official history museum has a collection of more than 100,000 objects, including Norman Rockwell's Saturday Evening Post *covers depicting "vignettes of daily life" (see p50).*

National Museum of American Jewish History
Located in Old City, this museum has a collection of nearly 10,000 artifacts, some dating to the 18th century, showcasing the history of Jews in America (see p46).

Old City

Society Hill and Penn's Landing

Independence Seaport Museum
A prominent seafaring museum, showcasing the submarine Becuna *and the cruiser* Olympia. *This is a view of the interior of the submarine* Becuna *(see pp64–5).*

| 0 meters | 500 |
| 0 yards | 500 |

Philadelphia's Architecture

Early architectural styles, derived from the
colonists' native Britain, can still be seen in the
older areas of Philadelphia. Colonial buildings
incorporated simple Georgian and Palladian
designs, which evolved into a bolder Federal style,
with touches of Roman and Greek classical styles.
The 19th century brought grander designs fueled
by the Victorian era and the French-influenced
Beaux-Arts style, which inspired many of the city's
architectural wonders along the Benjamin Franklin
Parkway. While modernist buildings crowd parts
of Center City, it is the scattering of postmodernist
skyscrapers that enliven the city skyline.

**Philadelphia Merchants' Exchange,
an example of the Greek Revival style**

**Betsy Ross House, a simple
Georgian-style structure**

GEORGIAN

Named after three British
kings called George, this
architectural style prolifer-
ated in early 18th-century
Britain and soon became popular in colonial Philadelphia.
Developed from the Roman
Palladian style and often
with columned façades, many
of the early Georgian-style
designs in the colonies were
less elaborate than their
English counterparts.
   Independence Hall *(see
pp42–3)* is a Georgian structure influenced by the style
of English master architect
Christopher Wren, while
Christ Church *(see p52)* is a
bold example of Georgian
ecclesiastical architecture.
colonial Georgian-style
homes include the Deshler-
Morris House, which was
George Washington's
summer retreat, and Cliveden,
both in Germantown *(see
pp106–107)*. Both houses

have columned doorways
and nine front windows. A
more simple home is the
Betsy Ross House *(see p52)*.

FEDERAL

In Colonial America, the
Georgian style quickly
evolved into a more sophisticated Federal style, often
with classical Greek and
Roman influences. Particularly
popular after the American
Revolution until about 1820,
this architectural style is
characterized by oval and
circular rooms, classical
entryway detailing, rounded
fanlights over doors, and
Palladian windows. Also
typical of this style are free-
standing mansions and town
houses with symmetrical
brick façades and shuttered
windows. Entrances are
often cut from granite slabs
and feature gently fluted
columns. The largest and
most elegant rooms of
Federal houses are usually

found on the second floor.
Some stately examples of
such architecture are Old
City Hall, Congress Hall, and
the east and west wings of
Independence Hall. Idyllic
Fairmount Park, next to the
Schuylkill River, has several
mansions built with this
architectural style, including
Sweetbriar, Strawberry
Mansion, and Lemon Hill,
which has oval rooms on all
three floors *(see pp108–109)*.

GREEK REVIVAL

Philadelphia's merchants'
Exchange *(see p54)*, with a
four-columned Corinthian
portico at one end and an
unusual, semi-circular
portico at the other, testifies
to the nation's infatuation
with Greek Revival archi-
tecture in the 1830s. It was
designed by the up-and-
coming architect William
Strickland, already noted for
designing the steeple atop
Independence Hall. He also

Strawberry Mansion, a Federal-style house in Fairmount Park

Parlor of the Victorian-style Ebenezer Maxwell House

drafted the architectural plan for another prominent Greek Revival structure, the imposing second Bank of the US (see p47), with sturdy stone columns on its Greek temple-like façade.

A smaller Greek Revival structure, which now houses the Atwater Kent Museum (see p50), was designed by John Haviland, a contemporary of Strickland. This was the first home of the Franklin Institute (see p85), where Strickland and other architects taught the new nation's first architecture classes.

Detail of Philadelphia Museum of Art façade

VICTORIAN

Ornate, Victorian-style façades were designed for Philadelphia buildings from the 1850s onwards. Victorian-era architecture is influenced by various styles, such as Second

Empire, Italianate, and Gothic Revival. For example, City Hall (see p72), with its colonnades and mansard roof, is a French Second Empire design. The Academy of Music (see p76), designed by prominent 19th-century architect and Philadelphia native Napoleon LeBrun, is Italianate in style, with period gas lamps on its high-windowed façade and lavish interiors. The Italianate Revival Athenaeum also has gas lamps on its walls. The city's only authentically restored Victorian home is the Ebenezer Maxwell House in Germantown (see pp106–107), which is capped with a high tower, a mansard, and gable roof design.

BEAUX-ARTS

American architects trained at the École des Beaux-Arts in France brought home this Greek- and Roman-influenced style of architecture, with elaborate detailing, balustrades, and prominent columns. Due to the grandiosity and size of these structures, Beaux-Arts became the favored style for court houses, government buildings, museums, and railroad terminals, and was used in many

late 19th- and early 20th-century buildings. The 1876 centennial celebration in Philadelphia ushered in Fairmount Park's Memorial Hall (see p109), dotted with bronze sculptures and topped by a glass and iron dome creating a spacious atrium.

With one of the city's most splendid Corinthian porticos, 30th Street Station (see p184) is an example of this grand style, as is the Philadelphia Museum of Art (see pp88–91). Displaying much of the same grandeur is the Free Library of Philadelphia (see p84), and the similar structure next to it, both with porticos sheltering imposing colonnaded façades. On a smaller scale, the nearby temple-like Rodin Museum (see p00) features columns and a portico topped with a balustrade.

Philadelphia's skyscrapers, Liberty One (left) and Mellon Bank Center

POSTMODERNIST

The late 20th century witnessed a rebellion against the box-like glass and steel structures built after World War II. Thus was born the postmodern era in architecture, which featured sleek modernism tempered by conservative and historical design. This is evident in the twin towers of Liberty Place (see p79) with their pointed apexes. Also in the same style are the top floors of the Bell Atlantic Tower, while the Mellon Bank Center building is crowned with a pyramid-like dome. The latest addition to the city's skyline is the cutting edge Comcast Center.

Colonnaded entrance of the Beaux-Arts style Philadelphia Museum of Art

Philadelphia's Best: Parks and Gardens

William Penn wanted his city to be "a green countrie towne" and included five squares in his original city grid. Today, three of these, Logan, Rittenhouse, and Washington Squares, are pleasant areas with trees and park benches. Along the Schuylkill River on the outskirts of Center City is Fairmount Park. Its 9,200 acres (3,700 ha) of parkland and gardens make it America's largest urban park. The area has biking and walking paths along the river and one of its tributaries, Wissahickon Creek, that runs within a gorge. Fairmount Park includes the peaceful Shofuso Japanese House and Garden and restored historic houses that were once the homes of the colonial elite. Beyond Philadelphia, near the Delaware state border, are the exquisite Longwood Gardens.

Morris Arboretum of the University of Pennsylvania

Located in the Chestnut Hill neighborhood, this scenic tract of land includes ponds, greenhouses, meadows, and gardens with thousands of rare plants and "trees-of-record" (see p95).

Longwood Gardens
22 miles (35 km)

Longwood Gardens

Industrialist Pierre S. du Pont designed this extravagant horticultural wonderland filled with spectacular choreographed fountains, whimsical topiaries, conservatories with exotic plants, and meadows and gardens replete with more than 11,000 varieties of indoor and outdoor plants (see p128).

Fairmount Park

This extensive greenbelt along the Schuylkill River and Wissahickon Creek is dotted with statues and features miles of running and biking paths (see p95).

0 kilometers   2

0 miles   2

Wissahickon Gorge
The country's only covered bridge within a major city is sited on a hiking trail in this gorge, whose forests and creek are home to over 100 bird species.

Logan Square
This grand square was once used as a burial ground and pastureland. Its center-piece is the majestic, multi-spouted Swann Memorial fountain designed by sculptor Alexander Stirling Calder (see p84).

Washington Square and Tomb of the Unknown Soldier
Named in honor of George Washington, the first president of the US, the centerpiece of this peaceful park is his statue, and the tomb of the unknown soldier of the Revolutionary War (see p60).

Rittenhouse Square
Center City's most popular park often fills with downtown workers who lunch under the trees. Reminiscent of New York's Central Park, it is flanked by upscale restaurants (see p78).

Welcome Park
Named after Penn's ship, this park was completed in 1982, three centuries after the founding of Philadelphia. Marble slabs depicting the city's original grid crisscross the park (see p55).

PHILADELPHIA THROUGH THE YEAR

Moderating mid-Atlantic coastal waters often temper the effects of extreme heat and harsh cold, making Philadelphia's summers enjoyable and the winters bearable. Spring flowers and warmer temperatures breathe new life into the city, with restaurants and cafés setting up tables outdoors, while city residents head to parks and riverfronts, anticipating summer festivals

Phillies logo

and excursions to beaches and lakes. Activities continue outdoors in fall, which heralds a rush of cool air and colorful foliage to Philadelphia's forested greenbelts. After Thanksgiving, activities tend to move indoors with a rush of Christmas shoppers to quaint boutiques and shopping malls. Sports and cultural activities are in full swing during the winter months, right through to spring.

School and college track teams compete at the Penn Relays

SPRING

Cherry blossoms bloom along the Schuylkill River in early spring, as Philadelphians flock to the Schuylkill river walk to enjoy the warmer weather. April also signals the start of the Philadelphia Phillies' baseball season.

MARCH

Cherry Blossom Festival *(late Mar)*. Features performances of traditional Japanese arts and culture at various locations throughout the city.
Philadelphia Flower Show *(mid-Mar)*, Pennsylvania Convention Center. Largest indoor flower show in the United States.
St. Patrick's Day Parade *(mid-Mar)*, Center City. A parade celebrating Philadelphia's strong Irish heritage.

APRIL

Philadelphia Antiques Show *(mid-Apr)*, 33rd Street Armory. Dealers from across the United States gather to display their unique finds.
Philadelphia Film Festival *(mid-Apr)*. Showcases the best in independent and foreign cinema.
Philadelphia Furniture and Furnishings Show *(mid-Apr)*, Pennsylvania Convention Center. Exhibition and sale of artisan-designed and manufactured furniture and home furnishings.
Penn Relays *(late Apr)*, Franklin Field. High school and college track stars compete in the longest uninterrupted collegiate

Juggler in action

track meet in the nation.
Equality Forum *(late Apr)*. Begun in the 1960s, this week-long gathering celebrates the cultural and political legacy of the gay, lesbian, bisexual, and transgender communities.
International Children's Festival *(late Apr–early May)*, Annenberg Center for the Performing Arts. Jugglers, folk singers, puppeteers, and dancers delight young audiences.
Philadelphia Phillies Baseball *(Apr–Sep)*, Citizens Bank Park. The season starts with many home games at the 43,500-capacity park.

Blooms at the Philadelphia Flower Show, a spring-time celebration

AVERAGE DAILY HOURS OF SUNSHINE

Hours
10
8
6
4
2
0

Jan Feb Mar Apr May Jun Jul Aug Sep Oct Nov Dec

Sunshine Chart
This chart shows the average daily number of hours of sunshine in Philadelphia each month. June, July, and August have long days with lots of sunshine. Spring and fall have lesser hours of sunshine, with the shortest days in winter, which can still have ample hours of bright sun on clear, cold days.

MAY

Broad Street Avenue Run *(early May)*, Olney to south Philadelphia. This 10-mile (16-km) run raises funds for the American Cancer Society.
Dad Vail Regatta *(second weekend)*, Schuylkill River at Kelly Drive. Largest collegiate regatta in the United States with more than 100 colleges and universities participating.
Jam on the River *(Memorial Day weekend)*, Penn's Landing. The biggest party on Memorial Day, it features rock and blues music.
Devon Horse Show and Country Fair *(late May and early Jun)*, Devon Fair Grounds. Equestrian talents on display at the country's oldest and largest event of its kind.
Mann Center for the Performing Arts *(May–Sep)*, Fairmount Park. Performances through the summer by the Philadelphia Orchestra, Philly Pops, and others.
Penn's Landing Festivals *(May–Sep)*. Concerts along with ethnic events for families.
Annual Student Exhibition *(May/Jun)*, Pennsylvania Academy of the Fine Arts. This century-old tradition displays the works of award-winning students.

SUMMER

Summer ushers in a variety of festivals and live music on Penn's Landing. Fairmount Park fills with picnickers and thousands jam roadways to the New Jersey shore. Philadelphians celebrate the nation's birth, which took place in their own city, on the Fourth of July with remembrances, concerts, parades, and a massive display of fireworks above the Philadelphia Museum of Art.

JUNE

Commerce Bank Philadelphia International Championship *(first week)*. Philadelphia Museum of Art to Manayunk. The country's largest one-day professional cycling race.
Bloomsday *(Jun 16)*, Rosenbach Museum & Library. James Joyce fans celebrate the day on which Leopold Bloom, the protagonist of Joyce's *Ulysses*, made his "odyssey" through Dublin.
Odunde Afrikan American Street Festival *(mid-Jun)*, South Street. Celebrates the Yoruba New Year, beginning with a procession to the Schuylkill River and ending with a lively street fair.
Manayunk Arts Festival *(late Jun)*, Main Street. The region's largest outdoor arts and craft festival.

Commerce Bank Philadelphia International Championship

Fourth of July fireworks over the Philadelphia Museum of Art

JULY

Sunoco Welcome America! (week leading up to Jul 4). A week-long celebration with a concert and free events.
Fourth of July Parade *(Jul 4)*, Center City. Parade followed by fireworks.
Let Freedom Ring *(Jul 4)*, Liberty Bell Center. Descendants of those who signed the Declaration of Independence tap the Normandy Bell, an exact cast of the Liberty Bell.
Philadelphia International Gay & Lesbian Film Festival *(mid–late Jul)*. Showcases gay and lesbian films.

AUGUST

Philadelphia Folk Festival *(late Aug)*, Schwenksville. Music, dance, and crafts fair.
Philadelphia Eagles Football *(Aug–Dec)*, Lincoln Financial Field. The season features several home games.
Philadelphia Fringe Festival *(late Aug–early Sep)*. Citywide. Avant-garde theater.

AVERAGE MONTHLY PRECIPITATION

mm												Inches
300												12
240												9
180												6
120												3
60												0
0	Jan	Feb	Mar	Apr	May	Jun	Jul	Aug	Sep	Oct	Nov	Dec

Rainfall Chart
This chart shows the average monthly rainfall and snowfall. The heaviest rain is in July and August, with a yearly average of 41 inches. Considerable snow falls in January and February. The annual snowfall average is 21 inches.

■ Rainfall (from baseline)

□ Snow (from baseline)

Rowers in Lancaster County in the fall

FALL

Summer gradually gives way to cooler temperatures by mid-September, as thousands of students flock to the city's more than 80 colleges and universities. The bright reds and yellows of fall foliage begin to make an appearance by the end of September, with dramatic colors in October and early November. Football season gets into high gear, as fans head out to watch the Philadelphia Eagles. Autumn also kicks off many cultural activities, signaling a new season for the city's world-class performing arts, opera, and symphony companies.

SEPTEMBER

Von Steuben Day Gala and Parade *(late Sep)*, Center City. Celebrates the city's German heritage and pays tribute to Baron Friedrich von Steuben, a general in the Revolutionary War.

Puerto Rican Day Parade *(last Sun)*, Center City. Celebrating Puerto Rican heritage with a festival and parade.
Philadelphia College Festival *(late Sep or early Oct)*. College Day concert in the Benjamin Franklin Parkway, plus various career fairs and cultural events.

OCTOBER

Pulaski Day Parade *(first Sun)*, Center City. Pays tribute to the Polish Revolutionary War hero, General Casimir Pulaski.
Columbus Day Parade *(second Sun)*, South Broad Street. The parade honors explorer Christopher Columbus and the Italian American community.
Philadelphia Open Studio Tours *(mid-Oct)*. Local artists throughout the city open their workshops for two weekends.
Philadelphia 76ers Basketball *(Oct–Apr)*, Wachovia Center. NBA basketball season begins with a number of home games.

Philadelphia Flyers Hockey *(Oct–May)*, Wachovia Center. The NHL hockey season kicks off with home games.
Terror Behind the Walls *(mid-Oct through Oct 31)*, Eastern State Penitentiary. A "haunted" house in the former prison celebrates Halloween.

NOVEMBER

Philadelphia Museum of Art Craft Show *(early Nov)*, Pennsylvania Convention Center. Features handmade textiles, jewelry, household wares, and more.
Philadelphia Marathon *(third Sun)*. A 26-mile (42-km) run through the city starts and ends at the Philadelphia Museum of Art.
Thanksgiving Day Parade *(fourth Thu)*. Benjamin Franklin Parkway. The oldest such parade in the country.

Colorful floats and giant balloons at the Thanksgiving Day Parade

AVERAGE MONTHLY TEMPERATURE

°C
30
20
10
0
-5

°F
86
68
50
32
23

Jan Feb Mar Apr May Jun Jul Aug Sep Oct Nov Dec

Temperature Chart
Spring is usually mild with some brisk days. Summer can be hot and muggy on certain days, although most days are comfortable. Fall brings clear and colder days. In winter, wind chills sometimes drop temperatures to below freezing, but many days are refreshingly chilly and bright.

Christmas lights at the Wanamaker Building

WINTER

Strings of sparkling lights illuminate streets, buildings, and trees throughout Center City and beyond, as Christmas shoppers throng the city's main shopping districts. New Year's Day brings the Mummers Day Parade, one of Philadelphia's most honored traditions, in which costumed revelers and string bands march down the street. Sports enthusiasts spend the winter months attending Philadelphia 76ers basketball and Flyers hockey games.

DECEMBER

Christmas Tree Lighting
(Wed after Thanksgiving), City Hall. Signals the start of the holiday season.
Philadelphia Holiday Festival *(dates vary)*. Citywide performances by Mummers string bands, festivities, lighting events, and even tax-free shopping for shoes and clothing.

Washington Crossing the Delaware River Reenactment *(Dec 25)*, Washington Crossing. Reenactment of this historic turning point in the American Revolutionary War.
New Year's Eve *(Dec 31)*, Penn's Landing. A night of celebrations with fireworks along the Delaware River.
The Nutcracker *(dates vary)*, Academy of Music. Part of Pennsylvania Ballet's season, productions of this ballet are put on before Christmas.

JANUARY

Mummers Day Parade
(Jan 1), Center City. A Philadelphia tradition, where up to 20,000 people in decorative costumes parade to the music of string bands.
Chinese New Year Celebrations *(dates vary)*, Chinatown. Parades and festivities for two weeks.
Welcome Spring *(mid-Jan through Mar)*, Longwood Gardens. Indoor displays of bulbs, trees, and flowers create the illusion of spring during the winter months.

FEBRUARY

Philadelphia International Auto Show *(first week)*, Pennsylvania Convention Center. Highlights the latest in classic and luxury cars.
Mardi Gras *(Fat Tuesday before Ash Wednesday)*, South Street. Day-long revelry and celebration.
African American History Month *(all month)*. Various events throughout the city.

PUBLIC HOLIDAYS

New Year's Day (Jan 1)
Martin Luther King Day (3rd Mon in Jan)
Presidents' Day (3rd Mon in Feb)
Memorial Day (Last Mon in May)
Independence Day (Jul 4)
Labor Day (1st Mon in Sep)
Columbus Day (2nd Mon in Oct)
Veterans Day (Nov 11)
Thanksgiving Day (4th Thu in Nov)
Christmas Day (Dec 25)

Mummers Day Parade, a Philadelphia New Year's Day tradition

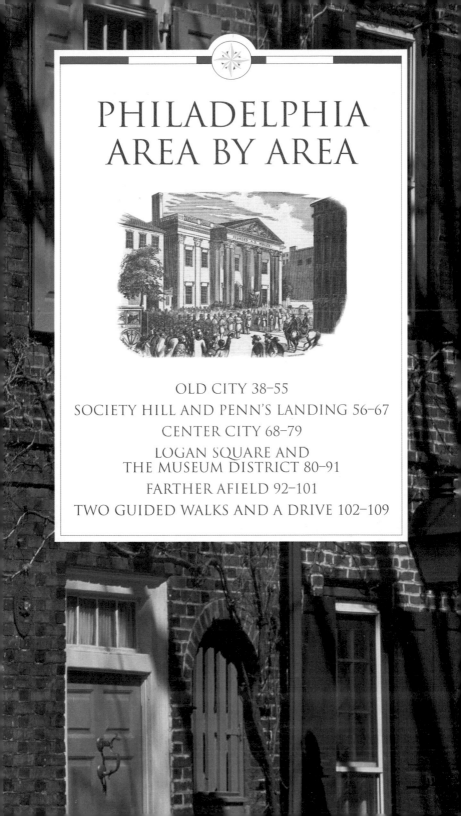

PHILADELPHIA
AREA BY AREA

OLD CITY

The foundations of Philadelphia, and all of the United States, are rooted in the neighborhood of Old City, which includes the Liberty Bell and Independence Hall, both of which form part of Independence National Historical Park. This area was settled by city founder William Penn and his fellow Quakers in the late 1600s. It later served as the seat of government for rebellious colonial patriots during the American Revolution in the 1770s. Today, well-preserved historical structures, buildings, and homes that date back to the 18th and 19th centuries, some still situated on narrow cobblestoned streets, stand alongside modern buildings and high-rises.

Plaque at Independence Hall

SIGHTS AT A GLANCE

Historical Buildings and Districts

Arch Street Friends
  Meeting House **7**
Betsy Ross House **20**
Bishop White House **27**
Carpenters' Hall **25**
Christ Church Burial Ground **8**
City Tavern **29**
Curtis Center and Dream
  Garden Mosaic **13**
Declaration House **15**
Elfreth's Alley **19**
First Bank of the US **24**
Franklin Court and B. Free
  Franklin Post Office **22**

Free Quaker Meeting House **4**
Independence Hall pp42–3 **1**
Philadelphia Merchants'
  Exchange **28**
Philosophical Hall and
  Library Hall **12**
Second Bank of the US **11**
Todd House **26**
US Mint **6**

Museums and Galleries

The African American Museum
  in Philadelphia **16**
Atwater Kent Museum **14**
Fireman's Hall Museum **18**
Independence Visitor Center **3**

Liberty Bell Center p44 **2**
*National Constitution
  Center pp48–9* **5**
National Liberty Museum **23**
National Museum of American
  Jewish History **9**

Places of Worship

Christ Church **21**
Congregation Mikveh Israel **10**
St. George's United Methodist
  Church **17**

Parks and Gardens

Welcome Park **30**

KEY

🟦 Street-by-Street map
  see pp40–41

🚆 SEPTA regional rail station

🅂 SEPTA subway stop

ℹ️ Visitor information

0 meters   500

0 yards   500

GETTING THERE

All sights are within walking distance of each other. Philly Phlash can be accessed along Market Street, and the local rail service makes stops at the Market East Station. The Market-Frankford line has two stops in Old City, at 2nd and Market, and 5th and Market. SEPTA buses 21, 38, and 42 also have stops in Old City.

◁ **The south face of Georgian-style Independence Hall, formerly known as the State House** *(see pp42-3)*

Street-by-Street: Independence National Historical Park

Known locally as Independence Mall, this urban park encompasses several well-preserved 18th-century structures associated with the American Revolution. The Declaration of Independence that heralded the birth of a new nation was written and signed in this historic area. Dominated by the tall brick tower of Independence Hall, the park includes the US Mint and several special-interest museums that explore Philadelphia's colonial and seafaring past, as well as its ethnic heritage. At least 20 of the buildings are open to the public.

Plaque commemorating Independence Hall

Christ Church Burial Ground ⑧

US Mint
This mint, the oldest in the country, struck its first coins in 1793. It also mints commemorative coins such as the Eisenhower dollar ⑥

ARCH STREET

5TH STREET

MARKE

★ National Constitution Center
This museum features interactive exhibits explaining the US Constitution. Visitors can walk among life-sized statues of the delegates who were present when this document was adopted in 1787 ⑤

7TH STREET

Free Quaker Meeting House ④

KEY

– – – Suggested route

STAR SIGHTS

★ National Constitution Center

★ Liberty Bell Center

★ Independence Hall

Independence Visitor Center

Located in what is called "America's most historic square mile," the Independence Visitor Center provides visitors with practical information and a cultural and historical orientation. Timed tickets for Independence Hall are available here ③

National Museum of American Jewish History
This unique museum celebrates the history of Jews in America through artifacts such as this mid-1700s Torah scroll and ark from the collection of Congregation Mikveh Israel ❾

LOCATOR MAP
See Street Finder maps 3 & 4

Arch Street Friends Meeting House ❼

Congregation Mikveh Israel ❿

Second Bank of the US
An extensive collection of portraits of people involved in the events of 1776 is on display at this Greek Revival building ⓫

★ **Liberty Bell Center**
Inscribed with the words, "Proclaim Liberty throughout all the Land," the Liberty Bell is said to have been rung when the Declaration of Independence was adopted. It is now housed in the new Liberty Bell Center ❷

Philosophical Hall and Library Hall ⓬

0 meters 50
0 yards 50

★ **Independence Hall**
The centerpiece of the park, this World Heritage Site was where the Declaration of Independence was ratified on July 4, 1776. The Declaration was signed in August the same year ❶

Independence Hall ❶

Independence Hall tower clock

This unadorned brick building and clock tower are the most important structures in Independence Hall National Park. Earlier designated the State House of Pennsylvania, it is the site of the drafting and signing of the US Constitution and the Declaration of Independence, the document that declared America's freedom from the British Empire in 1776. Designed by master carpenter Edmund Woolley and lawyer Andrew Hamilton, Independence Hall was completed in 1753, more than two decades after construction began. Today, the meeting rooms are simply furnished, as they were in the late 1700s, and park personnel re-create history by pointing out the Windsor-style chairs from which colonial leaders debated the contents of the Declaration.

Congress Hall
Congress met in this hall from 1790 to 1800. Presidential inaugurations were also held here for George Washington and John Adams.

West Wing

THE DECLARATION OF INDEPENDENCE

Following colonial resistance to British "taxation without representation," the first shots of rebellion rang out in 1775 at the battles of Concord and Lexington outside Boston. Within a year, a strong feeling for independence overwhelmed the colonies. Known for his powerful writing style, Thomas Jefferson, Virginia Delegate and future president, took on the task of drafting a document declaring independence. He eloquently asserted man's right to freedom and rebellion while listing colonial grievances against England's King George III. After making changes, the Continental Congress ratified the Declaration of Independence on July 4, 1776.

An original copy of the 1776 Declaration of Independence

★ **Great Essentials Exhibit**
On display here are original copies of the Declaration of Independence and the US Constitution, as well as this silver Syng inkstand, said to have been used during the signing of the documents.

★ Assembly Room
Amidst its simple desks and chairs, delegates of the Continental Congress debated and signed the new nation's Declaration of Independence in 1776. Eleven years later, the Constitution was drafted and signed here as well.

★ Rising Sun Chair
The chair used by George Washington during the 1787 Constitutional Convention depicts a symbolic sun rising over the new nation.

Long Gallery
Running the length of the second floor, this light-filled reception room also hosted 18th-century balls and banquets.

East Wing

INDEPENDENCE HALL

① Congress Hall
② Old City Hall
③ Philosophical Hall

KEY

▨ Illustrated Area
☐ Lawn

STAR FEATURES

★ Great Essentials Exhibit

★ Assembly Room

★ Rising Sun Chair

Liberty Bell Center ❷

Originally rung to signal Pennsylvania Assembly meetings in the State House (now Independence Hall) in the mid-1700s, the Liberty Bell is one of the world's greatest symbols of freedom, bearing the inscription "Proclaim Liberty throughout all the Land unto all the Inhabitants thereof." Famous for its irreparable crack, the 2,080-lb (940-kg) bell was moved to its new home in the Liberty Bell Center in 2003. The center details the bell's history and significance, and how it became an icon for other freedom struggles. Clearly visible on the bell is the unsuccessful "stop drilling" repair, where, in 1846, the edges of the fracture were filed down to reduce friction and stress in an effort to slow the growth of the crack.

VISITORS' CHECKLIST

Market St between 5th & 6th Sts.
Map 4 D3. *Tel* (215) 965-2305.
🚇 Market East Station. 🚍 5th
St. 🚌 Philly Phlash. ⏰ 9am–
5pm. ♿ www.nps.gov/inde

The Liberty Bell
The bell cracked the first time it was rung in 1753. Recast twice by Philadelphia's Pass and Stow Foundry, it was placed in the steeple of the State House (now called Independence Hall). It is said to have been first referenced as "Bell of Liberty" by 19th-century abolitionists.

Multimedia Display Gallery
This gallery displays old newspaper reports, videos, and photographs of people who have fought for liberty, such as the Dalai Lama and Nelson Mandela.

Curved wall   Entrance

Liberty Bell Center
The center is an elongated building where visitors first walk through a multimedia display gallery. This leads to the bell itself, set next to a large window with an excellent view of Independence Hall. A new commemorative installation, "The President's House", sits adjacent to the Liberty Bell. This was the official residence of the US President before the White House.

LIBERTY BELL TIMELINE

1752 Pennsylvania Assembly orders the bell from Whitechapel Foundry in England	**1835** Termed "Bell of Liberty" by abolitionists **1841–45** Cracks again in this period	**1944** Tapped during Normandy Invasion on June 6		**1988** Liberty Bell Medal created
1750	**1800**	**1850**	**1900**	**1950**	**2000**

1776 Possibly rung on July 8 after first public reading of the Declaration of Independence	**1976** Moved from Independence Hall to outside pavilion for country's bicentennial
1753 It cracks when first rung, and is recast twice	**1915** Tapped when transcontinental telephone service started **2003** Bell moved to new Liberty Bell Center

Independence Visitor Center ❸

6th & Market Sts. **Map** 4 D2.
Tel (215) 965-7676. 🚇 *Market East Station.* 🚌 *5th St.* 🚌 *Philly Phlash.* 🕐 *Oct– Jun: 8:30am–5pm Mon–Sun; Jul–Sep: open later.* 🔴 *Jan 1, Thanksgiving, Dec 25.* ♿ 🖥 🌐 *www.* independencevisitorcenter.com

One of the first stops for any visitor to Philadelphia should be the Independence Visitor Center. It was opened in 2001 as part of the Independence National Historical Park redevelopment project, which also included the Liberty Bell and National Constitution centers.

This expansive center offers information on more than 4,000 attractions in the city and the region. Apart from screening historical and orientation films, such as the short film *Independence* directed by John Huston, it has maps and brochures, touch-screen information kiosks, daily listings of events, and trip planning services. Both National Park Service rangers and City of Philadelphia tourism specialists provide assistance and advice about historical sights, attractions, shopping, and dining. A gift shop has all manner of souvenirs themed around Philadelphia.

Of particular interest at the center is a rotating exhibition of original engravings of

Plain brick façade of the 18th-century Free Quaker Meeting House

colonial Philadelphia by William Russell Birch, which were first published in 1800. Prints of his original engravings line the entrance corridor leading in from Market Street.

The center is the first stop for visitors to Independence Hall as well, since timed-entry tickets for the hall are available here on a first-come-first-served basis.

Free Quaker Meeting House ❹

Arch & 5th Sts. **Map** 4 D2.
🚇 *Market East Station.* 🚌 *5th St.* 🚌 *Philly Phlash.* 🕐 *1–5pm Wed– Sun.* 📷 ♿

This simple Georgian brick building was built in 1783 for Quakers who were compelled to bear arms in the American Revolution. Bearing arms meant going against the pacifist beliefs of the order,

which led inevitably to expulsion from the main Quaker community. A group of about 200 such people called themselves the "Free Quakers" and founded a meetinghouse of their own. However, in the years that followed, attendance dropped to perhaps a few dozen, and by 1834, only two Free Quakers, Betsy Ross and John Price Wetherill, still attended meetings. Shortly thereafter, the meeting-house was permanently closed. Since then, the building has served as a school, a library, and a warehouse.

Today, the building still contains two benches and a window from colonial times. Also on display is Betsy Ross's five-pointed star tissue pattern, which she is said to have used to shape stars to make the colonial-era American flag. Today, the descendants of

Free Quaker Meeting House

the original Free Quakers hold their annual meetings here to decide how to distribute funds generated by rental of the hall and how best to invest income for charitable purposes. Actors dressed in colonial garb give talks and interpretations of the building's history, and guides demonstrate how to cut a five-pointed star in one snip.

The Independence Visitor Center, in the middle of "America's most historic square mile"

National Constitution Center **❺**

See pp48–9.

US Mint **❻**

5th & Arch Sts. **Map** 4 D2. **Tel** *(215) 408-0112.* 🚆 *Market East Station.* 🚇 *5th St.* 🚌 *Philly Phlash.* ○ *9am–3pm Mon–Fri.* 🎫 *group tours by prior arrangement.* **www**.usmint.gov
Federal Reserve Bank of Philadelphia 6th & Arch Sts. **Tel** *(215) 574-6000.* ○ *photo ID required to enter.*

The Philadelphia mint, the oldest in the US, produces gold bullion coins and medals, and also makes most of the coins that Americans use everyday. The first US coins, minted in 1793, were copper pennies intended solely for commerce in the colonies. Today, 24 hours a day, five days a week, hundreds of machines and operators, in a room the size of a football field, blank, anneal, count, and bag millions of dollars worth of pennies, dimes, and quarters. The gift shop, open on a limited basis, sells commemorative coins and numismatic collectables.

A related exhibit, Money in Motion, is on display at the **Federal Reserve Bank of Philadelphia**, which is located one block west of the US Mint. It explains US monetary policy and history with the help of interactive computer screens and impressive exhibits.

Philadelphia's oldest Quaker meetinghouse, on Arch Street

Arch Street Friends Meeting House **❼**

320 Arch St. **Map** 4 E2. **Tel** *(215) 627-2667.* 🚆 *Market East Station.* 🚇 *2nd St.* 🚌 *Philly Phlash.* ○ *10am–4pm Mon–Sat.* 🛐 *10:30am Sun; 7pm Wed.* **www**.archstreetfriends.org

This brick structure is the oldest Quaker meeting house still in use in Philadelphia. Built in 1804, the site first served as a Quaker burial ground, but later accommodated victims of the yellow fever epidemic in the 1790s. Today, the house has a central hall and two adjacent meeting rooms. The East Room features Quaker artifacts and six dioramas depicting William Penn's life as a Quaker. The West Room contains worn wooden benches and now serves as the main meeting and worship hall.

Christ Church Burial Ground **❽**

5th & Arch Sts. **Map** 4 D2. **Tel** *(215) 922-1695.* 🚆 *Market East Station.* 🚇 *5th St.* 🚌 *Philly Phlash.* ○ *10am–4pm Mon–Sat, noon–4pm Sun (burial ground); 9am–5pm Mon–Sat, noon–5pm Sun (church).* 🎫 🚹 **www**.oldchristchurch.org

This crammed cemetery dates back to 1719, and is an expansion of the church's original graveyard. More than 5,000 people are buried here, most from colonial times. The burial ground is the final resting place of Benjamin Franklin, his wife Deborah, and their daughter and son-in-law Sarah Franklin and Richard Bache. Four older signers of the Declaration of Independence – Dr. Benjamin Rush, Francis Hopkinson, George Ross, and Joseph Hewes – are also buried here. Franklin's grave is on the perimeter of the grounds, and is visible through an iron grating. Passers-by toss pennies on the grave, both to show respect and to bring good luck. With headstones already deteriorating by the mid-19th century, all gravestone inscriptions were copied and published in

Headstone, Christ Church Burial Ground

1864 in order to preserve records of people interred in this graveyard.

National Museum of American Jewish History **❾**

Independence Mall East, 55 N 5th St. **Map** 4 D2. **Tel** *(215) 923-3811.* 🚆 *Market East Station.* 🚇 *5th St.* 🚌 *Philly Phlash.* ○ *10am–5pm Mon–Thur, 10am–3pm Fri, noon–5pm Sun.* ● *Sat, Jewish holidays.* 🚻 **www**.nmajh.org

The museum's mission of preserving and exploring the history of American Jews began in 1976. There were only 40 objects at that time but the collection has since grown to more than 10,000 artifacts, including posters,

Inspecting coins at the US Mint

photographs, books, and paintings. Of particular note are a 1789 prayer manuscript composed by Richmond Jews on the adoption of the US Constitution and a selection of mid-19th century Jewish cookbooks. On the grounds is the impressive *Religious Liberty*, a marble monument by American Jewish sculptor, Sir Moses Jacob Ezekiel, which was dedicated in 1876.

A new state-of-the-art facility, just steps from the museum, is due to open in 2010 and will include interactive exhibits and one of the nation's largest collections of Jewish Americana.

Federal-style façade of Library Hall, a reproduction of the 1789 original

Congregation Mikveh Israel ⑩

44 N 4th St. **Map** 4 E2. **Tel** (215) 922-5446. 🚇 Market East Station. 🚌 5th St. 🚐 Philly Phlash. ☐ 10am–5pm daily. 🔲 7:15am daily; Fri evening; 9am Sat. 🚻 www.mikvehisrael.org

Philadelphia's oldest Jewish congregation, Mikveh Israel, dates to before the 1740s. The congregation built its first synagogue in 1782, and moved into its current building in 1976.

Mikveh Israel's archival collection includes two pairs of Torah finials crafted by silversmith Myer Myers in 1772 and letters written by US Presidents George Washington and Abraham Lincoln. Past congregation members included colonial patriot and financier Haym Salomon; Nathan Levy, whose ship brought the Liberty Bell to America; and Rebecca Gratz, who founded educational and social institutions. The synagogue still holds a traditional service, which has remained virtually unchanged since the colonial era.

Redbrick exterior of Congregation Mikveh Israel

Second Bank of the United States ⑪

420 Chestnut St. **Map** 4 D3. **Tel** (215) 965-7676, (800) 537-7676. 🚇 Market East Station. 🚐 Philly Phlash. ☐ 11am–4pm Wed–Sun. 🚻 www.nps.gov/inde

Built between 1819 and 1824, this is one of America's finest examples of Greek Revival architecture. Once a repository that provided credit for federal government agencies and private businesses, it now houses a collection of 185 paintings from the late 18th and early 19th centuries. On view are portraits of colonial and federal leaders, military officers, explorers, scientists, and founding fathers.

Many of the portraits are by Charles Willson Peale (1741–1827), his brother James, and their respective children, who together form America's most distinguished family of artists. Peale began collecting portraits after the Revolutionary War. Today, 94 of his paintings, including likenesses of George Washington, Thomas Jefferson, and the Marquis de LaFayette,

the Continental Army's French ally, are on display, along with portraits by other artists.

Philosophical Hall and Library Hall ⑫

5th St between Chestnut & Walnut Sts. **Map** 4 D3. **Tel** (215) 440-3400. 🚇 Market East Station. 🚌 5th St. 🚐 Philly Phlash. ☐ Philosophical Hall: 10am–4pm Thu–Sun, varies with exhibits; Library Hall: 9am–4:45pm Mon–Fri (lobby exhibit). 🚻 www.amphilsoc.org

A Colonial-era "think tank," the American Philosophical Society was founded in 1743 by Benjamin Franklin to promote the study of government, nature, science, and industry. Built in 1789, the Federal-style Philosophical Hall was a meeting place for doctors, clergymen, and the founding fathers of the nation. Reopened in 2001 for the first time since the early 19th century, the hall today hosts art, history, and science exhibitions.

The society also owns Library Hall, once the home of the Library Company founded by Franklin in 1731. The company's vast collections served as the Library of Congress until 1800. The current building, a reconstruction of the 1789 original, stores some of the society's most precious works, including the title page of an 1859 manuscript of Darwin's *Origin of Species*, the journals of explorers Lewis and Clark, and Jefferson's handwritten Declaration of Independence.

National Constitution Center ⑤

The inscription "We the People" is boldly engraved on the massive Indiana limestone façade of this sprawling center, which was opened on July 4, 2003. It explains the US Constitution through more than 100 interactive and multimedia exhibits, including artifacts, sculptures, photographs, video, and film. Visitors can listen to President Franklin Delano Roosevelt's speeches or to actual arguments from Supreme Court cases at a replica of the Supreme Court Bench, or walk through a re-creation of the 19th-century Senate floor. The circular main hall also contains displays that illuminate the text of the Constitution and highlight the themes of liberty and freedom.

Washington's statue in Signers' Hall

Engraved Façade
"We the People," part of the opening words of the US Constitution, engraved on the façade of the center.

THE US CONSTITUTION

After the Revolutionary War, delegates from the original 13 states, except Rhode Island, gathered in Philadelphia for the Constitutional Convention in 1787. It took them nearly four months to draft a document creating a strong centralized government for the new nation. Adopted on September 17, the Constitution ensures individual liberties and defines distinct powers for Congress, the president, and the federal courts, while also establishing a system of "Checks and Balances" so that no branch of government can dominate the others.

A copy of the Constitution of the United States

F.M. Kirby Auditorium and Theater

Grand Hall Overlook

Terrace

Grand Hall Lobby
Flags of US states hang from the Grand Hall's second floor overlook, from where the lobby's two-story glass windowpanes provide a stunning view of Independence National Historical Park.

STAR EXHIBITS

★ "Freedom Rising"

★ American National Tree

★ Signers' Hall

Second
Floor

VISITORS' CHECKLIST

525 Arch St. **Map** 4 D2.
Tel (215) 409-6600. 🚇 *Market East Station.* 🚌 *5th St.* 🚐 *Philly Phlash.* 🕐 *9:30am–5pm Mon–Fri, 9:30am–6pm Sat, noon–5pm Sun.* ⬤ *Thanksgiving, Dec 25.*
🈳 ♿ 🍴 🛍 📷
www.constitutioncenter.org

★ **"Freedom Rising"**
The circular, 350-seat Kimmel Theater features "Freedom Rising," a multimedia production that narrates the story of the US Constitution. This 17-minute show is projected on a 360-degree screen.

★ **American National Tree**
With the "We the People" wall in the foreground, the circular American National Tree features the stories of 100 Americans who have influenced the Constitution. Each story exemplifies tolerance, diversity, and opportunity.

Box Office

First Floor

Main Entrance

KEY

▢ Richard and Helen DeVos Exhibit Hall

▢ Kimmel Theater

▢ Posterity Hall

▢ Signers' Hall

▢ F.M. Kirby Auditorium and Theater

▢ First Public Printing of the Constitution

▢ Non-exhibition space

CENTER GUIDE

The Grand Hall Lobby and Kimmel Theater are on the ground floor. Permanent displays and interactive exhibits are situated on the second floor in the circular DeVos Hall.

★ **Signers' Hall**
Walk among life-sized bronze statues of the 39 men who signed the Constitution (including that of Benjamin Franklin, seated in the front), and the three who dissented.

Curtis Center and Dream Garden Mosaic ⓑ

6th & Walnut Sts. **Map** 4 D3.
Tel (215) 238-6450. 🚇 Market
East Station. 🚏 5th St. 🚌 Philly
Phlash. ◯ 8am–6pm Mon–Fri,
10am–1pm Sat. ♿

This Beaux-Arts building is
where Cyrus Curtis kicked off
his publishing empire in 1883
with the founding of the
Ladies Home Journal. His
publishing company also
breathed new life into the
Saturday Evening Post,
and created popular
magazines such as
*American Home, Jack
and Jill, Holiday,* and
Country Gentleman.
 Inside the building is the
enormous *Dream Garden
Mosaic,* a 49ft x 15ft (15m x
4.5m) glasswork that domi-
nates the lobby. Designed
by Maxfield Parrish, the
mosaic was completed in
1916 by Louis Comfort
Tiffany and Tiffany Studios.
The artwork, depicting a
garden with trees and
streams, has more than
100,000 pieces of hand-
fired favrile glass. In
1998, it was sold to a
Las Vegas casino
owner, but the people
of Philadelphia resisted the
move. Local artists and histo-
rians helped in raising $3.5
million for the Pennsylvania
Academy of the Fine Arts
(see pp74–5) to buy back the
mosaic. It later underwent
painstaking restoration.

**Atwater Kent
exterior detail**

Atwater Kent Museum ⓮

15 S 7th St. **Map** 4 D3. **Tel** (215)
685-4830. 🚇 Market East Station.
🚏 8th St. 🚌 Philly Phlash.
◯ 1–5pm Wed–Sun. ● Jan 1,
Thanksgiving, Dec 25. 🎫 📷
www.philadelphiahistory.org

Philadelphia's official history
museum since 1938, the
Atwater Kent Museum has a
collection of 100,000 objects
and images spanning 300
years. Designed by John
Haviland in Greek Revival
style and completed in
1826, this was the original
home of The Franklin.
The nation's first architecture classes were taught
here. The building was
saved from demolition
in 1935 when A. Atwater
Kent purchased it for a
museum. Today, a colorful
walk-on map of the city
of Philadelphia covers the
entire first floor gallery.
Objects displayed in past
exhibitions have included
furniture used by President
George Washington while
living in Philadelphia,
Benjamin Franklin's
wine glass, and the
Wampum belt given to
William Penn by the
Lenni-Lenape *(see p18).*
The museum has an expan-
sive collection of *Saturday
Evening Post* covers showing
"vignettes of daily life" in
America by Norman Rockwell,
who created 322 images for
the Philadelphia-based magazine between 1916 and 1963.

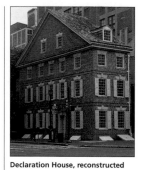

**Declaration House, reconstructed
in 1975 by National Park Service**

Declaration House ⓯

7th & Market Sts. **Map** 4 D2.
Tel (215) 965-7676, (800) 537-7676.
🚇 Market East Station. 🚏 8th St.
🚌 Philly Phlash. ◯ hours vary, call
to confirm.

The current brick structure of
Declaration House is a 1975
reconstruction of the
Georgian-style home where
Thomas Jefferson drafted the
Declaration of Independence
(see p42) from June 11 to 28,
1776. He had rented two
upstairs rooms from bricklayer
Jacob Graff, who had built
the house in 1775. Although
only a few blocks from
Independence Hall, the house
faced a field and stable, and
offered Jefferson a quieter
setting to write the Declaration.
 Today, along with a bust of
the famous American statesman and third president, the
house includes copies of
Jefferson's rough drafts of
the Declaration. The two

Dream Garden Mosaic, an enormous glass artwork gracing the Curtis Center lobby rooms upstairs contain period furnishings, and include re-creations of Jefferson's bedroom and parlor, where he wrote the document.

The African American Museum in Philadelphia ⑯

701 Arch St. **Map** 4 D2. **Tel** *(215) 574-0380.* 🚇 *Market East Station.* 🚊 *5th St.* 🚌 *Philly Phlash.* ⭕ *10am– 5pm Tue–Sat; noon–5pm Sun; Martin Luther King Day.* ⬤ *Mon, public hols.* **www**.aampmuseum.org

A Smithsonian affiliate, this museum is one of several founded in Philadelphia during the nation's bicentennial year. The museum is dedicated to "collecting, preserving, and interpreting the material and intellectual culture of African Americans" in the local area and the Americas. Since opening in 1976, the collection has swelled to more than 500,000 artifacts, including photographs, documents, fine and folk art, costumes, books, periodicals, and a number of other memorabilia.

Permanent and changing exhibitions recognize and celebrate important aspects of African-American life and history, including the Civil Rights movement, and contributions in diverse areas, such as the arts, entertainment, sports, medicine, politics, religion, law, and technology. A permanent exhibit features artifacts from and an overview of the ancient Nile Valley civilizations of Egypt, Nubia, and Aksum. Previous exhibitions at the museum have showcased African woodcarvings and textile designs while interpreting the traditions and ceremonies of several African countries. Others have focused on struggles against slavery and oppression, including the Haitian Revolution, which resulted in Haiti establishing the world's first Black

L'Ouverture **by Ulrick Jean-Pierre, African American Museum**

republic in 1804. The museum also organizes regular workshops and demonstrations.

St. George's United Methodist Church ⑰

235 N 4th St. **Map** 4 E2. **Tel** *(215) 925-7788.* 🚇 *Market East Station.* 🚊 *5th St.* 🚌 *Philly Phlash.* ⭕ *10am– 3pm Mon–Fri; Sun morning after worship; Sat by appt.*

The American Methodist movement began in St. George's United Methodist Church in 1769, making it the country's oldest Methodist church in continuous use. This simple brick structure, its inside walls adorned with a muted blue tint, has not changed much since it was remodeled in 1792. Colonial-era wooden pews and floorboards remain, as do the wrought iron candle chandeliers and candelabra, although now wired with electric lights. A two-room museum has 18th- and 19th-century artifacts, hymnals, bibles, and other important church keepsakes. They include a 1785 silver chalice from John Wesley, the founder of the movement, the original handwritten journals of Joseph Pilmoor, the first pastor of the church, and a bible from Francis Asbury, considered

Exhibit at the African American Museum

the father of the American United Methodist Church.

St. Augustine's Church across the street dates back to 1796. Burned down in 1844 by anti-Catholic rioters, the current building was designed by architect Napoleon LeBrun and rebuilt in 1847.

Fireman's Hall Museum ⑱

147 N 2nd St. **Map** 4 E2. **Tel** *(215) 923-1438.* 🚇 *Market East Station.* 🚊 *2nd St.* 🚌 *Philly Phlash.* ⭕ *9am– 5pm Tue–Sat.* **www**.mfrconsultants. com/pfd/museum.shtml

Housed in an old firehouse that was operational between 1902 and 1952, this unique museum narrates the history of firefighting in Philadelphia, back to colonial times. The building still contains the original brass sliding pole used for quick access to fire trucks. Several pieces of old equipment are on display, including an 1896 hook-and-ladder, a 1903 high-pressure Cannon Wagon, and a 1907 steam-powered pumper. Of special note are two well-preserved hand-pumpers, one from 1815, and the other from 1730, six years before Benjamin Franklin founded the nation's first fire department. Also on display are axes, saws, nozzles, old fire plaques indicating insured buildings, and leather fire hats from the early 19th century. A large stained-glass window memorializes fallen firefighters.

Façade of the Fireman's Hall Museum

Elfreth's Alley ⑲

N 2nd St between Arch & Race Sts. **Map** 4 E2. 🛈 *Elfreth's Alley Museum, 126 Elfreth's Alley, (215) 574-0560.* 🚇 *Market East Station.* 🚊 *2nd St.* 🚌 *Philly Phlash.* 🏛 ◻ *Mar–Oct: 10am–5pm Tue–Sat, noon–5pm Sun; Nov–Feb: 10am–5pm Thu–Sat, noon–5pm Sun.* 🎗 ◻ **www**. elfrethsalley.org

The oldest continuously occupied residential street in the country, this narrow cobblestoned lane is lined with 33 historic homes, most in simple Georgian style. Named after Jeremiah Elfreth, a blacksmith who built and rented out some of the first homes, the alley dates back to 1702, when it was a path used by carts hauling goods from the Delaware River docks. Its early occupants were tradespeople, artisans, and sea captains, while the industrial boom later brought in laborers and tailors.

The oldest homes are at 120 and 122, built between 1724 and 1728. The street's Mantua Maker's Museum House, at 126, has been restored to resemble the period between 1762 and 1794, when it was owned by sisters-in-law Mary Smith and Sarah Milton, makers of mantuas and dresses. The home at 124 is now a gift shop.

Halfway down the street is another smaller alley, Bladen Court, which includes three houses and a courtyard. Twice a year, in June and December, many Elfreth Alley residents open their homes for tours during Fete Days celebrations.

Betsy Ross House, where the first American flag was sewn

Betsy Ross House ⑳

239 Arch St. **Map** 4 E2. *Tel (215) 686-1252.* 🚇 *Market East Station.* 🚊 *2nd St.* 🚌 *Philly Phlash.* ◻ *Apr–Sep: 10am–5pm; Oct–Mar: 10am–5pm Tue–Sun.* ⬤ *Jan 1, Thanksgiving, Dec 25.* 🛗 *limited access.* **www**.betsyrosshouse.org

One of Philadelphia's most visited historic sites, this simple colonial home was where Quaker seamstress and upholsterer Betsy Ross is said to have sewn the first American flag – although no official documentation exists to prove it. Instead, the story was handed down through generations of her family. Nonetheless, the 1740 row house has been restored to around 1777, when Ross was supposedly commissioned by George Washington to create the "Stars and Stripes" for the struggling new nation. The home, with narrow stairwells and low ceilings,

is decorated with period antiques and reproduction pieces, but also has a few original items that once belonged to Ross, including her eyeglasses, a family bible, and an American Chippendale walnut chest-on-chest.

Christ Church ㉑

2nd St above Market St. **Map** 4 E2. *Tel (215) 922-1695.* 🚇 *Market East Station.* 🚊 *2nd St.* 🚌 *Philly Phlash.* ◻ *9am–5pm Mon–Sat; 12:30pm–5pm Sun.* ⬤ *Jan & Feb: Mon & Tue.* 🛈 *9am & 11am Sun, noon Wed.* **www**.oldchristchurch.org

Founded in 1695, Christ Church was Philadelphia's only Church of England parish for 66 years. The existing structure, built in 1754 in Georgian style, after Wren's London churches, was the town's tallest building at the time. Often called the "Nation's Church," it was where revolutionary leaders, including Benjamin Franklin, Betsy Ross, and George and Martha Washington, once worshipped. Plaques mark some pews used by the colonial elite.

Inside is the baptismal font in which William Penn was baptized, dating from the 14th century and donated by London's All Hallows Church in 1697. Bishop William White *(see p54)*, parish rector for 57 years, is buried in the chancel of the church.

Franklin Court and B. Free Franklin Post Office ㉒

Between 3rd & 4th Sts and Chestnut & Market Sts. **Map** 4 E3. *Tel (215) 965-7676, (800) 537-7676.* 🚇 *Market East Station.* 🚊 *2nd St.* 🚌 *Philly Phlash.* ◻ *court: hours vary; post office: 9am–5pm Mon–Sat.* 🛗

This expansive court, which cuts through an entire city block, is where Benjamin Franklin's home once stood. Although razed in 1812, a "Ghost House" frame depicts the exact positions of the house and adjacent print shop, while excavations underneath reveal

Elfreth's Alley, dating to the early 18th century

the original foundations. An underground museum has exhibits explaining Franklin's life and features a few original family artifacts. On the court grounds are several former residences once owned by Franklin, which now house artifacts, replicas and demonstrations of colonial printing and bookbinding operations, and the B. Free Franklin Post Office and Museum, which has an active post office. Another building houses the restored offices of *The Aurora*, the newspaper published by Franklin's grandson, Benjamin Franklin Bache.

Classical façade of the First Bank, designed by Samuel Blodgett

Tribute to valor – the National Liberty Museum

National Liberty Museum ㉓

321 Chestnut St. **Map** 4 E3. *Tel* *(215) 925-2800.* 🚉 *Market East Station.* 🚇 *2nd St.* 🚌 *Philly Phlash.* 🕐 *Jun–Aug: 10am–5pm; Sep–May: 10am–5pm Tue–Sun.* 🔴 *Jan 1, Thanksgiving, Dec 25.* 🎫 *for adults.* 🚻 *www.*liberty*museum.org*

Through exhibits heralding freedom and diversity, the National Liberty Museum takes an unconventional approach to its mission of defusing violence and bigotry. The museum honors 1,000 people worldwide who have stood up against repression. On display are life-sized dioramas of South Africa's Nelson Mandela in his jail cell, and concentration camp victim Anne Frank's Amsterdam bedroom, in which she hid

from the Nazis. Another display has photographs of every rescue worker who died in the September 11, 2001 attacks. With more than 100 glass artworks, the museum is the only one in the world to use glass as a symbol for freedom, and has a two-story structure, the *Flame of Liberty*, by Dale Chihuly, as its centerpiece.

First Bank of the United States ㉔

116 S 3rd St between Chestnut & Walnut Sts. **Map** 4 E3. *Tel (215) 965-7676.* 🚉 *Market East Station.* 🚇 *2nd St.* 🚌 *Philly Phlash.* 🔴 *closed to the public.*

The dispute over building the First Bank instigated the new nation's first debate on the interpretation of the US Constitution (*see pp48–9*),

which neither allowed nor prohibited the building of a federal bank. Alexander Hamilton, treasury secretary from 1789 to 1795, led the charge to provide the nation with a firm financial footing and a means to pay off the Revolutionary War debt. Chartered by President Washington and Congress in 1791, the bank building was completed six years later, with its classical design signifying culture and political maturity.

In 1811, Congress voted to withdraw the charter. The building was then occupied by Girard Bank through the 1920s, and finally taken over by the National Park Service in 1955. Original brick rooms and sheet iron vault doors still remain in the building, which will house the Civil War and Underground Museum of Philadelphia in 2010.

BENJAMIN FRANKLIN

One of America's finest statesmen, Benjamin Franklin wore many hats as a printer, inventor, author, philosopher, postmaster, and diplomat. Born in Boston in 1706, Franklin moved to Philadelphia in 1723. He established the first library and fire department in the city, and upgraded its postal services. Franklin also founded the University of Pennsylvania and the Pennsylvania Hospital. In the Revolutionary War, he presided over the 1776 Constitutional Convention and helped draft the

Benjamin Franklin (1706–90)

Declaration of Independence (*see p42*). He won favor with the French who would come to America's aid against the British. In 1787, he signed the US Constitution, and died in Philadelphia three years later. In 2006, the city honored Franklin with a year-long celebration of his 300th birthday.

Carpenters' Hall ㉕

320 Chestnut St. **Map** 4 E3. **Tel**
(215) 925-0167. 🚉 *Market East
Station.* Ⓢ *5th St.* 🚌 *Philly Phlash.*
🕙 *10am–4pm daily.*
⬤ *Jan 1, Thanksgiving, Dec 25.*
www.carpentershall.org

As the name suggests, this
two-story structure was built
for the Carpenters' Company,
the country's oldest trade
guild, established in 1724. It
played an important role in
the Revolutionary War,
secretly hosting the First
Continental Congress in 1774.

Today, the Carpenters' Hall
houses displays of original
Windsor chairs, used during
the Congress, and colonial-era
carpenters' tools. Two rebuilt
structures share the grounds –
Pemberton House, named
after a Quaker merchant, is
now a gift shop, while the
New Hall Military Museum
displays weapons of the
colonial army and navy. The
original 1791 building housed
War Department offices.

Georgian-style Carpenters' Hall,
designed by Robert Smith in 1770

Todd House ㉖

4th & Walnut Sts. **Map** 4 D3.
Tel *(215) 965-7676.* 🚉 *Market East
Station.* Ⓢ *5th St.* 🚌 *Philly Phlash.*
🎟 *compulsory; free tickets available
at Independence Visitor Center on
first-come, first-served basis.* ♿

This Georgian-style home
reflects the way the middle
class lived in late 18th-century
Philadelphia. What makes
Todd House particularly
interesting is its famous

Reconstructed dining room of Bishop White House

resident, Dolley Payne, who
later married James Madison,
the fourth president of the
US. Built in 1775, the home
was occupied by Dolley and
her first husband, lawyer John
Todd, both Quakers, from
1791 to 1793. Dolley lost
Todd and their infant son in
1793 during the city's yellow
fever epidemic. The following
year, she met Madison during
an arranged meeting.

Today, the three-story home
has been restored to when
John and Dolley Todd lived
here, with furnishings that
reflect subtle Quaker conserv-
atism. Period items include
replicas of Dolley's dressing
table, and John Todd's first-
floor law library, which contained more than 300 volumes.

Bishop White House ㉗

309 Walnut St. **Map** 4 E3. **Tel** *(215)*
965-7676. 🚉 *Market East Station.*
Ⓢ *5th St.* 🚌 *Philly Phlash.* 🎟
compulsory; free tickets available at
Independence Visitor Center on first-
come, first-served basis. ♿

The residence of Bishop
William White for nearly 50
years, this three-story Federal
structure, built in 1786, is an
excellent example of a late
18th-century upper-class
Philadelphia home. Dr. White,
the first Episcopal Bishop of
Pennsylvania and rector of
Christ Church *(see p52)* and
St. Peter's Episcopal Church
(see p61), often entertained
the colonial elite here, including George Washington and

Benjamin Franklin. The house
has been restored, and period
and original family pieces
decorate the rooms, including
whale oil lamps on the fireplace mantel and an assortment of silver pieces in the
dining room. Chair placement
and bookcases in Dr. White's
upstairs study have been
accurately reconstructed,
thanks to a painting of the
room commissioned after his
death. An inside privy, which
remains today, is indicative of
the home's upper-class status.

Philadelphia Merchants' Exchange,
designed in Greek Revival style

Philadelphia Merchants' Exchange ㉘

143 S 3rd St at Walnut St. **Map** 4 E3.
Tel *(215) 965-7676.* 🚉 *Market East
Station.* Ⓢ *2nd St.* 🚌 *Philly Phlash.*
🕘 *9am–5pm (lobby exhibit).*
www.phlx.com

The oldest stock exchange
building in the country, this
imposing edifice is one of

Old City's finest architectural gems. Completed in 1834, it was designed in Greek Revival style by the up-and-coming architect William Strickland, already noted for designing the new steeple atop Independence Hall *(see pp42–3)* and for his work on the Second Bank of the US *(see p47)*. Strickland's admiration of classical Greek design is reflected by the columned Corinthian portico at one end and the unusual, semi-circular portico at the other.

With the financial district shifting to Center City in the late 19th century, the building soon became neglected. The National Park Service took it over in 1952, making it a part of Independence National Historical Park. Today, the Park Service maintains offices in the building. Although the exchange is closed to the public, visitors are permitted to enter the lobby and view a small exhibit that details the history and architecture of the exchange.

City Tavern ㉙

138 S 2nd St between Walnut & Chestnut Sts. **Map** 4 E3. *Tel* (215) 413-1443. 🚇 *Market East Station.* 🚌 *2nd St.* 🚌 *Philly Phlash.* 🕐 *from 11:30am; reservations taken until 8:30pm* 🚻 *www.citytavern.com*

Recalling the atmosphere of an authentic London tavern, the City Tavern also boasted the second largest ballroom in the colonies when it first opened in 1773.

City Tavern, still a popular dining spot in Philadelphia

However, just a year later, with the Revolutionary War in the offing, the three-story building was used by members of the First Continental Congress as an unofficial gathering place. Later, in 1777, when he became the leader of the Continental Army, Washington used the tavern as his headquarters.

After the Revolutionary War, the Constitutional Convention held its closing banquet here in 1787. Frequented by the likes of George Washington, Thomas Jefferson, and other colonial notables, it was once called "the most genteel tavern in America," by John Adams, the second president of the United States.

However, by the 1790s, the City Tavern had lost its prominence and served as a merchants' exchange until 1834, when it was partially destroyed by fire. The original structure was finally demolished in 1854 to make way for new brownstone buildings.

After careful research, the National Park Service reconstructed the tavern in 1975. Today, the inn is almost identical to the original, with serving staff in period dress and colonial-style dishes on the menu. These include such delicacies as sweet potato biscuits, said to be a favorite of Jefferson, turkey pot pie based on Martha Washington's recipe, West Indies pepperpot soup, and ales brewed according to Washington's and Jefferson's original recipes.

Statue of William Penn

Welcome Park ㉚

S 2nd St at Walnut St (2nd St & Sansom St Alley). **Map** 4 E3. 🚇 *Market East Station.* 🚌 *2nd St.* 🚌 *Philly Phlash.*

Named after the ship that ferried Penn and the first Quakers from England to the New World, the *Welcome*, this open city square is dedicated to the city's founder, William Penn. It was constructed in 1982 to commemorate the 300th anniversary of the founding of the colony of Pennsylvania. The centerpiece of the park is a smaller version of Penn's statue from City Hall *(see p72)*. Emblazoned along the south wall of the park is a timeline of Penn's life and the events leading to the creation of the new colony. The park is located where the Slate Roof House – Penn's home and the Pennsylvania Seat of Government from 1700 to 1701 – once stood. This postmodernist square is made of concrete crisscrossed by marble slabs, depicting the main streets of the original city grid planned by William Penn and his surveyor Thomas Holmes.

At the park's north end sits the Thomas Bond House, named after the surgeon who, in 1751, along with Benjamin Franklin and others, founded Pennsylvania Hospital, the nation's first public hospital *(see p67)*. The restored 1769 Georgian-style home is now a bed-and-breakfast *(see p134)*.

Welcome Park, dedicated to city founder William Penn

SOCIETY HILL
AND PENN'S LANDING

Detail, Old St. Mary's Church

Villiam Penn first stepped ashore on the banks of the Delaware River at what is today known as Penn's Landing, the eastern edge of this neighborhood. An elongated and tree-lined promenade, Penn's Landing includes a plaza for concerts, historic ships and dinner boats along the piers, and the Independence Seaport Museum.

Heading west, several walkways lead to Society Hill, a well-preserved area with churches, synagogues, and 18th-century homes. The area's southern border, South Street, contrasts with the more serene Society Hill, indulging in the excitement derived from a trendy and eclectic mix of cafés, restaurants, shops, nightclubs, and bars.

SIGHTS AT A GLANCE

Historical Buildings and Districts
New Market and Head House Square **15**
Penn's Landing **14**
Pennsylvania Hospital **17**
Physick House **6**
Powel House **12**
South Street and Walkway **16**

Parks and Gardens
Rose Garden and Magnolia Garden **9**
Washington Square **1**

Places of Worship
Mikveh Israel Cemetery **18**
Mother Bethel AME Church **2**
Old Pine Street Church **3**
Old St. Joseph's Church **10**
Old St. Mary's Church **8**
Society Hill Synagogue **7**
St. Peter's Episcopal Church **4**

Museums and Galleries
Independence Seaport Museum pp64–5 **13**
Polish American Cultural Center Museum **11**
Thaddeus Kosciuszko National Memorial **5**

GETTING THERE
Most sights here are a 5- to 15-minute walk from Independence Mall. Philly Phlash buses run May–Oct and are accessible on Market Street, while the Market-Frankford line has stops at 2nd and Market, 5th and Market, and 8th and Market. SEPTA bus 42 runs along Spruce and Walnut Streets.

KEY

▨ Street-by-Street map *see pp58–9*

S SEPTA subway stop

| 0 meters | 250 |
| 0 yards | 250 |

◁ **Penn's statue outside Pennsylvania Hospital, founded in 1751 (see p67)**

Street-by-Street: Society Hill and Penn's Landing

Flowers laid at the Tomb of the Unknown Soldier

This historic neighborhood dates back to 1682 when William Penn chartered the "Free Society of Traders" to help develop a fledgling Philadelphia. The area was home to many notable colonial figures and members of the new Federal government, which was formed after the Revolutionary War. In the late 1950s, the Philadelphia Redevelopment Authority saved hundreds of 18th- and early 19th-century homes from likely demolition, selling them to private citizens who agreed to restore them. Today, a walk through the neighborhood reveals surviving narrow streets and courtyards, and houses in a mix of architectural styles, including Georgian, Federal, Greek Revival, and Beaux-Arts.

Mother Bethel AME Church
Founded in 1791, this site is the oldest piece of land continuously owned by African Americans. A lower level museum includes the tomb of founder Richard Allen ❷

Old Pine Street Church
The cemetery of "the Church of the Patriots" also contains the grave of Eugene Ormandy, director of the Philadelphia Orchestra from 1938 to 1980 ❸

KEY

‒ ‒ ‒ Suggested route

0 meters   100

0 yards   100

STAR SIGHTS

★ Powel House

★ Washington Square and Tomb of the Unknown Soldier

St. Peter's Episcopal Church
Completed in 1761, this Anglican church has an unusual double-ended interior, with the altar at one end, and the pulpit at the other ❹

★ **Washington Square and Tomb of the Unknown Soldier**
This peaceful square has the nation's only tomb dedicated to the unknown Revolutionary War soldier ❶

LOCATOR MAP
See Street Finder maps 3 & 4

SOCIETY HILL AND PENN'S LANDING

Rose Garden

Old St. Mary's Church ❽

Magnolia Garden
This garden was established as a tribute to George Washington, who liked magnolias ❾

Polish American Cultural Center Museum ⓫

5TH STREET

4TH STREET

SPRUCE STREET

CYPRESS ST

Society Hill Synagogue ❼

Physick House ❻

Thaddeus Kosciuszko National Memorial ❺

★ **Powel House**
This restored Georgian house was the home of Samuel Powel, the last mayor of colonial Philadelphia and the city's first after the Revolutionary War. Visitors to the house included George and Martha Washington ⓬

Old St. Joseph's Church
Founded in 1733 by English Jesuits, this was the first Catholic church in the city. The present structure, dating from 1838, has a graceful curving balcony and fine stained-glass panels, such as this, depicting the Virgin ❿

Washington Square, one of the five original squares in Penn's grid

Washington Square and Tomb of the Unknown Soldier ❶

Walnut St between 6th & 7th Sts.
Map 4 D3. 🚇 Market East Station.
Ⓢ 5th, 8th, 9th-10th Sts. 🚌 42, Philly Phlash.

One of the five original squares in Penn's city grid, Washington Square, named after the nation's first president, is a pleasant park with benches and towering trees. This quiet space is also hallowed ground, having served as a cemetery for 90 years until the late 18th century. More than 2,000 Revolutionary War soldiers and prisoners of war were buried in massive pits here. Congressman John Adams described the pathos in a letter to his wife Abigail in 1777, writing that he spent an hour "in the Congregation of the dead" and that "I never in my whole life was affected with so much melancholy." In 1793, mass graves were again dug for victims of the city's yellow fever epidemic. Today, the park's centerpiece is the Tomb of the Unknown Soldier, with a statue of Washington, which was erected in the 1950s as a tribute to those who fought in the

Washington's statue at Washington Square

Revolutionary War. The tomb includes the remains of a revolutionary soldier who was buried on the site.

Mother Bethel AME Church ❷

419 Richard Allen Ave, corner of 6th & Lombard Sts. **Map** 4 D4. **Tel** (215) 925-0616. 🚇 Market East Station. Ⓢ 5th St. 🚌 42, Philly Phlash. ◯ 10am–3pm Tue–Sat only by appt. **www**.motherbethel.org

Standing on the oldest piece of land to be continuously owned by African Americans in the US, Mother Bethel traces its roots to former slave Richard Allen (1760–1831), the first Bishop of the African Methodist Episcopal Church. Allen began preaching in 1786 at St. George's United Methodist Church (see p51), where he successfully built up a black parish. He founded his own church in 1794, by buying and moving a blacksmith's shop to the current site, and using the anvil as his pulpit. The current structure, built in 1889, still contains the original curved pews and stained-glass windows.

In 1830, the church hosted the first national convention for African Americans, and for years was a stop along the Underground Railroad, the

system set up by abolitionists to transport fugitive slaves to Canada and the free states. Today, a museum in the lower level houses the tomb of Allen and his wife Sarah, along with historic church artifacts, including the original pews from the blacksmith shop.

Old Pine Street Church ❸

412 Pine St. **Map** 4 D4. **Tel** (215) 925-8051. 🚇 Market East Station. Ⓢ 2nd, 5th Sts. 🚌 42, Philly Phlash. 📷 10am–3pm Mon–Sat, call in advance. ✝ 9:30am Sun. ♿ limited access. **www**.oldpine.org

The only remaining colonial Presbyterian place of worship in Philadelphia today, Old Pine Street Church was founded in 1768. Designed in Georgian style by Robert Smith, it was later remodeled into an imposing columned Greek Revival building. George Duffield, the church's first pastor, served as chaplain to the Continental Congress of 1774 and second US President John Adams and Dr. Benjamin Rush, the "Father of American Psychiatry," were parishioners here, earning it the moniker "Church of the Patriots."

In 1777, occupying British forces used the church as a hospital and stable, also burying 100 Hessian soldiers in a mass grave outside the church wall. Today, there are more than 3,000 tombs in the surrounding cemetery, including that of Eugene Ormandy, conductor of the Philadelphia Orchestra from 1938 to 1985.

Detail of a gravestone from the Old Pine Street Church graveyard

Interior and altar of St. Peter's Episcopal Church

St. Peter's Episcopal Church ❹

313 Pine St. **Map** 4 D4. **Tel** (215) 925-5968. 🚇 Market East Station. Ⓢ 2nd, 5th Sts. 🚌 42, Philly Phlash. ◯ 8am–4pm Mon–Fri; 11am–5pm Sat; 1–3pm Sun. ✝ 9am, 10am & 11am Sun. ♿ www.stpetersphila.org

Opened for worship in 1761, St. Peter's was founded by Society Hill Anglicans who were members of a then over-crowded Christ Church *(see p52)*, and who wanted a church closer to their homes. Christ Church and St. Peter's functioned as one parish until 1832, with Bishop White *(see p54)* serving as rector of both churches.

St. Peter's, built in Georgian style by Robert Smith, has a unique design. The placement of the wine-glass pulpit and altar at opposite ends of the building, and the seats in boxed pews facing either way, give the church no definitive front or back. In 1842, well-known architect William Strickland designed the land-mark tower and spire that still house bells from London's Whitechapel Foundry, which had forged the first Liberty Bell in 1753 *(see p44)*.

Buried in the graveyard are several important colonial Americans, including portrait painter Charles Willson Peale, naval hero Stephen Decatur, and George M. Dallas, vice president of the US from 1845 to 1849, after whom counties were named in Texas, Iowa, Arkansas, and Missouri.

Thaddeus Kosciuszko National Memorial ❺

301 Pine St. **Map** 4 D4. **Tel** (215) 597-9618. 🚇 Market East Station. Ⓢ 2nd St. 🚌 42, Philly Phlash. ♿ limited access. ◯ noon–4pm Wed–Sun. www.nps.gov/thko

Remembered as the "Hero of Two Continents," General Thaddeus Kosciuszko fought for freedom in both his native Poland and colonial America. During the Revolutionary War, he designed and built fortifi-cations at Saratoga and West Point that proved critical to American victories over the British troops.

After the war, Kosciuszko returned to Poland in 1784 and took part in its fight for independence from Russia, but he was wounded and imprisoned by the Russians. He was released only upon the condition that he leave Poland. He then returned to Philadelphia to recuperate from his war wounds for nine months in this Society Hill house. His upstairs room has been restored and furnished with period pieces similar to those he owned. It also contains his medals, walking crutch, and a sable fur given to him on his release by Russia's Tsar Paul I. While nursing his injuries, Kosciuszko spent most of his time reading, sketching, and receiving guests, including his close friend and then US Vice President, Thomas Jefferson.

Physick House ❻

321 S 4th St. **Map** 4 D4. **Tel** (215) 925-7866. 🚇 Market East Station. Ⓢ 2nd, 5th Sts. 🚌 42, Philly Phlash. ◯ noon–4pm Thu–Sat; 1–4pm Sun. ✓ www.philalandmarks.org

Named after Dr. Philip Syng Physick, the "Father of American Surgery" and grand-son of silversmith Philip Syng, who designed the inkwell used during the signing of the Declaration of Independence *(see p42)*, this is one of the few free-standing colonial homes that remain today. Built in 1786 by wine importer Henry Hill, this Federal-style house has what is believed to be the largest fanlight in colonial Philadelphia over its door. After acquiring the home in 1815, Physick set up his medical practice, treating such prominent patients as Dolley Madison *(see p54)* and President Andrew Jackson.

Physick lived there until his death in 1837, and the house has been restored to that period. Original, locally quarried Pennsylvania Blue Marble can be seen in the hall and on fire-place mantels. Family pieces, such as an

Physick House entrance fanlight

unusual mid-18th-century oval wooden case that belonged to William Penn's grandson, a British Wagstaff grandfather clock belonging to Physick's father, and original silver items are also displayed. Physick's medical instruments can be seen in an upstairs room, and include surgical tools and medicine chests with bottles.

Interior of Physick House, containing original colonial-era furnishings

Society Hill Synagogue **❼**

418 Spruce St. **Map** 4 D4. **Tel** *(215) 922-6590.* 🚇 *Market East Station.* 🚋 *5th St.* 🚌 *42, Philly Phlash.* 🕐 *9am–4pm Mon–Thu; call in advance.* ✡ *Fri night & Sat morning.* ♿ *www.societyhillsynagogue.org*

Originally built as a Baptist church, this impressive structure was designed by 19th-century architect Thomas Ustick Walter, who was most noted for his design of the dome and House and Senate wings of the US Capitol in Washington DC. The original structure was built in Greek Revival style in 1830, but two decades later, Walter was again commissioned to design a new Italianate façade, much of which remains today. The building was home to Baptist worshippers for more than 80 years, until a group of Romanian Jews acquired it in 1912.

By 1916, the building was known as the Great Romanian Synagogue. The name, written in Yiddish, is still visible over the entrance. In the mid-1960s, it became the new home of Society Hill Synagogue, which is an active congregation rooted in the texts and practices of conservative Judaism.

Old St. Mary's Church **❽**

252 S 4th St. **Map** 4 D4. **Tel** *(215) 923-7930.* 🚇 *Market East Station.* 🚋 *5th St.* 🚌 *42, Philly Phlash.* 🕐 *9am– 5pm Mon–Fri.* ✝ *Sun.* ♿ *www. ushistory.org/tour/tour_stmary.htm*

Founded to take on parishioners from an over-crowded Old St. Joseph's Church, this redbrick church was built in 1763. Together, the two houses of worship served the city's Catholic population as one parish until the 1820s. Old St. Mary's witnessed several significant events in the years leading up to the birth of the nation. During the American Revolutionary War, members of the Continental Congress attended services here. The first public religious commemoration of the Declaration of Independence took place here in 1779, on the third anniversary of its adoption. Following the British surrender at Yorktown in 1781, the church held a Thanksgiving service, with the flags of the conquered army laid on the altar steps. In 1810, Old St. Mary's was enlarged to its present size and became the first Catholic cathedral of the new diocese of Philadelphia. Its graveyard, dating to 1759, contains the tombs of Commodore John Barry, "Father of the American Navy," and the first to capture a British ship during the

Detail from Old St. Mary's Church

Revolutionary War, Thomas Fitzsimons, one of the signers of the Constitution, Mathew Carey, 18th-century American publisher and bookseller, and Michael Bouvier, the great-great-grandfather of first lady Jacqueline Kennedy Onassis.

Roses in full bloom in Society Hill's Rose Garden

Rose Garden and Magnolia Garden **❾**

Locust St between 4th & 5th Sts. **Map** 4 D3. 🚇 *Market East Station.* 🚋 *5th St.* 🚌 *42, Philly Phlash.*

These two public gardens, directly across each other on Locust Street, are nestled within shaded and quiet courtyards, characteristic of Society Hill's charm. The Rose Garden stretches through the center of the entire block, all the way up to Walnut Street. It commemorates the signers of both the Declaration of Independence and the US Constitution. The funding to plant roses, which flower during spring and summer, is povided by The Daughters of the American Revolution, an organization whose members are drawn from the direct descendants of those who fought in the Revolutionary War. Inside the garden is a section of a cobblestoned street dating back to 1800.

The Magnolia Garden was established as a tribute to George Washington, who had often expressed an interest in horticulture and, in particular, magnolia trees. Different varieties of magnolias are planted around the restful garden, whose centerpiece is a small fountain.

Italianate façade of Society Hill Synagogue

Interior of Old St. Joseph's Church with its unusual curving balcony

Old St. Joseph's Church ⑩

321 Willings Alley. **Map** 4 D3. **Tel** (215) 923-1733. 🚇 Market East Station. 🚌 5th St. 🚌 42, Philly Phlash. ⏰ 9:30am–4pm Mon–Fri (to 6:30pm Sat), 7:30am–2pm Sun. ✝ noon Mon–Sat, 7:30am & 9:30am Sun. 🚻 www.oldstjoseph.org

Located in a narrow alleyway, Old St. Joseph's was Philadelphia's first Catholic church. Reverend Joseph Greaton, an English Jesuit, founded it in 1733. In 1734, efforts were made to thwart Roman Catholic church services, but these were unsuccessful, with religious freedom for all assured by Penn's 1701 Charter of Privileges.

The old chapel was replaced by a larger building in 1757, and six years later, Old St. Mary's was built a block away to handle the growing number of members. St. Joseph's current structure dates from 1838 and features a grand columned altar and a curved balcony at the sanctuary's front end. On the ceiling is the fresco, *The Exaltation of Saint Joseph into Heaven*, painted by 19th-century Italian artist Filippo Costaggini, whose work can also be seen in the US Capitol in Washington DC.

Polish American Cultural Center Museum ⑪

308 Walnut St. **Map** 4 E3. **Tel** (215) 922-1700. 🚇 Market East Station. 🚌 2nd, 5th Sts. 🚌 42, Philly Phlash. ⏰ May–Dec: 10am–4pm Mon–Sat; Jan–Apr: 10am–4pm Mon–Fri. ⚫ public hols. ⬛ www.polishamericancenter.org

Through portraits and memorabilia from Poland, this small museum's mission is to promote awareness and appreciation of Polish culture and history. It honors Poles who have made significant contributions to history, ranging from figures such as Nicholas Copernicus, the astronomer, and composer Frédéric Chopin, to such modern-day luminaries as the late Pope John Paul II and politician and Nobel Peace Prize winner Lech Walesa. Of particular note are displays on the heroes of the American Revolutionary War, Thaddeus Kosciuszko and General Casimir Pulaski, the namesake of an annual city parade that celebrates Polish heritage (see p34). Also on display is traditional Polish folk art – festive garb, Easter eggs, decorative paper cutouts, and wooden plates.

Portrait of General Pulaski, Polish American Cultural Center Museum

Powel House ⑫

244 S 3rd St. **Map** 4 E4. **Tel** (215) 627-0364. 🚇 Market East Station. 🚌 2nd St. 🚌 42, Philly Phlash. ⏰ noon–5pm Thu–Sat, 1–5pm Sun. 🎫 compulsory. www.philalandmarks.org

This grand Georgian home built in 1765 is an exquisite example of how the colonial elite lived. Samuel Powel, one of the wealthiest men in colonial America, was its second owner, purchasing it in 1769 when he was about to marry Elizabeth Willing. Powel was Philadelphia's last mayor before the Revolutionary War and the first after the nation's birth. He died in 1793, a victim of the city's yellow fever epidemic.

The Powels used their lavish home to entertain the country's most important citizens, including Benjamin Franklin, George Washington, and John Adams, the second president of the US. Original features that remain today include a Pennsylvania Blue Marble fireplace on the first floor, the stairwell of Santo Domingo mahogany, and the cypress front door. Noteworthy furnishings include a small scale from Benjamin Franklin, original china and a sewing cabinet gifted to Mrs. Powel by the Washingtons, Gilbert Stuart portraits, and original silhouettes of Washington cut on cobalt blue paper by Samuel Powel at a social event. Outside the house is a peaceful garden dating back to the late 1700s.

Powel House, an elegant upper-class colonial-era residence

Independence Seaport Museum �013

Olympia exhibit

Located on Penn's Landing waterfront, the mandate of this museum is to preserve US maritime history and traditions with a special focus on Delaware Bay and the Delaware River and its tributaries. Displays combine artifacts and paintings of naval encounters, along with computer games, large-scale ship models, and audiovisuals that include sounds of ship horns and accounts by sailors and shipbuilders. The museum re-creates the Benjamin Franklin Bridge as a three-story replica that spans a carpeted Delaware River. Exhibits include a replica of the bridge of the destroyer USS *Lawrence*, and of steerage compartments in which many immigrants traveled to America. There is an active boatbuilding workshop, and berthed nearby are the World War II submarine *Becuna*, commissioned in 1944, and the *Olympia*, Admiral George Dewey's flagship in the 1898 Spanish-American War.

Waterfront Museum
This expansive facility is the centerpiece of Penn's Landing.

Museum Library

Submarine Becuna

This World War II vessel with torpedo launching tubes was the submarine flagship of the Southwest Pacific Fleet, which was under the command of General Douglas MacArthur.

First Floor

What Floats Your Boat? is an interactive exhibit exploring the science, art, and history of boats.

★ Workshop on the Water
Craftspeople build and restore traditional boats of the 19th century at this workshop dedicated to the skills and traditions of wooden boatbuilding and sailing in the Delaware River Valley and the New Jersey shore.

MUSEUM GUIDE
The first floor houses most of the exhibits, the museum shop, and visitor information. The second floor includes On the Rivers, On the Shores and the Quarterdeck Gallery with the Olympia exhibit. The Olympia and the Becuna are berthed outside the museum.

KEY

■	Workshop on the Water
■	What Floats Your Boat?
■	Home Port Philadelphia
■	Divers of the Deep
■	River Gallery
■	Quarterdeck Gallery
■	On the Rivers, On the Shores
■	Non-exhibition space

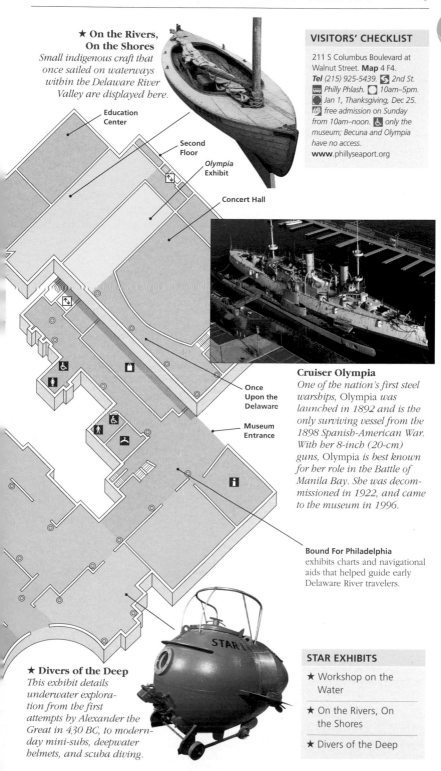

★ On the Rivers, On the Shores
Small indigenous craft that once sailed on waterways within the Delaware River Valley are displayed here.

Education Center

Second Floor

Olympia Exhibit

Concert Hall

Once Upon the Delaware

Museum Entrance

Cruiser Olympia
One of the nation's first steel warships, Olympia *was launched in 1892 and is the only surviving vessel from the 1898 Spanish-American War. With her 8-inch (20-cm) guns,* Olympia *is best known for her role in the Battle of Manila Bay. She was decommissioned in 1922, and came to the museum in 1996.*

Bound For Philadelphia
exhibits charts and navigational aids that helped guide early Delaware River travelers.

★ Divers of the Deep
This exhibit details underwater exploration from the first attempts by Alexander the Great in 430 BC, to modern-day mini-subs, deepwater helmets, and scuba diving.

STAR EXHIBITS
★ Workshop on the Water

★ On the Rivers, On the Shores

★ Divers of the Deep

Small boats at Penn's Landing marina with the Benjamin Franklin Bridge in the background

Penn's Landing ⑭

Western shore of the Delaware River between Market & South Sts.
Map 4 F3. 🚉 *Market East Station.*
Ⓢ *2nd St.* 🚌 *21, Philly Phlash.*

A popular waterfront on the Delaware River, Penn's Landing is where city founder William Penn first stepped onto his new colony in 1682 (*see p18*). Development of the docks seen today began in 1967, before which it was an unappealing stretch of land. Among its attractions are grassy areas with trees, walkways, and an amphitheater where summer festivals and concerts are held. Several vessels are anchored at the docks, including the century-old sailing ship *Moshulu* (*see p148*), the dinner cruise boat *Spirit of Philadelphia*, the 1883 three-masted barkentine *Gazela*, once a Portuguese fishing boat, and the paddle-boat charter *Liberty Belle*.

Nearby is the Independence Seaport Museum (*see pp64–5*) with its two historic vessels – the cruiser *Olympia* and the submarine *Becuna* – docked in a small harbor.

Penn's Landing offers outstanding waterfront views of the Ben Franklin and Walt Whitman Bridges, and the Camden Waterfront, where *Battleship New Jersey* is moored. Along the Chestnut Street overpass is the impressive Irish Memorial, a bronze sculpture with 35 life-sized figures, which honors the

more than one million people who died and the others who fled Ireland during the Great Hunger of the 1840s.

New Market and Head House Square ⑮

2nd St between Pine & Lombard Sts.
Map 4 E4. 🚉 *Market East Station.*
Ⓢ *2nd St.* 🚌 *42, Philly Phlash.*

One of the oldest in America, this covered marketplace was established in 1745. Called the "Shambles," meaning butcher shop, it was the second public marketplace in colonial Philadelphia – the first was located at the eastern end of High Street, now called Market Street. It was where vendors sold fresh produce, meat, poultry, and fish two days a week. The original New Market stretched two blocks from Pine Street to South Street and was flanked

by two firehouses, known as head houses. The two firehouses once contained fire gear and apparatus for three volunteer fire companies.

Today, only the firehouse at 2nd and Pine Streets remains. Built in 1805, it is thought to be the country's oldest existing firehouse. New Market was restored in the 1960s, and has since housed the Crafts and Fine Arts Fair on summer weekends.

South Street and Walkway ⑯

South St. **Map** 4 E5. 🚉 *Market East Station.* Ⓢ *2nd St.* 🚌 *42, Philly Phlash.*

Known as Cedar Street in colonial times, and bordering on what was then New Market and Head House Square, South Street remains a marketplace of sorts today, but with an emphasis on pop culture and counterculture.

South Street, promising revelry and an exciting atmosphere

The South Street Head House District, which stretches from Front to 11th Streets and includes some surrounding streets, is an eclectic melting pot of more than 300 shops, galleries, cafés, restaurants, bars, and more. Eateries range from pizzerias and sushi bars to vegetarian cafés and fine-dining restaurants, while shops sell everything from jewelry and fine art to funk culture items and grunge-style clothing. There are also body piercing and tattoo parlors, jazz clubs, and rocking nightclubs. The strip often overflows with younger revelers on weekend nights that usually extend into the early hours of the morning. A walkway over I-95 (also called the Delaware Expressway) links Columbus Boulevard to South Street, offering fine views of Penn's Landing, and *Battleship New Jersey* across the Delaware River.

Pennsylvania Hospital's surgical amphitheater

Exterior of Pennsylvania Hospital with a statue of William Penn

Pennsylvania Hospital ⑰

800 Spruce St. **Map** 3 C4. *Tel (215) 829-6799.* 🚆 *Market East Station.* 🚇 *8th St.* 🚌 *42, Philly Phlash.* 🕐 *8:30am– 4:30pm Mon–Fri.* 📖 *book in advance.* ♿ **www.pahosp.com**

Founded by surgeon Thomas Bond and Benjamin Franklin in 1751 to care for the "sick-poor and insane," Pennsylvania Hospital was the nation's first public hospital. The old section, the Pine Building, was built in stages. The wings are Georgian, the east wing being completed in 1755, and the west in 1796. The Federal center section was built in 1804 and includes the Great Court, the area open for self-guided tours.

Inside the center section is artist Benjamin West's masterpiece, *Christ Healing the Sick in the Temple*, which was delivered to the hospital in 1817, along with portraits of colonial physicians, including Dr. Philip Syng Physick *(see p61)* and Benjamin Rush, well-known for his contributions to the field of psychiatry. In the Great Court are the hospital's early fire pumper, purchased in 1803, and the musical planetarium clock constructed by colonial clockmaker and astronomer, David Rittenhouse, in 1780.

On the second floor is a medical library founded in 1762 with a collection of more than 13,000 volumes, some dating back to the 15th century. The library, located in this room since 1807, houses the country's most complete collection of medical books published between 1750 and 1850. Under a skylight on the top floor is the nation's first surgical amphitheater, called the "dreaded circular room," which was used for operations from 1804 to 1868. Outside, an 18th-century statue of William Penn stands over a peaceful courtyard overflowing with wisteria shrubbery.

Mikveh Israel Cemetery ⑱

44 N 4th St. **Map** 3 C3. *Tel (215) 922-5446.* 🚆 *Market East Station.* 🚇 *8th St.* 🚌 *42, Philly Phlash.* 🕐 *10am–5pm Tue–Sat, and by appt.* **www.**mikvehisrael.org

This burial ground, the oldest Jewish cemetery in the city and one of the oldest in America, was founded in 1740 after shipper and merchant Nathan Levy sought a place to bury one of his children according to Jewish law. Governor Thomas Penn, son of William Penn, granted land here and deemed it a Jewish graveyard. Levy, whose ship brought the Liberty Bell to Philadelphia, is also buried here. Other notables include members of the prominent Gratz family, including philanthropist Rebecca Gratz, the inspiration for the eponymous character in Sir Walter Scott's novel *Ivanhoe*, fur trader Aaron Levy, founder of Aaronsburg, Pennsylvania, rabbis of the congregation, and financier Haym Salomon. His grave is unmarked, only noted by a memorial at the entrance. Jewish soldiers of the Revolutionary War, the War of 1812, and the Civil War are also buried here. The cemetery was walled in the late 18th century to protect it from people "setting marks and firing shots."

Marker at Mikveh Israel cemetery

CENTER CITY

T his sprawling, modern downtown district is Philadelphia's financial and business center. The city's tallest skyscraper, Comcast Center, is situated west of City Hall, on 17th Street and JFK Boulevard. At the neighborhood's eastern end is Chinatown, flanking the Pennsylvania Convention Center and the adjacent Reading Terminal Market, with Center City's

Classical urn at Rittenhouse Square

major department store nearby. Along Broad Street, the central north-south artery, are 19th-century buildings that house the Masonic Temple and the Pennsylvania Academy of the Fine Arts in the north, while the theater district is located in the south. In Rittenhouse Square, some of the city's most extravagant apartment buildings and hotels tower over town homes that line quiet streets.

SIGHTS AT A GLANCE

Historical Buildings and Districts
Chinatown **7**
City Hall **4**
Liberty Place **15**
Library Company of Philadelphia **8**
Masonic Temple **3**
Reading Terminal Market **5**
Rittenhouse Square **13**

Places of Worship
Arch Street United Methodist Church **2**
St. Mark's Episcopal Church **14**

Museums and Galleries
College of Physicians of Philadelphia/Mütter Museum **16**
Rosenbach Museum and Library **17**

Cultural Venues
Academy of Music **9**
Kimmel Center for the Performing Arts **10**
Pennsylvania Academy of the Fine Arts pp74–5 **1**
Pennsylvania Convention Center **6**
Suzanne Roberts Theatre **11**

0 meters 500
0 yards 500

KEY

Street-by-Street map
See pp70–71

SEPTA regional rail station

SEPTA subway stop

Greyhound bus terminal

Visitor information

GETTING THERE
The Market-Frankford subway has stops east to west along Market Street, while the Broad Street line makes stops north to south. Rail stops include Suburban and Market East Stations. SEPTA buses 21, 38, and 42 run east to west along Market, Chestnut, and Walnut Streets.

◁ **High-rise office buildings dominating the skyline in Center City, Philadelphia's business district**

Street-by-Street: Center City

City Hall sits in the heart of Center City, where Market Street and Broad Street – the city's main east-west and north-south arteries – converge. Most of this area, dominated by 19th- and 20th-century architecture, was developed well after the American Revolutionary War. Diagonally across from City Hall is JFK Plaza, where Philadelphia's famous LOVE statue stands next to a pool and fountain, providing respite from the area's heavy commercial activity. Just a block north of City Hall are the landmark Masonic Temple and the Pennsylvania Academy of the Fine Arts.

The Union League of Philadelphia on Broad Street, is a classic French Renaissance-styled building.

JFK Plaza features Robert Indiana's iconic 1960s LOVE artwork.

★ City Hall
A 37-ft (11-m) high statue of William Penn stands atop this Beaux-Arts building, one of the largest and most elaborate city halls in the country ❹

0 meters	250
0 yards	250

KEY

— — — Suggested route

STAR SIGHTS

★ City Hall

★ Pennsylvania Academy of the Fine Arts

★ Reading Terminal Market

The Wanamaker Building is designed in Beaux-Arts style with a restrained Renaissance exterior. It is built around a soaring central atrium, which houses an enormous pipe organ. The building hosts an annual holiday light-and-sound show and is home to Macy's department store.

★ Pennsylvania Academy of the Fine Arts
America's oldest fine art museum was founded in 1805 by portrait artist Charles Willson Peale. Its collection spans three centuries ❶

LOCATOR MAP
See Street Finder maps 1, 2, & 3

Arch Street United Methodist Church
This Gothic Revival church is the square's oldest structure ❷

Masonic Temple
Home to the Grand Lodge of Freemasons, the building has an ornate Romanesque Revival façade ❸

Pennsylvania Convention Center
Opened in 1993, the center has vast amounts of exhibition and ballroom space ❻

★ Reading Terminal Market
Once the largest arched-roof train shed in the world, this is now one of the best farmers' markets in the country ❺

Pennsylvania Academy of the Fine Arts ❶

See pp74–5.

Arch Street United Methodist Church ❷

55 N Broad St. **Map** 2 F4.
***Tel** (215) 568-6250.* 🚉 *Suburban
Station.* 🅂 *15th St, City Hall.*
🚌 *Philly Phlash.* 🕐 *10am–3pm
Mon–Fri.* 🕍 *8:30am & 11am Sun.*
🛆 **www**.archstreetumc.org

This Gothic Revival marble
building, constructed in two
sections between 1864 and
1870, is the oldest structure
on William Penn's original
Center Square. The church
was founded in 1862 during
the American Civil War and
was still being built when the
funeral procession of President
Abraham Lincoln passed by it
in 1865. It was designed by
Quaker Addison Hutton,
whose architectural plan
called for a radical change
from the unadorned and plain
Quaker meetinghouses of
the 18th and 19th centuries.
  The original construction
included the installation of a
2,322-pipe organ by J.C.B.
Standbridge, Philadelphia's
leading builder of organs.
The organ has been restored
twice, once in 1916 and again
in 1959. The sanctu-
ary's spacious

**Philadelphia's Masonic Temple, an
architectural masterpiece**

atrium is detailed with a
Victorian stenciling pattern
and stained glass. Today, a
diverse congregation from the
Center City neighborhood
worships at the church.

Masonic Temple ❸

1 N Broad St. **Map** 2 F4. ***Tel** (215)
988-1900.* 🚉 *Suburban Station.* 🅂
15th St, City Hall. 🚌 *Philly Phlash.* 🌑
Jul–Aug: Sat; Mon, public hols. 🎫 *by
donation.* 🎟 *11am, 2pm, & 3pm Tue–
Fri, 10am & 11am Sat (call to verify
times).* 🛆 **www**.pagrandlodge.org

An architectural jewel,
dedicated as the Grand Lodge
of Free and Accepted Masons
of Pennsylvania in 1873, this
remarkable building contains a
number of ornate meeting halls
in various styles. Among them,
the Oriental Hall's (1896)
ornamentation and coloring

have been copied from
the Alhambra in Granada,
Spain; the Renaissance
Hall (1908) follows an
Italian Renaissance motif;
while the Egyptian Hall
(1889) takes its inspiration
from the temples of
Luxor, Karnak, and Philae.
High arches, pinnacles,
and spires form the Gothic
Hall, and the cross-and-
crown emblem of Sir
Knights – "Under this sign
you will conquer" – hangs
over a replica of the
Archbishop's throne in
Canterbury Cathedral,
Great Britain.
  The halls were created to
honor the building trades,
and much of the stone and
tilework are imperceptibly
faux finished – an attestation
to the skill of the men who
made them. President George
Washington, a Freemason,
wore his Masonic apron when
he laid the cornerstone of the
US Capitol in Washington DC.
The apron is on display, along
with other Masonic rarities, in
a museum on the first floor.

City Hall ❹

Broad & Market Sts. **Map** 2 F4.
***Tel** (215) 686-2840.* 🚉 *Suburban
Station.* 🅂 *15th St, City Hall.* 🚌 *38,
Philly Phlash.* 🏛 *building and
tower:12:30pm Mon–Fri; tower:
every 15 mins from 9:30am–4:30pm
Mon–Fri.* 🛆 **www**.phila.gov

Built on Penn's original Center
Square, this imposing marble,
granite, and limestone landmark is the largest and perhaps
the nation's most ornate city
hall. The building, which took
30 years to build and was
completed only in 1901, is
designed in French Second
Empire style with a mansard
roof and prominent 548-ft
(167-m) high tower. City Hall
was the nation's tallest occupied building until 1909. The
tower, with four clocks and a
37-ft (11-m) tall statue of
Penn, was the city's highest
structure until 1987 *(see box)*.
  Philadelphia artist Alexander
Milne Calder designed the
60,000-lb (27-ton) statue, the
largest atop any building in the
world. Calder also designed

NO BUILDING HIGHER THAN
WILLIAM PENN'S STATUE

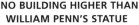
**City Hall with
Penn's statue**

While skyscrapers sprang up across America
in the 20th century, Philadelphia maintained
a "gentlemen's agreement" not to build higher
than 491 ft (150 m) – lower than the statue
of William Penn on top of City Hall. Honoring
Penn and the city's colonial heritage, the rule
remained unchallenged for almost a century.
But lured by new revenues and jobs, the
agreement was broken in 1987 when the
61-story One Liberty Place *(see p79)* was
built. It towers over City Hall by more than
400 ft (122 m). Within just five years, several
other skyscrapers followed, including Two
Liberty Place, the Mellon Bank Center, the
Bell Atlantic Tower, and, in 2008, the city's
tallest skyscraper, the Comcast Center.

Ornamental, French-influenced City Hall in the midst of Center City

more than 250 other sculptures in the building, including the tower's bronze eagles, and the bronze figures of Native American and Swedish settlers.

Inside, rooms not to be missed include the Mayor's Reception Room, and Conversation Hall, which has statues of George Washington and other colonial notables. The Council Caucus Room, with its grand domed ceiling, features carvings representing the four seasons as stages in life. An elevator takes visitors to a deck on the tower that offers spectacular city views while on the ground level the visitor center stocks maps and brochures of the city's sights.

Jars of preserves at Reading Terminal Market

Reading Terminal Market ❺

12th & Arch Sts. **Map** 3 B2. **Tel** (215) 922-2317. 🚇 Market East Station. 🚊 11th St. 🚌 Philly Phlash. ◯ 8am–6pm Mon–Sat. ◯ Jan 1, Easter, Jul 4, Memorial Day, Thanksgiving, Dec 25. ♿ www.readingterminalmarket.org

Once a Center City railroad terminal and marketplace, Reading Terminal Market is now considered by many to be one of the finest farmers' markets in the United States. It was created in 1892, after two farmers' markets on this site were leveled to make space for a new train terminal. These markets were relocated beneath the new train shed. So modern was the market for its time that people came from as far off as the New Jersey shore to buy fresh Lancaster County produce. Over the years, the market gradually declined and was nearly destroyed in the 1970s. New construction routed the city's trains around the old terminal in the 1980s, and the market was refurbished in the early 1990s.

Today, the revitalized Reading Terminal Market houses more than 80 vendors, six days a week, selling an extensive variety of free-range meats and poultry, seafood, country vegetables, pastas, Amish specialties, and baked goods, as well as other items such as books, clothing, flowers, jewelry, crafts, unique spices, and hard-to-find specialties and ethnic foods. Several stands also offer freshly-made and prepared foods, ranging from Pennsylvania Dutch country breakfasts to soul food.

Pennsylvania Convention Center ❻

Between Market & Race Sts and 11th & 13th Sts. **Map** 2 F3. **Tel** (215) 418-4700, (800) 428-9000. 🚇 Market East Station. 🚊 11th St, 13th Sts. 🚌 38, Philly Phlash. ◯ for conventions; Head House entrance open 24 hrs. **www**.paconvention.com

A sprawling 1.3 million sq ft (120,774 sq m) of meeting and exhibition space make up one of the country's most unique convention centers. The building's Grand Hall, above Reading Terminal Market, was once a bustling train terminal for the Reading Railroad. Reopened in 1994, the hall retains its Victorian features, including the majestic ceiling that had once made it the largest single-arch train shed in the world. Much of the original wooden roof and milk-glass windows remain, now casting natural light onto the terrazzo marble floor with simulated tracks where commuter trains once awaited passengers. Visitors can enter through the old railroad headhouse (now part of the Philadelphia Downtown Marriott) on the Market Street side for a peek at the Grand Hall, where a storyboard outlines its history.

Scattered throughout the multiblock complex is a vast and diverse collection of contemporary paintings, sculptures, and other artworks rendered by nearly 60 artists. Expansion of the center, now underway, will be complete by 2011.

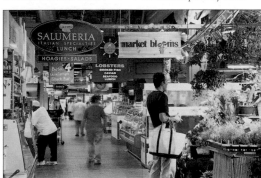

Colorful wares for sale at Reading Terminal Market

Pennsylvania Academy of the Fine Arts ❶

Founded by Colonial painter and scientist Charles Willson Peale and sculptor William Rush in 1805, the Pennsylvania Academy of the Fine Arts is America's oldest art museum and fine arts school. Its galleries display works by some of the world's best-known artists. One of them, the classical stylist Benjamin West (1738–1820), a Quaker from Pennsylvania, helped organize the British Royal Academy in 1768. Former student, the Impressionist Mary Cassatt (1844–1926), and modern abstractionist Richard Diebenkorn (1922–93), among others, share its wall space. The academy's main building, the distinctive National Historic Landmark Building, with its ornate arched foyer, is considered one of the finest examples of Victorian architecture in America. The contemporary Samuel M.V. Hamilton Building, with new galleries, opened in 2005 as part of the museum's 200th anniversary celebrations.

National Historic Landmark Building
Designed by Furness and Hewitt, the academy's main building opened during the nation's centennial in 1876.

Sculpture Exhibit
The 1873 marble sculpture Semiramis, by William Wetmore Story (1819–95).

National Historic Landmark Building Second Floor

★ The Cello Player
One of America's greatest painters, Thomas Eakins (1844–1916) taught at the academy from 1876 to 1886. This penetrating study of a cello player, capturing a moment of intense concentration, was painted in 1896. Rudolph Hennig, a leading musician, posed for it.

STAR EXHIBITS

★ The Cello Player

★ The Fox Hunt

★ Pantocrator

★ The Fox Hunt
This 1893 masterpiece by naturalist painter Winslow Homer (1836–1910), considered one of the greatest American artists of the 19th century, is among the academy's vast collections.

★ **Pantocrator**
Vincent Desiderio's monumental 2002 oil-on-linen triptych, 8 ft (2.5 m) tall and 17 ft (5 m) wide, is part of the Academy's collection of contemporary American art.

Samuel M.V. Hamilton Building Second Floor

Upper Foyer Gallery

Samuel M.V. Hamilton Building
Adjacent to the National Historic Landmark Building, this contemporary structure doubles the academy's available display space, and includes a sculpture study center and a painting deck.

Samuel M.V. Hamilton Building First Floor

Entrance

Lower Foyer Gallery

Fisher Brooks Gallery
This expansive new space on the first floor of the Samuel M.V. Hamilton Building houses the academy's post-World War II collection and also holds special exhibitions.

KEY

▢	Fisher Brooks Gallery
▢	Foyer Galleries
▢	18th–20th century art
▢	Exhibit gallery
▢	Tuttleman Sculpture Gallery
▢	Non-exhibition space

GALLERY GUIDE
The grand staircase of the National Historic Landmark Building leads up to the gallery level on the second floor, which displays sculpture and 18th- to early 20th-century works, including portraiture, Impressionist, American genre, and landscape paintings. The Samuel M.V. Hamilton building houses contemporary artworks after 1945.

Ornamental gate at the entrance of Chinatown

Chinatown ❼

North of Arch St at 10th St.
Map 3 C1. 🚇 Market East Station.
🚋 11th St. 🚌 Philly Phlash.

This thriving neighborhood
spans an area nearly four
blocks wide and includes
more than 50 restaurants, a
score of grocery stores, and
other shops and boutiques.
Chinatown's origin dates to
the 1860s when the first
Chinese laundry was
established in the area.
It witnessed rapid
growth after World
War II owing to
a huge influx
of immigrants.
   In the US's third
largest Chinatown,
behind those found
in New York and
San Francisco,
visitors can still find
a variety of Asian fare including
traditional eel, squid, and
duck dishes, and Chinese
cultural gifts such as porcelain,
wooden Buddhas, and
dragons. The colorful
Friendship Gate, with ornate
dragons and Chinese art, is
at 10th and Arch Streets and
should not be missed.

**Dragon figurine in a
Chinatown shop**

Library Company
of Philadelphia ❽

1314 Locust St. **Map** 2 F5. **Tel** (215)
546-3181. 🚇 Suburban Station.
🚋 Walnut-Locust. 🚌 21, 42.
🕐 9am–4:45pm Mon–Fri.
www.librarycompany.org

Founded as the country's
first lending library by
Benjamin Franklin in 1731,
the Library Company has the

distinction of being America's
oldest cultural institution.
Its extraordinary collection
of historic books, papers
and images – numbering
more than 500,000 books,
75,000 graphics, and 160,000
manuscripts – documents
American culture from the
colonial era through the
19th century.
   The **Historical Society of
Pennsylvania**, housed on
the same block as Library
Company, was founded
in 1824 and is one of
the oldest historical
societies in the US.
Its stockpile has
600,000 printed
items, and more
than 19 million
manuscripts and
graphic materials
from the 17th
century onwards.

🏛 **Historical Society
of Pennsylvania**
1300 Locust St. **Tel** (215) 732-6200.
🕐 12:30pm–5:30pm Tue & Thu, 12:
30pm–8:30pm Wed; 10am–5:30pm
Fri (last admittance at 4:45pm).
🔴 public hols. 🚻 **www**.hsp.org

Academy of
Music ❾

S Broad & Locust Sts (240 N Broad
St). **Map** 2 E5. **Tel** (215) 893-1999.
🚇 Suburban Station. 🚋 Walnut-
Locust. 🚌 21, 42, Philly Phlash.
🕐 for performances. 🎟 tickets sold
one hour before a performance &
until half-an-hour after the last performance begins; tickets also sold at
the Kimmel Center 10am–6pm.
🎫 by appt; call (215) 893-1935.
www.academyofmusic.org

Often referred to as the
"Grand Old Lady of Locust
Street," the Academy of Music
was the city's foremost
performing arts venue before
the construction of the
Kimmel Center in 2001. It
remains the country's oldest
grand opera house still in use.
   Designed by Philadelphia
architects Napoleon LeBrun
and Gustavus Runge, the
Victorian Italianate style structure took two years to build
and was completed in 1857.
The interior's horseshoe design
offers greater visibility to the
audience seated on both sides
of the balconies, which are
supported by Corinthian-style
columns. While the façade has
ornate gas lamps, the main hall
still has a glittering, 5,000-lb
(2,300-kg) crystal chandelier,
originally with 240 gas burners,
and later wired for electricity.
Statues representing Poetry
and Music crown the prosceni-
um arch. The former home
of the Philadelphia Orchestra
– which now performs in the
Kimmel Center – the academy
today hosts the Pennsylvania
Ballet and the Opera Company
of Philadelphia *(see p164)*.

The Academy of Music, home to Philadelphia's opera and ballet

The Kimmel Center's glittering, modern façade

Kimmel Center for the Performing Arts **⓿**

260 S Broad St. **Map** 2 E5. **Tel** *(215) 790-5800, (215) 893-1999 (tickets).* 🚇 *Suburban Station.* 🚊 *Walnut-Locust.* 🚌 *21, 42, Philly Phlash.* ⏲ *10am–6pm; later for performances.* **www.**kimmelcenter.org

The centerpiece of the city's performing arts district, this modern complex opened in December 2001 after three years of construction. Covering an entire city block, it includes two separate venues in a spacious atrium under a 150-ft (46-m) high barrel-vaulted glass roof. The center is named after philanthropist and businessman Sidney Kimmel, who made the single-largest private donation towards the complex.

The cello-shaped Verizon Hall, whose acoustics have been designed specifically for the Philadelphia Orchestra, seats more than 2,500 people. The Perelman Theater seats 650 people and has a rotating stage for chamber music, dance, and theatrical shows.

Other highlights include an expansive lobby with a stage for separate functions, an education center for performing arts classes, and a smaller studio and theater. The center's glass-enclosed roof garden offers great city views and an upper balcony houses a high-end restaurant.

Suzanne Roberts Theatre **⓫**

480 S Broad St. **Map** 3 A4. **Tel** *(215) 982-0420.* 🚇 *Suburban Station.* 🚊 *Lombard-South.* 🚌 *21, 42.* 📷 ♿

The newest addition to the Avenue of the Arts is the Suzanne Roberts Theatre, now home to the Philadelphia Theater Company. The theater is named after former actress, playwright, director, and philanthropist Suzanne Roberts, who, for more than 40 years, has devoted her energy and talent to the city's theater community. It is housed in a modern facility that boasts a dramatic glass façade, two-story lobby, mezzanine level reception areas, and a 365-seat auditorium with state-of-the-art lighting and sound facilities. A second, 100-seat flexible stage is used for more intimate performances.

Rosenbach Museum and Library **⓬**

2008-2010 DeLancy Pl at 20th St. **Map** 2 D5. **Tel** *(215) 732-1600.* 🚇 *Suburban Station.* 🚊 *Lombard-South.* 🚌 *21, 42.* ⏲ *10am–5pm Tue–Sun, 10am–8pm Wed.* ⬤ *Mon, public hols.* 📷 ♿ **www.**rosenbach.org

Home to Dr. Rosenbach, one of America's most prominent rare book and manuscript dealers, this 1865 townhouse with a museum and research library sits on a quiet and shaded Rittenhouse street. Dr. Abraham Simon Wolf Rosenbach (1876–1952) and his brother Philip ran their company during the first half of the 20th century, combining great scholarship and business acumen. Apart from books, they also bought and sold 18th- and 19th-century artifacts such as silver, furniture, sculptures, drawings, and paintings.

So precious were many of their acquisitions that the brothers kept them for their own collection, which includes 30,000 books and 300,000 manuscripts and letters. Some of these are displayed today, including manuscript pages of James Joyce's *Ulysses*, over 100 personal letters of George Washington, and three of President Lincoln's speeches in manuscript form. In the house are the brothers' original possessions, including Chippendale furniture, gold-plated silver, and portraits by American artist Thomas Sully.

The museum's Maurice Sendak Gallery showcases the works and personal collections of the celebrated children's author, Maurice Sendak, best known for his 1963 classic *Where the Wild Things Are.*

Suzanne Roberts Theatre, Avenue of the Arts

Shaded walkway and benches at Rittenhouse Square, a favored outdoor park

Rittenhouse Square ⑬

Walnut St between 18th & 19th Sts. Map 2 D5. 🚇 *Suburban Station.* Ⓢ *Walnut-Locust.* 🚌 *21, 38, 42, Philly Phlash.*

One of Center City's most popular outdoor parks, on any sunny day shaded Rittenhouse Square teems with local residents and downtown workers relaxing under the trees. One of the five public areas planned by Penn in his 1682 city grid, it was originally known as Southwest Square. It was renamed in 1825 in honor of David Rittenhouse (1732–96), first director of the US Mint, astronomer, clockmaker, and a descendant of Wilhelm Rittenhouse, who established the nation's first papermill near Wissahickon Creek in 1690.

In the mid-19th century, the first house was built opposite the square, which soon became a prominent public garden. The park was given its present-day appearance in 1913 by French American Beaux-Arts architect Paul Cret, who also designed the Barnes Foundation's gallery building and the Valley Forge memorial arch. Benches line the many walkways that crisscross the park and lead to the small fountain and reflecting pool at its center. Flowers add color in spring and summer. Since its development, the square has been a desirable address in town. Extravagant

high-rise apartments and hotels, and upscale restaurants and cafés surround the square, reminiscent of a New York City park scene.

St. Mark's Episcopal Church ⑭

1625 Locust St. **Map** 2 E5. *Tel* (215) 735-1416. 🚇 *Suburban Station.* Ⓢ *Walnut-Locust.* 🚌 *21, 38, 42, Philly Phlash.* 🕐 *daily.* 📷 *only by appointment.* **www.** saintmarksphiladelphia.org

Founded by a local group of Anglican worshippers in 1847, St. Mark's Episcopal Church is one of the nation's

Downtown Philadelphia's Gothic-style St. Mark's Episcopal Church

best examples of Gothic Revival architecture. The parishioners raised $30,000 and hired John Notman, a prominent Philadelphia architect, to design and build a new church in the medieval designs of the 14th- and 15th-century high Gothic period. The church was opened in 1849 during the early development of the Rittenhouse Square neighborhood.

Inside is a baptistry made of inlaid Italian marble and colorful panels in a spacious sanctuary that is reminiscent of an old English church.

Not to be missed is the adjoining structure, the spectacular Lady Chapel. It was donated by Rodman Wanamaker as a memorial to his wife, who died in 1900 and is buried in the chapel's crypt. The 12 panels in this chapel have ornate carvings depicting scenes from the life of St. Mary the Virgin. Its ornate and beautiful marble altar, encased in silver, was made by Carl Krall and is one of only three such in the world. Still used for mass, it is the most well-known of St. Mark's ecclesiastical treasures. In 1937, the organ, considered to be one of the best examples of tonal construction in the nation, was dedicated to the church.

Liberty Place ⑮

16th & Chestnut Sts. **Map** 2 E4.
Tel (215) 851-9055. 🚇 Suburban
Station. 🚇 Broad St. 🚌 Philly
Phlash. ⬤ 9:30am–7pm Mon–Sat;
noon–6pm Sun. ♿ **www**.
shopsatliberty.com

This gleaming, modern office
complex, which sprawls over
a vast area, is built on two
city blocks and anchors what
were once Philadelphia's
tallest skyscrapers. Designed
by Murphy and Jahn
Associates and built by
Rouse & Associates, the two
steel towers with sapphire
blue glass sheathing have a
postmodern architectural
aesthetic. Built in 1987 with
pyramidal tops and spires
reminiscent of New
York's Chrysler
Building, the 945-ft
(288-m) One Liberty
Place tower was
the first structure

to break the 86-year gentlemen's agreement not to build
higher than the height of the
hat on Penn's statue on top of
City Hall *(see p72)*. The 61-story
One Liberty Place stretches
almost 100 ft (30 m) higher
than its 58-story companion
tower Two Liberty Place,
which houses the national
headquarters of the CIGNA
Insurance Corporation and
new luxury condominiums.

The mall complex that
connects the two towers
houses 60 stores that cover
the needs and fashion
desires of Center City office
workers, running the gamut
from specialty food shops,
chic boutiques, and trendy
shoe shops to more practical outlets such as book-
stores and newsstands.
A food court has sev-
eral vendors dishing
up everything from
spicy Cajun dishes
to smoothies.

**Joseph Hyrtl's collection of 139
skulls, Mütter Museum**

College of Physicians of Philadelphia/Mütter Museum ⑯

19 S 22nd St. **Map** 1 C4. *Tel* (215)
563-3737. 🚇 Suburban Station.
🚇 15th St. 🚌 21, 38, 42. ⬤
10am–5pm. ⬤ Jan 1, Thanksgiving,
Dec 25. 📷 **www**.collphyphil.org

A non-profit society founded
in 1787 "to advance the
Science of Medicine," the
College of Physicians provides
health education to medical
professionals and the public
through the C. Everett Koop
Community Health Information
Center, the Historical Medical
Library, the Free Library, and
computerized databases.

For a visitor, the college's
most fascinating resource is
the Mütter Museum. Named
after professor of surgery
Thomas Mütter, who in 1858
donated 2,000 specimens he
had used for teaching, the
museum displays some curious
and unusual items, including
preserved specimens and wax
anatomical and pathological
models. These were used for
educational purposes in the
mid-1800s, when diseases and
genetic defects were identifi-
able only by their physical
manifestations.

Key exhibits include the
skull collection of Joseph
Hyrtl, a 19th-century Viennese
anatomist, a plaster cast of the
original Siamese twins, Chang
and Eng, who died in 1874,
and When the President is the
Patient, one of the only major
exhibitions in the US to focus
on the long, hidden history
of illness in the White House.
Memorabilia from famous
scientists and physicians is
also on display.

One Liberty Place, with Two Liberty Place behind it

LOGAN SQUARE AND THE MUSEUM DISTRICT

Logan Square, with its multispouted Swann Memorial Fountain, is the centerpiece of the Museum District, bordered by the Schuylkill River on the west and the Cathedral of Saints Peter and Paul on the east. Benjamin Franklin Parkway, often referred to as the Champs Elysées of Philadelphia, is the route

Detail, Philadelphia Museum of Art façade

for most parades held in the city. It runs through the heart of this area and is flanked by buildings with imposing architectural styles, reminiscent of the ancient temples of Greece and Rome. To the north is the Eastern State Penitentiary, a fortress-turned-museum that once housed some of the country's most notorious criminals.

SIGHTS AT A GLANCE

Historical Buildings and Districts
Eakins Oval **8**
Fairmount Waterworks **10**
Free Library of Philadelphia **1**
Logan Square **2**
Thomas Eakins House **12**
Boathouse Row *(see p96)*

Museums and Galleries
Academy of Natural Sciences **4**
Eastern State Penitentiary **11**
The Franklin **6**
Moore College of Art and Design **5**
Philadelphia Museum of Art pp88–91 **9**
Rodin Museum **7**

Places of Worship
Cathedral of Saints Peter and Paul **3**

GETTING THERE
The easiest way to get around the Museum District is by Philly Phlash buses, which run along Benjamin Franklin Parkway to the Philadelphia Museum of Art (Mar–Nov only). SEPTA bus 38 runs from Center City along Market Street, and then up 22nd Street to Logan Square before turning onto the Parkway toward the Museum of Art. Regional trains stop at either Suburban or 30th Street Stations, while the subway stops are at 15th and 30th Streets. Once at Logan Square, most of the sights are within walking distance.

KEY
- Street-by-Street map See pp82–3
- SEPTA regional rail station
- SEPTA subway stop

0 meters 500
0 yards 500

◁ **The Swann Memorial Fountain located in the center of Logan Square**

Street-by-Street: Logan Square and the Museum District

Central to this neighborhood is the Benjamin Franklin Parkway – a grand boulevard lined with trees and grassy areas stretching from Center City to the Philadelphia Museum of Art. Statues and sculptures around the museum add to the area's European flair. Imposing structures housing many of the city's other key museums were built along the Parkway and around Logan Square in the 19th and early 20th centuries. Today, they hold some of the world's most prized antiquities, artworks, and natural history collections. Among them are the Rodin Museum and The Franklin, named after the scientist and statesman.

Fairmount Water Works

Stately temple-like façades that once housed the nation's first municipal water-pumping station now serve as home to a diving, entertainment, and interpretive education center, as well as a fine dining restaurant **❿**

Statue of George Washington

Eakins Oval

Ornate fountains and statues are the centerpieces of this traffic circle named after the 19th-century Philadelphia artist Thomas Eakins **❽**

★ The Franklin

A massive statue of Benjamin Franklin sits in the atrium of this popular interactive science museum. The museum highlights Franklin's discoveries in technology and also houses a planetarium and IMAX theater **❻**

WINTER STR

RACE STR

STAR SIGHTS

★ The Franklin

★ Philadelphia Museum of Art

★ Rodin Museum

Academy of Natural Sciences

The oldest continuously operating natural history museum in the Western hemisphere has dinosaur fossils among its more than 17 million specimens **❹**

Moore College of Art and Design ❺

LOCATOR MAP
See Street Finder maps 1 & 2

★ **Philadelphia Museum of Art**
*The country's third largest fine art museum, sited in a
landmark building, has vast collections of paintings,
sculptures, and decorative arts showcasing more
than 2,000 years of human creativity* **9**

★ **Rodin Museum**
*This small museum has more
than 130 sculptures by Auguste
Rodin, including* The Thinker.
*This is the largest collection
of his works outside France* **7**

**Free Library of
Philadelphia**
*Founded in the 1890s,
the library moved to
its permanent home
in the Beaux-Arts
Main Library
Building in 1927* **1**

Logan Square
*Originally called Northwest Square, Logan Square
is now centered by the Swann Memorial Fountain
and flanked by the Free Library of Philadelphia* **2**

**Cathedral of
Saints Peter
and Paul** **3**

KEY

- - - Suggested route

| 0 meters | 200 |
| 0 yards | 200 |

The Beaux-Arts façade of the Free Library of Philadelphia

Free Library of Philadelphia ❶

1901 Vine St. **Map** 2 E2. **Tel** (215) 686-5322. 🚇 Suburban Station. Ⓢ Race-Vine. 🚌 38, Philly Phlash. ◯ 9am–9pm Mon–Wed, 9am–5pm Thu–Sat, 1–5pm Sun. ◑ Sun in summer, public hols. 📷 tour starts at Rare Book Dept at 11am. ♿ www.library.phila.gov

Opened in 1894, the Free Library first occupied three rooms in City Hall. It relocated a few times before moving into its current Beaux-Arts building in 1927. Constructed of Indiana limestone with a granite base, it is similar in appearance to the adjacent building that houses the Philadelphia city courts.

Today, the library has up to 1.75 million volumes, and its key collections include maps, children's books, social sciences and history books, and the largest public library chamber music collection in the eastern US. The Rare Book Department is also one of the nation's largest, with holdings that span 4,000 years and include Sumerian cuneiform tablets, medieval manuscripts, incunabula, early American children's books, and letters and manuscripts from authors such as Charles Dickens and Edgar Allen Poe (see p94).

Logan Square ❷

19th St at Benjamin Franklin Parkway. **Map** 2 D3. 🚇 Suburban Station. Ⓢ Race-Vine. 🚌 38, Philly Phlash.

Part of William Penn's original grid plan, Logan Square (then known as Northwest Square) was initially used as a burial ground, then for pastureland, and later for public executions. It was renamed Logan Square in 1825 in honor of Penn's secretary James Logan. The square changed dramatically during the 1920s, when the construction of the Benjamin Franklin Parkway turned it into a traffic circle, which is why it is today also referred to as Logan Circle.

At its center is the Swann Memorial Fountain, designed by Alexander Stirling Calder in 1924. It features three statues, meant to represent the city's three main waterways – the Delaware and Schuylkill Rivers, and Wissahickon Creek. Today, the shaded area is a popular spot along the Parkway, with children often dipping in the fountain on hot summer days.

Cathedral of Saints Peter and Paul ❸

18th St at Benjamin Franklin Parkway. **Map** 2 E3. **Tel** (215) 561-1313. 🚇 Suburban Station. Ⓢ Race-Vine. 🚌 38, Philly Phlash. ◯ 7am–4:30pm Mon–Sat. 🕇 daily. ♿

This grand cathedral, with a copper dome more than 60 ft (18 m) high, is a prominent city landmark. Designed by architects John Notman and Napoleon LeBrun, the Victorian Italianate basilica with Renaissance features was modeled after the Lombard Church of St. Charles in Rome and completed in 1864. The sanctuary is shaped in the form of a cross with a white marble floor, a marble altar, and six marble columns rising more than 40 ft (12 m) along the curved walls of the apse. Stained-glass windows add a touch of beauty to the main altar area, side altars, and the eight side chapels. Of particular note is the organ, one of the largest in the city, with 75 pipes and four manuals. The cathedral is now the seat of Philadelphia's Roman Catholic Archdiocese.

Window of the Cathedral of Saints Peter and Paul

Logan Square's Swann Memorial Fountain, named after the founder of the Philadelphia Fountain Society

Exhibit at Dinosaur Hall, Academy of Natural Sciences

Academy of Natural Sciences ④

1900 Benjamin Franklin Parkway. **Map** 2 D3. *Tel* (215) 299-1000. 🚉 Suburban Station. 🚇 Race-Vine. 🚌 38, Philly Phlash. ⏰ 10am–4:30pm Mon–Fri, 10am–5pm Sat & Sun. ⊙ Jan 1, Thanksgiving, Dec 25. ♿ **www**.acnatsci.org

A natural history museum and research library, the Academy of Natural Sciences was founded in 1812 by seven naturalists, who pooled their fossils and specimens to foster education and research about the earth's diverse species. Its collection has since swelled to 17 million specimens. Exhibits are housed on four levels, and include mounted animals, ranging from birds native to Pennsylvania to bison from North America and cape buffalo from Africa. Dinosaur Hall is a favorite with children, while the live butterfly exhibit is a reproduction of a tropical rainforest. The animals in the Live Animal Center cannot survive in the wild and are thus used for teaching purposes.

Moore College of Art and Design ⑤

20th St & Benjamin Franklin Parkway. **Map** 2 D3. *Tel* (215) 965-4000. 🚉 Suburban Station. 🚇 Race-Vine. 🚌 38, Philly Phlash. ⏰ galleries: 10am–5pm Tue–Fri, noon–4pm Sat & Sun. ⊙ Mon, public hols. ♿ **www**.moore.edu

This school is the first and only women's art and design college in the United States, and one of only two in the world. It was founded as the Philadelphia School of Design for Women in 1848 by Sarah Worthington Peter (1800–77). Her aim was to educate women for careers that would lead to financial independence, and in accordance with that, the original curriculum provided training in the new fields spawned by the Industrial Revolution, such as textile design. Today, the college offers nine undergraduate degree programs in fine arts and design.

Two galleries of the college are open to the public. Rotating exhibitions highlight the works of alumnae and women artists. The Paley Gallery exhibits national and international artists, while the Levy Gallery showcases local artists and provides a center for exploration and experimentation for emerging and established talent. Past shows have featured work by Mary Cassatt, Karen Kilimnik, and Jacqueline Matisse.

The Franklin ⑥

222 N 20th St at Benjamin Franklin Pkwy. **Map** 2 D3. *Tel* (215) 448-1200. 🚉 Suburban Station. 🚇 Race-Vine. 🚌 38, Philly Phlash. ⏰ museum: 9:30am–5pm daily; IMAX theater: 10am–6pm daily (to 9pm Fri & Sat). ♿ **www**.fi.edu

The oldest science and technology institution in continuous use in North America, this museum was founded in 1824. Named after Benjamin Franklin *(see p53)*, the institute's first location was in the building that now houses the Atwater Kent Museum *(see p50)*. The current building opened in the 1930s and contains a spacious rotunda with a 21-ft (6-m) tall marble statue of Franklin. Exhibits highlight Franklin's accomplishments in medicine, astronomy, meteorology, and optics. Among the museum's attractions are Electricity Hall,

Franklin's statue in the museum atrium

which showcases his discovery of electricity, the Giant Walk-Through Heart with interactive devices *(see p26)*, and the Train Factory, which has an original Baldwin steam locomotive.

The KidScience exhibit, for five to eight year olds, is designed to teach basic principles of science. Children are taken on a fictional journey across *The Island of the Elements* where they learn about Light, Water, Earth, and Air.

Moore College of Art and Design, housed in a modern building

Rodin's sculpture, The Thinker, outside the Rodin Museum

Rodin Museum **7**

22nd St at Benjamin Franklin Parkway. **Map** 2 D2. **Tel** (215) 568–6026. Suburban Station. Spring Garden. 38, Philly Phlash. 10am–5pm Tue–Sun. Mon, public hols. www.rodinmuseum.org

French sculptor Auguste Rodin's (1840–1917) most famous artwork, *The Thinker*, sits outside the columned façade that leads into the courtyard of this small, temple-like museum. With nearly 130 sculptures, it contains the largest collection of Rodin's work outside of Paris.

Opened in 1929, the Rodin Museum's entrance showcases the impressive, 20-ft (6-m) high *The Gates of Hell*, which Rodin worked on for 37 years until his death. Inside is the life-sized sculpture of six heroes of the Middle Ages, known as *The Burghers of Calais*. Other notable works include *Apotheosis of Victor Hugo*, a sculpture of the French writer, and different sculptures of kissing lovers, known as *Eternal Springtime*.

Eakins Oval **8**

Benjamin Franklin Parkway. **Map** 1 C1. 30th St Station. Spring Garden. 38, Philly Phlash.

Named after prominent Philadelphia artist Thomas Eakins, this oval was part of the Benjamin Franklin Parkway project in the 1920s. Located opposite the entrance to the Philadelphia Museum of Art, Eakins Oval has a prominent equestrian statue of President George Washington at its center. The center also features a fountain, which has figurines of wild animals surrounding four statues that symbolize four of the country's major rivers – the Delaware, Mississippi, Hudson, and Potomac. Two smaller fountains flank the large central one – the Ericsson fountain, named for the engineer who designed the USS *Monitor*, a Union naval vessel of the Civil War, and another named after Fairmount Park Commission chairman Eli Kirk Price (1797–1884) who led efforts to build the parkway. Today, the oval is at the center of a traffic circle and includes a shaded green area with park benches and a parking lot.

Washington's statue at Eakins Oval

Philadelphia Museum of Art **9**

See p91.

Fairmount Water Works **10**

640 Waterworks Dr. **Map** 1 B1. **Tel** (215) 685-4908. 30th St Station. Spring Garden. 38, Philly Phlash. 10am–5pm Tue–Sat, 1–5pm Sun. Mon, public hols. www. fairmountwaterworks.org

Situated on the elevated banks of the Schuylkill River, these impressive Greek Revival buildings were constructed between 1812 and 1871 to supply drinking water to Philadelphia – the first American city to take on providing water as a municipal responsibility. When it opened in 1822, its cutting-edge technology of the time – huge water wheels, turbines, and pumps – and the beauty of the site made it a destination point for engineers and visitors from the US and Europe.

Water pumping ended in 1909, and today the restored buildings house old pumping apparatus and an interpretive center with a number of fascinating interactive exhibits. Water In Our World challenges children and adults alike to learn about water resources. Other exhibits include a real-time fish migration up the river, a virtual helicopter tour of the watershed, and a computer simulation of historic technology.

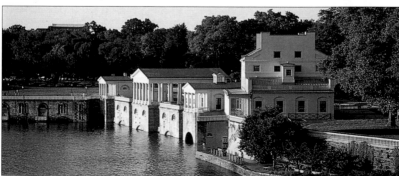

Fairmount Waterworks, now a National Historic Landmark

Reconstruction of Al Capone's cell at the Eastern State Penitentiary

Eastern State Penitentiary ⑪

22nd St at Fairmount Ave. **Map** 2 D1.
Tel (215) 236-3300. ⑤ Spring
Garden ⑲ 38, Philly Phlash ◯
10am–5pm daily. ● Jan 1, Easter,
Thanksgiving, Dec 24, 25, & 31. ⑫
children under 7 not allowed. ⑫ ⑤
www.easternstate.org

Named the "House" by inmates
and guards, the Eastern State
Penitentiary was a revolutionary concept in criminal justice.
Prior to its opening, convicts
lived in despicable conditions
and suffered brutal physical
punishments. The Philadelphia
Quakers proposed an alternative in the form of a facility
where a lawbreaker could be
alone to ponder and seek
penitence for his misdeeds.
This led to the opening of the
penitentiary in 1829. During
incarceration, with sentences
seldom less than five years,
prisoners were hooded when
outside their cells to prevent
interaction with others.

The prison, with its fortress-
like Gothic Revival façade, had
a single entrance and 30-ft
(9-m) high boundary walls.
Inside, seven cellblocks extended from a central rotunda,
and each solitary cell had a
skylight and private outdoor
exercise yard. In the early 20th
century, the isolation form of
imprisonment was abandoned,
and more cellblocks were
added. Over the years, the
prison has housed several
infamous personalities including the gangster Al Capone.

Officially closed in 1971, it
is now a National Historic
Landmark and museum.

Today, the structure's chipped
walls and aging cellblocks
host changing exhibitions from
its collections of old artifacts
and photographs. The prison
also conducts tours, with
audio excerpts from former
guards and inmates, and each
Halloween it hosts *Terror
Behind the Walls*, a "haunted"
house experience *(see p34)*.

Thomas Eakins House ⑫

1729 Mt Vernon St. **Map** 2 E1.
Tel (215) 685-0750. ⑤ Spring
Garden ⑲ 38, Philly Phlash.
◯ hours vary.

This brick row house was
home to the artist Thomas
Eakins for most of his life,
with the exception of the time
he spent abroad: first in Paris
studying art at the École des
Beaux-Arts from 1866 to 1868,
and then traveling to Spain in
1869 before returning home
in 1870. One of the country's
most renowned Realist
painters of the late 19th and
early 20th centuries, Eakins'
works often reflected life in
Philadelphia through portraits
and family paintings, as well
as through his popular city
and nature paintings, which
included sculling and sailing
scenes on the Schuylkill and
Delaware Rivers.

Today, the Thomas Eakins
House is home to the city's
Mural Arts Program. Changing
exhibitions in the building's
galleries highlight artwork
created by Philadelphia's
youth participating in the
Mural Arts and other
outreach programs.

**Façade of Thomas Eakins House,
home to the Mural Arts Program**

MURAL ARTS PROGRAM

Philadelphia has America's largest collection of colorful,
outdoor and indoor murals, which are emblazoned on
walls all across the city. Through artists' visions and the
sheer manpower of inspired local youth, more than 2,700
variegated and vibrant murals have been painted since the
Mural Art Program's inception in 1984 as an anti-graffiti
initiative. With extensive
preparation including
scaffolding and under-
coating, a typical mural
is completed within two
months and can cost as
much as $20,000. The
murals often highlight
famous community
leaders, role models,
artistic cityscapes, and
themes of culture,
history, diversity, and
anti-drug messages.

**Murals on city walls, a tradition in the
city of Philadelphia**

Philadelphia Museum of Art ❾

Beaux-Arts roof detail

Founded in the country's centennial year of 1876, Philadelphia's most prominent museum attracts major exhibitions to supplement its superlative permanent collections. More than 200 galleries showcase works of art spanning more than 2,000 years, with some Asian exhibits dating from the third millennium BC. The medieval cloister court-yard and fountain on the second floor is very popular, as are the French Gothic chapel and the pillared temple from Madurai, India. In addition to outstanding collections of Old Master, Impressionist, and Postimpressionist paintings, Pennsylvania Dutch and American decorative arts are also featured with American art. Scattered throughout the museum are computerized stations with information on the exhibits.

Mask of Shiva
A 9th-century copper alloy artifact from India.

★ Sunflowers
Impressionist painter Vincent van Gogh (1853–90) is perhaps best known for his series of sunflower paintings. This version was painted just 18 months before his death.

East Entrance

Great Stair Hall

Van Pelt Auditorium

West Entrance

Ground Floor

KEY

- ☐ Julien Levy Gallery
- ☐ Modern and Contemporary Art
- ☐ European Paintings, Sculpture, Decorative Arts, and Architecture
- ☐ Special Exhibition Galleries
- ☐ American Art
- ☐ Arms and Armor
- ☐ Dutch Ceramics
- ☐ Middle East and Asian Art
- ☐ Non-exhibition space

MUSEUM GUIDE
The ground floor contains prints, drawings, photographs, and ceramics, while the first floor displays Impressionist, Post-impressionist, American, and contemporary art. The second floor has collections of European and Asian art. First Floor refers to the floor above ground level.

The West Entrance of the Philadelphia Museum of Art

VISITORS' CHECKLIST

26th St & Benjamin Franklin
Parkway. **Map** 1 C1. **Tel** (215)
763-8100. 🚊 30th St Station.
🚌 Philly Phlash. 🕙 10am–5pm
Tue–Sun; 10am–8:45pm Fri. 🕙
Mon, public hols. 💷 pay what
you wish on Sundays. 🚻 🛍 🍴
🚹 🅿 **www**.philamuseum.org

★ Ming Dynasty Ceramics
*Delicate ceramics, fine hardwood
furniture, and other objects of the Ming
Dynasty are on display in the Chinese
gallery, including this 15th-century
bowl, the* Three Friends.

Second Floor

**Cloister with Elements from the Abbey
of Saint-Genis-des-Fontaines**
*Surrounded by marble arcaded walkways
and centered by a rare fountain, this cloister is based on medieval French design.*

First Floor

American Art
*The museum has an
impressive collection
of American art that
includes* Noah's Ark,
*painted in 1946
by Edward Hicks
(1780–1849).*

**★ Thomas Eakins
Collection**
Portrait of Dr. Samuel D.
Gross (The Gross Clinic)
(1875) by Thomas Eakins,
acclaimed Philadelphian
artist, forms a part of the
museum's collection of
works by local artists.

STAR EXHIBITS

★ Sunflowers

★ Ming Dynasty Ceramics

★ Thomas Eakins
Collection

Exploring the Philadelphia Museum of Art

Stained glass roundel, France (1246–48)

The Museum of Art is home to over 300,000 objects from Europe, Asia, and the Americas, spanning more than 4,000 years. Its key exhibits include European paintings, from medieval and Renaissance to Impressionist and Postimpressionist pieces. Modern art collections feature works by Pablo Picasso and Henri Matisse, while Asian art includes furniture and ceramics. American art sections contain extensive works by Philadelphia artists Thomas Eakins and Charles Willson Peale, and the museum's collections of prints, drawings, and photographs feature works by 19th- and 20th-century US and European artists. It also has one of the oldest and largest collections of costumes and textiles in America.

Ruben's *Prometheus Bound* (1618) is a centerpiece painting combining historical and mythological subjects.

The first floor has some excellent Impressionist and Postimpressionist paintings by artists such as Renoir, Monet, Cezanne, Pissarro, and van Gogh. Works include Renoir's *Great Bathers* (1884–87), van Gogh's *Sunflowers* (1889), Cezanne's *Large Bathers* (1906), and Monet's *Poplars* (1891), to name just a few.

Fra Angelico's *Dormition of the Virgin* (c. 1427)

AMERICAN ART

One of the finest public holdings of American art, this collection is sourced from the Philadelphia area. Decorative arts, paintings, and sculptures include 18th- and 19th-century silver, ceramics, and porcelain, as well as Pennsylvania German items including toys, textiles, furniture, and illuminated folk art called fraktur. Impressive bookcases, desks, chairs, and chests made in colonial Philadelphia, along with other decorative arts, demonstrate the cultural links

EUROPEAN PAINTINGS, SCULPTURE, DECORATIVE ARTS, AND ARCHITECTURE

Most of the museum's second floor is devoted to European art from 1500 to 1850. In addition, it has rooms with sculpture, furniture, descriptive interiors, and original façades that highlight periods of European history from 1100 to 1800. The Portal from the Abbey Church of Saint-Laurent dates to 1125. Its imposing stone arched walls were once the main entrance to the Augustinian abbey church of Saint-Laurent in France.

The Cloister with Elements from the Abbey of Saint-Genis-des-Fontaines is based on one in a late 13th-century abbey in Roussillon in

Jester Vase (1894) by Marc-Louis-Emmanuel Solon

southwestern France. Other decorative arts include ceramic vases, stained and painted glass, stone sculptures, and metal and wooden objects ranging from candelabra to mahogany furniture and glass goblets. Key European paintings include masterpieces by Fra Angelico, Sandro Botticelli, Rogier van der Weyden, Peter Paul Rubens, and Nicolas Poussin, as well as classic European views and land- and cityscapes by 18th-century verdute artists Canaletto, his nephew and pupil Bernardo Bellotto, and Francesco Guardi. Renaissance portraits and religious paintings include Jan van Eyck's *Saint Francis of Assisi Receiving the Stigmata* (1428–30), Botticelli's *Stories of Saint Mary Magdalene* (1484–91) and Joos van Cleve's *King Francis I* (1525).

The Staircase Group (1795) by Charles Willson Peale

Japanese ceremonial teahouse, surrounded by a bamboo garden

MODERN AND CONTEMPORARY ART

The museum's modern art collection began with acquisitions of works by Pablo Picasso and Constantin Brancusi in the 1930s. Today key holdings include Picasso's *Self-Portrait* (1906) and *Three Musicians* (1921), encompassing his decade-long study of Synthetic Cubism. Works by Marcel Duchamp include the *The Large Glass* (1915–23), applied on two planes of glass with lead foil, fuse wire and dust, and the 1912 *Nude Descending a Staircase (No. 2)*, a mechanical portrayal of a subject with Cubist qualities. Salvador Dali's surrealistic 1936 painting *Soft Construction of Boiled Beans (Premonition of Civil War)* and Henri's Matisse's *Mademoiselle Yvonne Landsberg* (1914) also form part of the collection.

COSTUMES AND TEXTILES

Acquisitions from the 1876 Centennial Exposition initiated the museum's costume and textile collections. The first textiles showcased designs and techniques used in India, Europe, and the Middle East. The collections grew in the early 20th century with the addition of 18th- and 19th-century French textiles, and today number over 20,000 objects, including fashionable Philadelphia apparel, Pennsylvania Dutch quilts, weaving pattern books, and colonial-era clothing. One of the most famous costumes is the wedding dress worn by Princess Grace of Monaco, a Philadelphian. Other items include African-American quilts, 20th-century hats, 19th-century needlework, church embroideries and vestments, and three-century old Japanese Noh robes, dating from between 1615 and 1867.

between European and early American lifestyles and designs. Key paintings include Charles Willson Peale's *Rachel Weeping* (1772) and *The Staircase Group* (1795), in which he painted his sons ascending a staircase. Thomas Eakins' works, including *The Gross Clinic* (1875), are the most significant part of the museum's collection of 19th-century paintings. Sculptures and sketches by the renowned artist are also housed here. Other paintings include Winslow Homer's *A Huntsman and Dogs* (1891) and Edward Hick's *Noah's Ark* (1846).

MIDDLE EAST AND ASIAN ART

Within the second-floor galleries of Asian Art are exquisite carpets, delicate jade carvings, porcelains, ink paintings, and sculptures forming part of the museum's collections of Southeast Asian, Korean, Chinese, Japanese, Persian, and Turkish art.

The Chinese Ming Dynasty (1368–1644) is represented by a room brought from China, the imposing Reception Hall from a Nobleman's Palace, and ceramics and hardwood

Bird Tree, Pennsylvania (1800–1830)

furniture. Works by Japanese artists from the 12th to 20th centuries include exquisitely painted scrolls and screens, decorative arts, and fine modern designs. A centerpiece exhibit is *Evanescent Joys*, a ceremonial teahouse acquired from Japan in 1928. Korean art includes ceramics, lacquer, and sculpture, of which an example is a rare 15th-century cast-iron tiger. Also on display are outstanding Persian and Turkish carpets, including the showpiece 16th- to 17th-century *Tree Carpet*. The carpets were gifted by collectors Joseph L. Williams and John D. McIlhenny in the 1940s and 50s. The museum's Indian art collection includes *Nandi, the Sacred Bull of Shiva*, a 13th-century schist carving from Mysore, and the impressive Pillared Hall from Madurai. Reconstructed from the ruins of three temples, its granite pillars are the only examples of stone architecture from India in an American museum.

Gala Ensemble, Italy (late 19th to early 20th century)

FARTHER AFIELD

The growth of neighborhoods away from the city's historic center only began in the 19th century, with the exception of areas such as Germantown and Fairmount Park, which were distinct areas in colonial times. These are home to some of the city's most renowned sights, including the University of Pennsylvania just beyond the Schuylkill River.

Statue at Fairmount Park

Fairmount Park runs along the river, leading to the chic neighborhoods of Manayunk and Chestnut Hill, while just over the city's western border is the Barnes Foundation with a huge collection of Impressionist paintings. Sights to the south include the Italian Market and the Mummers Museum, while to the east are the varied attractions of the Camden Waterfront.

SIGHTS AT A GLANCE

Historical Buildings and Districts
Boathouse Row and Kelly Drive ⑥
Camden Waterfront ⑮
Chestnut Hill ❸
Edgar Allen Poe National Historic Site ❶
Fort Mifflin ⑭
Germantown ❷
Italian Market ⑪
Main Street Manayunk ❹
University of Pennsylvania and University City ❽
Walt Whitman House ⑯

Parks, Gardens, and Zoos
Fairmount Park ❺
Philadelphia Zoo ❼

Museums and Galleries
Barnes Foundation pp98–9 ❿
Mario Lanza Institute and Museum ⑫
Mummers Museum ⑬
University of Pennsylvania Museum of Archaeology and Anthropology ❾

KEY

▨	Main sightseeing area
▢	Urban area
✈	Airport
═	Highway
▬	Major road
═	Minor road
—	Railway
- -	State border

0 kilometers   4
0 miles   4

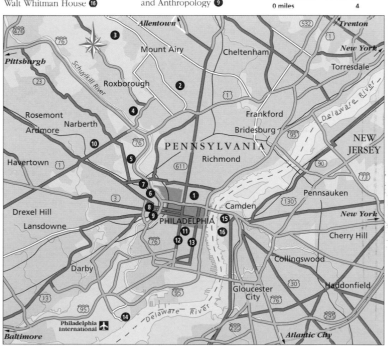

◁ **Turrets punctuate the roofline of Rosemont College, near Philadelphia**

Three-story brick house rented by Edgar Allan Poe in the mid-1840s

Edgar Allan Poe National Historic Site ❶

532 N 7th St. *Tel (215) 597-8780.* ⑤ *Spring Garden.* 🚌 *47.* ⭘ *9am–5pm Wed–Sun.* ⬤ *Mon, Tue; Jan 1, Veterans Day, Thanksgiving, Dec 25.* ♿ *limited.* **www**.nps.gov/edal

The great American writer Edgar Allan Poe (1809–49) lived in Philadelphia for six years from 1838 to 1844 in several residences. This three-story brick house was his rented residence for about a year between 1843 and 1844, and his only home that remains today in the city.

The inside, with original walls and creaking wooden floors, is empty as there are no accurate descriptions of what the house looked like during Poe's time, and none of his personal belongings have survived. The visitor area, though, has exhibits and a video highlighting his life and a room decorated as depicted in his essay "The Philosophy of Furniture."

In fact, Poe's years in the city were some of his most productive with the publishing of "The Murders in the Rue Morgue," "The Gold Bug," and "The Tell-Tale Heart." Poe fans seem to think that the house's basement may have inspired him to write "The Black Cat." One wall has brick columns similar to where, in the story, the murderer had entombed his victim. The raven statue outside is a tribute to one of his poems, "The Raven."

Germantown ❷

Centered by Germantown Avenue at Chelten Ave. 🚉 *R8 SEPTA regional rail to Chelten Ave station.* 🚌 *23.*

A few miles northwest of Philadelphia, this neighborhood was first inhabited in 1683 by German settlers wooed by Penn's promise of religious freedom. Its most prominent historical period was during and after the American Revolutionary War. It was the site of the Battle of Germantown in 1777, when British troops withstood an attack by the Continental Army, forcing the Americans to retreat to Valley Forge for the winter *(see pp20–21).* In 1793, President Washington and his family moved here to escape the yellow fever epidemic in the city. Several historic homes in this now urban neighborhood have been preserved and are open to visitors *(see pp106–107).*

At its center is Market Square, a busy marketplace in colonial times and now a small park dominated by a Civil War memorial. Flanking the square are the Deshler-Morris House, and the **Germantown Historical**

Society Museum and Library. The center's museum features rotating exhibitions chosen from among its 20,000 historical artifacts and documents, some of which date back to the 1600s. To its north is the **Awbury Arboretum**, a landscaped area with gardens, ponds, and a Victorian estate originally owned by a Quaker family. The neighborhood is best visited during the day as it is less safe at night.

🏛 **Germantown Historical Society Museum and Library**
5501 Germantown Ave. *Tel (215) 844–1683.* ⭘ *9am–1pm Tue, 1–5pm Thu & Sun.* 🎞 ♿

🌿 **Awbury Arboretum**
1, Awbury Rd. *Tel (215) 849-2855.* ⭘ *dawn–dusk.* ♿ *limited access.*

Chestnut Hill ❸

Centered by Germantown Ave at Chestnut Hill Ave. 🚉 *R7 or R8 SEPTA regional rail to Chestnut Hill stations.*

What began as a settlement of farmhouses and taverns in the mid-1700s is now one of Philadelphia's most upscale neighborhoods. Located on the city's northern border, Chestnut Hill is an urban village bisected by Germantown Avenue. Its shaded, cobblestoned streets

Boutiques and cafés line the sidewalks of Chestnut Hill

are lined with boutiques, fine-food restaurants, cafés, and galleries. Within its hilly terrain are the Wissahickon Gorge greenbelt and the **Morris Arboretum of the University of Pennsylvania**, an immense area that includes thousands of rare plants and "trees-of-record," greenhouses, ponds, and meadows. Some of the other attractions in this area include the **Woodmere Art Museum**, which is housed in a Victorian mansion and features a collection of more than 300 paintings and sculptures. The **Chestnut Hill Historical Society** has a collection of more than 15,000 items that date from the 1680s to the present, including artifacts, documents, and photographs.

🌸 **Morris Arboretum of the University of Pennsylvania**
100 Northwestern Ave. **Tel** (215) 247-5777. ⏰ 10am–4pm daily (to 8:30pm Thu), 10am–5pm Sat & Sun. 🅿️ ♿ www.morrisarboretum.org

🏛 **Woodmere Art Museum**
9201 Germantown Ave. **Tel** (215) 247-0476. ⏰ 10am–5pm Tue–Sat, 1–5pm Sun. 🅿️ ♿
www.woodmereartmuseum.org

🏛 **Chestnut Hill Historical Society**
8708 Germantown Ave. **Tel** (215) 247-0417. ⏰ 9:30am–2:30pm Tue & Fri; appointments preferred. www.chhist.org

Main Street Manayunk ❹

Main St, Manayunk. **Tel** (215) 482-9565. 🚆 R6 SEPTA regional rail Manayunk Station. 🚌 61.
www.manayunk.com

Once an industrial urban village, this neighborhood has been revitalized in recent years with trendy stores, galleries, restaurants, and cafés lining the fashionable Main Street. In 1824, it changed its name to Manayunk, from the Lenape word *manaiung*, which means, "Where we go to drink." With the completion

of the Manayunk Canal, the early 19th-century town grew into a thriving mill and industrial town. Today, the old mills are home to upscale apartments and an eclectic mix of storefronted shops. Main Street comes to life especially on weekends when sidewalk café tables fill up. The pedestrian walk along the canal is also popular with walkers and bikers.

Fairmount Park ❺

On both sides of the Schuylkill River & along Wissahickon Creek. **Tel** (215) 683-0200. 🚆 30th St Station. 🚇 Spring Garden. www. phila.gov/fairpark

Stretching along the shores of the Schuylkill River and Wissahickon Creek, Fairmount Park forms part of an extensive greenbelt. Its grassy fields and dense wooded areas are dotted with statues and criss-crossed by miles of hiking paths. The most popular path runs parallel to Kelly and Martin Luther King Jr. drives and stretches 8 miles (13 km) along both sides of the river.

West of the Schuylkill River is the Mann Center for the Performing Arts, an outdoor amphitheater and summer home of the Philadelphia Orchestra *(see p164)*. The nearby **Horticulture Center** has elongated ponds with fountains, while the **Shofuso Japanese House and Garden** is a 17th-century-style Shoin

Rose at Morris Arboretum

Outdoor seating at a café along Manayunk's Main Street

mansion that has a koi pond. The grand Memorial Hall, a centerpiece during the country's centennial celebration, was formerly the city's art museum. It was dedicated by President Ulysses S. Grant, but is now home to the **Please Touch Museum** for children *(see p170)*.

Other key attractions include 18th- and early 19th-century mansions that were once the rural homes of prominent colonial families *(see pp108–109)*.

🌸 **Horticulture Center**
Tel (215) 685-0096. ⏰ Apr–Oct: 8am–6pm; Nov–Mar: 8am–5pm. 🅿️ ♿

🌸 **Shofuso Japanese House and Garden**
Tel (215) 878-5097. ⏰ May–Oct: 10am–4pm Tue–Fri, 11am–5pm Sat & Sun. ⏰ Nov–Apr. 🅿️

🏛 **Please Touch Museum**
Tel (215) 963-0667. ⏰ 9am–5pm Mon–Sat, 11am–5pm Sun.

Geese at Fairmount Park, part of Philadelphia's greenbelt

Boathouse Row and Kelly Drive ❻

West of Philadelphia Museum of Art along Kelly Drive. 🚇 *30th St Station.* 🚌 *38, Philly Phlash.*

This row of quaint stone and brick boathouses is home to what's affectionately known as the "Schuylkill Navy," namely rowing and sculling clubs patronized by area universities and high schools. Situated on the river's eastern shore, some feature Victorian Gothic architecture and date back to the 19th century. These boathouses, and others farther upstream, host the country's largest intercollegiate sculling contest in May, the annual Dad Vail Regatta *(see p33)*.

At one end of Boathouse Row is the Azalea Garden, where people picnic under the magnolias and large oaks. At the other end is the small 1887 lighthouse that once flashed beacons to warn barges and steamboats of the nearby Fairmount dam. Also close to Boathouse Row is Icelandic sculptor Einar Jonsson's 1918 statue of Thorfinn Karlsefni, the Viking explorer who is said to have landed in America a millennium ago. At night, strings of lights illuminating the boathouses reflect

Hummingbird at Philadelphia Zoo

off the river, creating an idyllic scene often highlighted on calendars and postcards. A popular path along Kelly Drive offers miles of walking and biking on both sides of the Schuylkill River.

Philadelphia Zoo ❼

3400 Girard Ave. *Tel (215) 243-1100.* 🚇 *30th St Station.* 🚋 *34th St.* 🚌 *38.* ⬜ *Mar–Nov: 9:30am–5pm daily (to 4pm Dec–Feb).* ⬤ *Jan 1, Jun 9, Thanksgiving, Dec 24, 25, & 31.* 📷 **www**.philadelphiazoo.org

Boasting Victorian gardens and historic architecture, including the country home of William Penn's grandson John, the Philadelphia Zoo was opened in 1874. The zoo is the country's oldest and is home to more than 1,600 exotic animals from around the world.

The zoo houses several rare species such as naked mole rats and blue-eyed lemurs. A walk-through giant otter habitat shows these animals at their playful best. The magnificent big cats – clouded leopards, lions, tigers (including rare white tigers), and jaguars – are kept in near-natural habitats or inside the Bank of America Big Cat Falls exhibit, in weather-protected cages that provide a close-up view. Other features are an open birdhouse with uncaged finches and hummingbirds; the Reptile and Amphibian House with venomous king cobras, giant tortoises, and alligators basking in a tropical paradise; and a large reserve area for ten primate species. The Zooballoon takes passengers aloft for panoramic views of the city.

University of Pennsylvania and University City ❽

Main Campus between Chestnut St & University Ave and between 32nd & 40th Sts. *Tel (215) 898-5000.* 🚆 *SEPTA R1 regional rail to University City Station.* 🚋 *34th St.* 🚌 *42.* **www**.upenn.edu

This highly regarded Ivy League school has the honor of being America's first university. Founded by Benjamin Franklin in 1749, the University of Pennsylvania started classes two years later, beginning what would become the nation's first liberal arts curriculum. The university is also home to the country's first medical school, student union, and the oldest collegiate football field still in use.

Today, with more than 20,000 students enrolled in undergraduate, graduate, and professional school programs, it is often listed among America's top ten universities. Its vast urban campus features

Scenic Boathouse Row along Schuylkill River, to the west of the city

Shaded walkway at the University of Pennsylvania campus

19th-century buildings along grassy areas and shaded walkways, including Locust Walk, its main pedestrian street. Among the notable sculptures on the campus are two of Franklin along Locust Walk, one with the statesman and inventor seated on a bench.

The Penn campus is located within University City, a revitalized neighborhood with one of the Philadelphia area's most ethnically diverse and educated populations. It has Victorian-era homes, as well as its own brand of galleries, cafés, and restaurants. Within University City are also several medical centers and other institutions of higher learning, including Drexel University.

University of Pennsylvania Museum of Archaeology and Anthropology **⑨**

3260 South St. **Tel** (215) 898-4000.
R1 University City Station. 34th St. 42. 10am–4:30pm Tue–Sat, 1pm–5pm Sun. Mon, public hols; Sun in summer.
www.museum.upenn.edu

A world-class museum with nearly one million artifacts, this institute is one of Philadelphia's best. The museum's expansive 90 ft (27 m) rotunda is the largest unsupported masonry dome in the

country, and features Chinese art and early Buddhist sculpture. The museum's collections have been gathered since its founding in 1887 through more than 400 archaeological digs and research expeditions around the world. More than 30 galleries spread over three floors house impressive remnants of civilizations past and present spanning the earth, including a 13-ton (28,650-lb)

A flower stall at the Italian Market

granite Sphinx of Rameses II from 1200 BC, well-preserved mummies, an Etruscan warrior helmet from the 7th century BC, Zapotec figures from Mexico, African stringed musical instruments, and an Alaskan Umiak, a whaling boat with a skin hull.

Barnes Foundation **⑩**

See pp98–9.

Italian Market **⑪**

Along 9th St between Christian & Wharton Sts. Ellsworth-Federal. 47. 9am–5pm Tue–Sat, 9am–2pm Sun. Mon.
www.phillyitalianmarket.com

Under numerous awnings and corrugated tin roofs, this open-air market is the largest and oldest of its kind in the country. The market dates to the late 1800s, when Italian immigrants sold meats and produce, and Jewish merchants sold clothing. Although still predominantly Italian, today it comprises a mix of nationalities. The sights and sounds of the market, however, have not changed much from a century ago. Several stalls offer fresh fruit and vegetables, butcher shops sell prime cuts, poultry and game meats, while seafood vendors stack fish and shellfish on ice. Other specialties include pastas, cheeses from all over the world, spices, coffees, and teas. Bakeries have pastries ranging from ricotta-filled Italian cannolies to Amish baked goods. Food stands and cafés dish up Philly cheesesteaks, pizzas, and traditional Italian dishes.

Mural depicting the Italian Market and Frank Rizzo, 1970s city mayor

Barnes Foundation ❿

Floral motif, chest detail

Established in 1922 by pharmaceutical magnate Albert C. Barnes, the Barnes Foundation has one of the world's best displays of Impressionist, French Modern, and Postimpressionist paintings. There are more than 800 works on view, including 181 by Renoir, 69 by Cezanne, and 60 by Matisse, among others by artists such as Modigliani, Rousseau, van Gogh, and Picasso. Other exhibits include ancient Egyptian and Greek art, American furniture, and African sculpture. Grouped into 96 ensembles, the collection is displayed without labels and with little regard for chronology, so as to highlight artistic affinities between diverse works. The collection is in keeping with the foundation's aim of promoting "the advancement of education and the appreciation of the fine arts." The foundation is currently in the process of being relocated to Center City.

★ **The Postman**
Painted by Vincent van Gogh in 1889 in Arles, France, this is a portrait of postman Joseph Roulin. The foundation is home to seven van Gogh paintings.

Gardanne
Paul Cezanne, the renowned French artist, painted this scenic landscape of the town of Gardanne in the mid-1880s. 69 of Cezanne's works are at the Barnes, helping to make it one of the finest Impressionist collections in the world.

★ **Arboretum and Gardens**
The arboretum has a diverse collection of plants and trees, and highlights one of the foundation's aims of imparting education in horticulture.

Lower Level

Entrance

STAR EXHIBITS

★ The Postman

★ Arboretum and Gardens

★ After the Concert

★ Card Players and Girl

GALLERY GUIDE
Artworks can be viewed on both the first and second floors. Galleries in the foundation display various paintings and sculptures that highlight different themes. An artist's oeuvre is not necessarily displayed together.

KEY

	Second floor
	First floor
	Non-exhibition space

Gallery Building Exterior
Designed by Paul Philippe Cret, the French Renaissance structure is adorned with Doric columns and African motifs.

VISITORS' CHECKLIST

300 N Lath's Lane, Merion.
Tel (610) 667-0290. ☐ R5,
Merion. ☐ 44 from Center City.
☐ by reservation only. Sep–Jun:
9:30am–5pm Fri–Sun; Jul–Aug:
9:30am–5pm Wed–Sun.
☐ public hols. ☐ ☐ ☐
www.barnesfoundation.org

Second Floor

22
21
23
19

★ **After the Concert**
The Barnes has over 180 works by Pierre-Auguste Renoir, including this one, which was completed by the famous French Impressionist in 1877. Renoir painted several thousand works over 60 years, even while suffering from severe arthritis toward the end of his life.

1
14
13
8
9
11
12
10

First Floor

★ **Card Players and Girl**
Often referred to as the father of modern art, Paul Cezanne complet-ed this painting in 1892. Cezanne's compositions and use of color greatly influenced 20th-century art.

Main Gallery
The expansive Main Gallery has a vaulted ceiling and large windows. Extending across the top of one wall is The Dance, *a mural by Matisse that was specially commissioned for this room by Dr. Barnes in 1931.*

Art Deco façade of the three-story Mummers Museum

Fort Mifflin 🔞

Fort Mifflin Rd near Island Ave.
Tel *(215) 685-4192.* ☐ *Apr–Nov:
10am– 4pm Wed–Sun.* ● *public hols;
Dec–Mar, except for groups.* 🏷 ▮
www.phila.gov/recreation/
historical/fortmifflin.html

Historic Fort Mifflin, with
its well-preserved ramparts
and soldiers' barracks, is the
only fort in Philadelphia.
Surrounded by a moat, it overlooks the Delaware River and
offers views of the city skyline, and the nearby and often
noisy Philadelphia airport.

Construction of the fort
began with the installation of
sturdy granite walls in 1771 –
the only remnants of the original fortification that remain
today – and the fort stayed in
continuous use through the
Korean War in the 1950s.

Its most prominent moment,
however, was during the
Revolutionary War, when the
Continental troops in the fort
managed to keep the British
at bay for seven weeks. This
allowed Washington to retreat
to Valley Forge and thwarted
British efforts to open a supply route along the Delaware
River for their troops who
had occupied Philadelphia.

Today, Fort Mifflin is a
popular tourist attraction. The

Mario Lanza Institute and Museum 🔞

Columbus House, 712 Montrose St.
Tel *(215) 238-9691.* Ⓢ *Ellsworth-
Federal.* 🚌 *47.* ☐ *11am–3pm
Mon–Sat.* ● *Sun, public hols.* ▯
www.mario-lanza-institute.org

Housed in a former church
rectory, the museum honors
the world-famous
Philadelphia tenor and
movie star, Mario Lanza
(1921–59). Lanza devel-
oped an interest in
opera as he grew
up, and his talents
were soon recog-
nized. His career
flourished and
best-selling recordings and
starring roles in several major
films of the 1940s and 50s,
such as *The Great Caruso* and
For The First Time.

Through posters, newspaper
clippings, photographs, and
other memorabilia, the
museum charts his life from
his childhood to his death in
Rome from a heart attack.
The museum shop sells many
of the 460 songs Lanza
recorded during his career.

Mario Lanza bust

Mummers Museum 🔞

1100 S 2nd St. *Tel* *(215) 336-3050.*
🚌 *57.* ☐ *May–Sep: 9:30am–
4:30pm Tue–Sat (to 9:30pm Thu);
Oct–Apr: 9:30am–4:30pm Tue–Sun.*
● *Mon, public hols.* 🏷 ▯ ♿
www.mummersmuseum.com

Opened during the nation's
bicentennial year in 1976, this
museum celebrates the city's
Mummers tradition and annual
New Year's day Mummers
Parade where thousands of
people strut to the rhythm of
marching string bands *(see
p35).* Permanent and rotating
exhibits showcase the
museum's extensive collections. Artifacts from past
parades are displayed to
re-create the excitement of
the event. They include floats,
musical instruments used in
the parades, and plumed and
sequinned costumes. The
museum's library has newspaper clippings dating
back to the late 19th
century, and more than
6,000 manuscripts,
photographs, works
of art, and films that
highlight the parade's
history and tradition.
Every Thursday, May
through September,
string bands perform a free
concert at 8pm so that visitors
can sample the sounds of
the Mummers celebrations.

<table>
<tr><td>

MUMMERS TRADITION AND PARADE

The Mummers tradition dates to the late 1600s when Swedish
and Finnish settlers ushered in the new year with parades and
masquerades. Others soon joined in with the use of costumes
based on Greek celebrations of King Momus, the Italian feast
of Saturnalia, and the British Mummery Play. Today, the parade
features the Comics, who dress as hobos and clowns and poke
fun at the crowds; the Fancies, who dazzle in sequined out-
fits; the Fancy Brigades, who perform themed shows; and
the String Bands, where marchers play banjos, drums, and
glockenspiels. The parade is followed by the Fancy Brigade
Finale, held at the Pennsylvania Convention Center.

Costumed revelers at a Mummers Day parade

</td></tr>
</table>

Moat around 18th-century Fort Mifflin, Philadelphia's lone fort

former soldiers' barracks now house a small museum and a diorama depicting the siege of 1777. On display are tools, cannonballs, and grapeshot from the Revolutionary War, as well as items from the American Civil War, when Confederate soldiers, Union deserters, and civilian lawbreakers were imprisoned at the fort.

Camden Waterfront ⓯

Delaware River, NJ. **Tel** (856) 757-9400. 🚇 PATCO Speedline from Center City, New Jersey Transit. 🚌 New Jersey Transit. ⛴ RiverLink Ferry. **www**.camdenwaterfront.com

This spacious riverfront area in New Jersey, opposite Penn's Landing, has gardens, a music venue, an IMAX theater, and other attractions.

One of the biggest draws is the **Adventure Aquarium**. It boasts one of the largest tanks in North America and contains over 5,000 aquatic creatures, such as sharks, seals, and stingrays. Nearby is the floating museum, the **Battleship New Jersey**, with nine 16-inch (40-cm) guns in three triple turrets. One of the nation's most decorated battleships, she served in World War II and the Vietnam War. The waterfront is also home to the 6,500-seat Campbell's Field, which hosts the Camden Riversharks baseball team. For concerts, head to the 7,000-seat Susquehanna Bank Center, an indoor and outdoor amphitheater. The **RiverLink Ferry** (see p186) offers a scenic ride across the Delaware River to and from Penn's Landing.

Adventure Aquarium, exterior detail

🐟 **Adventure Aquarium**
1, Aquarium Dr. **Tel** (856) 365-3300. ⏰ 9:30am–5pm daily. 📷 🖥 🅿
www.adventure aquarium.com

🏛 **Battleship New Jersey**
Clinton Street at the waterfront. **Tel** (856) 966-1652. ⏰ Jan–Feb: 10am–3pm Fri–Mon; Mar–Apr & Sep 2–Dec: 9:30am–3pm daily; May–Sep 1: 9:30am–5pm daily. 📷 **www**.battleshipnewjersey.org

⛴ **RiverLink Ferry**
Tel (215) 925-5465. ⏰ Memorial Day–Labor Day: 9am–6pm daily; May & Sep: Sat & Sun. 📷 ♿ **www**.riverlinkferry.org

---

Walt Whitman House ⓰

328 Mickle Boulevard, NJ. **Tel** (856) 964-5383. 🚇 PATCO Speedline, New Jersey Transit. 🚌 New Jersey Transit. ⛴ RiverLink Ferry. ⏰ only by appointment: 10am–noon, 1–4pm Wed–Sat.

This modest, two-story house two blocks east of the Camden Waterfront is the only home that renowned American poet Walt Whitman (1819–92) ever owned. He lived here from 1884 until his death in 1892.

Whitman left Washington DC after suffering a stroke in 1873, coming to live with his brother George in Camden. When his brother decided to move to a nearby rural area, Whitman opted to stay on here. With the surprising success of the 1882 edition of his most famous volume of poetry, *Leaves of Grass*, he was able to purchase this home. Already a prominent poet, Whitman was visited in Camden by famous writers, such as Charles Dickens and Oscar Wilde, and Philadelphia artist and friend Thomas Eakins (see p87), who photographed and painted the aging poet.

Today, the house, a National Historic Landmark, contains some of Whitman's personal belongings, letters, and old photographs, including the earliest known image of the poet from 1848.

USS New Jersey, berthed at the dock adjacent to the Tweeter Center at Camden Waterfront

TWO GUIDED WALKS
AND A DRIVE

Philadelphia's colonial history around Society Hill and Independence National Historical Park, also called "America's most historic square mile," is best explored on foot. However, for those who wish to explore other historical

Maritime painting in the Seaport Museum

areas, this section introduces some neighborhoods that can be explored through a guided walk or drives.

The first is a walking tour around the Penn's Landing area along the scenic Delaware River. This tour includes stops at Gloria Del (Old Swedes') Church, the oldest church in Pennsylvania, and the Irish, Korean, and Vietnam memorials. The second

walk explores colonial-era homes along Germantown, which was settled in 1683. This 90-minute walk includes the "White House," where the first president of the US, George Washington, and his family stayed to escape the city's 1793 yellow fever epidemic. The third is a drive through Fairmount Park, close to the Philadelphia Museum of Art on the banks of the Schyulkill River. This tour also highlights historic homes, many of which were once the summer retreats of the colonial elite. This drive includes splendid panoramic views of the city skyline at Belmont Plateau.

Germantown
(see pp106–107)

Fairmount Park
(see pp108–109)

Penn's Landing
(see pp104–105)

KEY

···· Suggested route

═ Highway

▬ Major road

— Minor road

◁ One of the rowing teams of the "Schuylkill Navy" brings its boat ashore at Boathouse Row *(see p96)*

A Two-Hour Walk Along Penn's Landing

Penn's Landing's plaza, walkways, marina, and Christopher Columbus Park provide the setting for a scenic walk along the Delaware River, the natural boundary between the states of Pennsylvania and New Jersey. Docked along the riverside are some of Philadelphia's historic ships and popular dinner cruise boats, as this area is now a thriving commercial and entertainment zone. The walk, which starts in the neighborhood of Old City and includes historic sights, stretches south along the river to the Gloria Dei Church and then doubles back to include the city's monuments to the Vietnam War and Korean War.

Penn's statue at Welcome Park ①

Independence Seaport Museum ⑥, showcasing US maritime heritage

dates back to the mid-19th century and now contains a bank, restaurants, and a newspaper office.

Turn right onto Chestnut Street and stop in front of 126 Chestnut ③. A time capsule is buried at the site and a plaque on the sidewalk reads: "From the people of the Bicentennial to the Tricentennial – our mementos to be opened by the Mayor of Philadelphia on July 4, 2076."

Cross Front Street to the Irish Memorial ④, a memorial to those who suffered during the Irish Potato Famine (1845–50).

Corn Exchange National Bank, with a unique domed clock tower ②

Welcome Park to Irish Memorial

The walk begins in Welcome Park ① (see p55) at 2nd Street and the Sansom Street alley. Dedicated to William Penn, the park is located where his home, the Slate Roof House, once stood. Pass by the historic Thomas Bond House Bed and Breakfast (see p134) along 2nd Street to Chestnut Street, where the Corn Exchange National Bank building ② sits across the street. Designed in Colonial Revival style, the structure

Irish Memorial to Christopher Columbus Park

Pass over I-95 and enter Penn's Landing ⑤ (see p66). Head down the curving walkway toward the river for great views of the Ben Franklin Bridge and the Camden Waterfront (see p101), home to the Adventure Aquarium and the Battleship New Jersey.

Walk past the RiverLink Ferry port and the Independence Seaport Museum ⑥ (see pp64–5), where the museum's cruiser *Olympia* and submarine *Becuna* are berthed. A dead-end walkway stretches out into the Delaware River offering splendid views of the river and the Ben Franklin Bridge. Continue around the marina to Christopher Columbus Park ⑦, which has as its centerpiece a tribute dedicated in 1992 to the 500th anniversary of the explorer's voyage to America. Across from the *Olympia* and *Becuna* is the Penn's Landing Visitor Center.

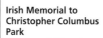

Detail of Irish Memorial Sculpture ④

Christopher Columbus Park to Korean War Memorial

Continue south along the waterfront to the *Moshulu* ⑧, a 1904 four-masted sailing ship that is now a floating restaurant (see p148). The *Spirit of Philadelphia*, a dinner cruise ship, is also berthed here. Then walk along Columbus

Camden Waterfront, across Penn's Landing and along the scenic Delaware River ⑤

Exterior of the restored Gloria Dei (Old Swedes') church, founded in 1677 ⑨

was completed in 1700, with the steeple added in 1703. Now an Episcopal parish, the church still contains the original marble baptismal font and carved wooden cherubim holding a bible, which were brought to the New World by the Swedish colonists. Among those buried in the church cemetery are soldiers of the Revolutionary War.

Head back up Columbus Boulevard and cross back over I-95 using the South Street overpass. Turn right on Front Street and continue to the Vietnam War Memorial ⑩. It pays tribute to the city's 80,000 veterans who served in the Vietnam War (1960–75), and has the names of more than 600 of those killed etched in stone. Cross Spruce Street and enter Foglietta Plaza, whose centerpiece is the Korean War Memorial ⑪ with the names of 603 local veterans killed or declared missing in action during the Korean War (1950–53).

Boulevard past the old Municipal Piers 38 and 40. Cross the boulevard at Christian Street to reach the Gloria Dei (Old Swedes') Church ⑨, the oldest in the state. Swedish Lutherans, who settled here in 1643, founded the church in 1677, before the arrival of William Penn. The brick building standing today

A 90-Minute Walk of Historic Homes in Germantown

Once a small country town a few miles northwest of Old City, Germantown *(see p94)* is now one of Philadelphia's oldest neighborhoods. It was settled in 1683 by immigrants from the Rhine Valley in Germany, who were attracted by Penn's promise of religious freedom. Within a century it evolved into a retreat for wealthy Philadelphia families. The homes on this walk, along cobblestoned Germantown Avenue, have been well preserved by the active Germantown Historical Society and are National Historic Landmarks. The stop-offs should be made during the day, as the area is best avoided at night. The route can be easily driven through, and tourism markers make the homes easy to find.

The Deshler-Morris House, now a National Park Service property ③

Germantown Historical Society and Visitor Center ①

Germantown Historical Society Museum and Library to Deshler-Morris House

The walk starts at the Germantown Historical Society Museum and Library ①. This museum traces Germantown's history, in addition to selling maps of the region. The museum's rotating exhibits are culled from the society's 20,000-artifact collection of paintings, kitchenware, toys, and period clothing. Exit the center, turn left on Germantown Avenue, and walk a few blocks to

Grumblethorpe ②, built in 1744 and home of wine merchant John Wister. Sally, his daughter, lived here during the American Revolution and kept a diary recording her impressions of the turbulent times. British General James Agnew died here after being mortally wounded in the fierce Battle of Germantown in 1777 *(see p21)* and a bloodstain remains on the first floor. The Georgian Grumblethorpe displays items that belonged to the family and the gardens outside still retain their 19th-century appearance.

Head back up Germantown Avenue to one of the community's most famous homes, the Deshler-Morris House ③. The house is situated opposite the Visitor Center and Market Square, which has a Civil War monument as its centerpiece. Built in the mid-1700s by Quaker David Deshler, the home served as the headquarters of British General William Howe during the

Chelten Avenue 250m

Battle of Germantown. After the Revolutionary War, the building became known as the Germantown "White House" when President Washington and his family lived here to escape the 1793 yellow fever epidemic. Today, the house exhibits period furnishings and original paintings by colonial artists Gilbert Stuart and Charles W. Peale.

Grumblethorpe, home to one family for 160 years ②

Back parlor of the Wyck House and Garden ④

Deshler-Morris House to Ebenezer Maxwell Mansion

Continue up Germantown Avenue several blocks to the Wyck House and Garden ④, owned for three centuries by nine generations of the same Quaker family. It contains the family's belongings, collected from 1689 until 1973, including antiques, books, and manuscripts that highlight the family's history and its devotion to the Quaker faith.

Turning left on Walnut Lane, walk two blocks to turn right on Greene Street to the Ebenezer Maxwell Mansion ⑤. Built in 1859, it is the city's only authentically restored Victorian residence. It features original

19th-century stenciled designs in the upstairs rooms, Rococo furniture in the dining room and parlor, and various other period items that reflect life in the 1860s.

Ebenezer Maxwell Mansion to Cliveden

Turn right on Tulpehocken Street back to Germantown Avenue and turn left for the Johnson House ⑥, built in 1768. This stone house was

Ebenezer Maxwell Mansion ⑤, a 19th-century Victorian house

owned by three generations of an abolitionist Quaker family, who made it into the city's only stop on the Underground Railroad that led slaves to freedom in Canada and the northern states *(see p60).*

Continuing up Germantown Avenue, the next home on the walk is Upsala ⑦. Built around 1740 and expanded in 1800, the home is an outstanding example of Federal architecture, with wooden and marble mantels inside *(see p28).* This house is where the Continental Army made its stand during the Battle of Germantown on October 4, 1777. Across the street is Cliveden ⑧. Built in 1767, it is one of the finest surviving colonial homes in the city. During the Battle of Germantown, British troops occupied the Georgian-style Cliveden and repulsed the colonial army. Chipped bricks from rifle shots are still evident on the home's façade, and one room has an original musket ball hole from the battle that raged in the street outside. Reenactments of the battle are held on the grounds on the first Saturday of every October.

The study at Cliveden, an example of a colonial-era house ⑧

KEY

••• Suggested route

S Parking

0 meters   400

0 yards   400

A Three-Hour Drive Around Fairmount Park Historic Mansions

Prominent colonial Philadelphia families took note of the trees and rolling hills in the landscape just west of the city along the Schuylkill River, and built mansions in what is today Fairmount Park *(see p95)*. Some of the homes had working farms with grazing lands and orchards, while others were upscale summer retreats. The park was established when the city began purchasing these properties in the mid-19th century, thus preserving scenic land and the homes in their architectural splendor. They are open for tours and are best seen as part of a driving tour. Those without vehicles can take a trolley tour conducted by Fairmount Park.

One of the many statues in Fairmount Park

Boathouse Row along Kelly Drive

Lemon Hill to Laurel Hill

Begin the drive from the parking lot at the Philadelphia Museum of Art's West Entrance ①. Turn left at the traffic light onto Kelly Drive, then drive straight on. At the seated statue of President Lincoln ②, take the fork to the right, and then make a sharp left to reach Lemon Hill ③. The house was named after the lemon trees that once grew here when Revolutionary War financier and signer of the Declaration of Independence Robert Morris owned the land. A later owner, Henry Pratt, built the mansion in 1800. The oval rooms, with curved doors, fanlights, and fireplaces on all three levels, are Federal elements, while the Palladian windows are

Georgian remnants. Return to the Lincoln statue, and turning right, continue up Kelly Drive past Boathouse Row. At the statue of Ulysses S. Grant turn right onto Fountain Green Drive and then left for Mount Pleasant ④. Once described by President John Adams as "the most elegant seat in Pennsylvania," this Georgian house has ornate woodwork and classical motifs in the entrance hall and stairway. Returning to Fountain Green Drive, which merges with

Reservoir Drive, continue to Ormiston ⑤. Built in the 1790s in Georgian style, the house has an original Scottish oven and an open fireplace. Events and rotating exhibits at Ormiston highlight the area's British heritage.

Drive down Reservoir Drive and turn left onto Randolph Drive. Continue to Edgeley Drive for Laurel Hill ⑥, a 1767 Georgian-style country house with a two-story octagonal wing, perched on a prominent bluff overlooking the river.

Mount Pleasant, built between 1762 and 1765 ④

Woodford, a National Historic Landmark ⑦

Laurel Hill to Memorial Hall

Continue through an intersection that has an equestrian statue of an American Indian, and onto Dauphin Drive. Turn left before 33rd Street onto Greenland Drive to reach Woodford ⑦, built in 1758 by William Coleman, a merchant and friend of Benjamin Franklin. The Georgian house has an array of exquisite colonial decorative arts and furniture, donated by Naomi Wood, a Philadelphian collector. Continue up Greenland Drive a short distance to Strawberry Mansion ⑧, with its Federal-style center

wing built by Judge William Lewis in 1789. Two large wings, in Greek Revival style, were added later. The house displays Empire and Federal period furnishings. Key exhibits include a doll collection and a well-preserved Victorian dollhouse. Drive down Strawberry Mansion Drive, turn right at Woodford Drive, and cross the Strawberry Mansion Bridge. Make a quick left onto West River Drive, continue for about a mile (1.6 km) and turn right onto Black Road toward the Smith Civil War Memorial ⑨. Turn right at the Memorial onto North Concourse Drive to reach Memorial Hall ⑩. Built in Beaux-Arts style, it was the city's first art museum and now houses the Please Touch Museum for children *(see p170)*.

Memorial Hall to Sweetbriar

Returning to the Smith Civil War Memorial, turn left, and then make a quick right onto Cedar Grove Drive and head to Cedar Grove ⑪, a house that was built elsewhere and reassembled in Fairmount Park. This Georgian house has an unusual two-sided wall of closets on the second floor, and much of its original, early Pennsylvania furniture. It is now maintained by the Philadelphia Museum of Art. For the last stop, turn right after Cedar Grove towards the

TIPS FOR DRIVERS

Starting point: *Philadelphia Museum of Art, West Entrance parking lot.*
Length: *5 miles (8 km) to visit homes, then another 2 miles (3 km) back to the museum.*
Stop-off points: *Homes open to the public can be visited, depending on opening hours and time.*
Trolley tour: *Visitors on foot can take a park trolley tour, leaving from the Philadelphia Museum of Art and the Independence Visitor Center (6th & Market Sts). Tel (215) 925-8687.* ☒ ▣ *May–Dec 15: 10:30am & 1:45pm Wed–Sun.*

Sweetbriar, a three-story house built in Federal style ⑫

Federal-style Sweetbriar ⑫, the home of merchant Samuel Breck, built in 1797. The Etruscan Room is decorated in keeping with Breck's interest in classical forms and ancient Etruscan wall painting.

Other historic homes such as Chaminoux, Ridgeland, and the Belmont Mansion are not open for visitors to tour.

KEY

··· Suggested route

🅿 Parking

Cedar Grove, built as a summer home in 1750 ⑪

BEYOND
PHILADELPHIA

Exploring Beyond Philadelphia

To the west of Philadelphia, the area encompassing Lancaster County is known as the Pennsylvania Dutch Country, and is made up of bucolic hills and farmland as far as the eye can see. The region is home to the Amish *(see p115)* who wear traditional clothing and are often seen riding in horse-drawn buggies. Farther west is the town of Hershey, home of the chocolates, and Gettysburg, site of the American Civil War's bloodiest battle. To the east, the glitzy casinos of Atlantic City are just over an hour's drive away, and a little farther is the idyllic beach resort of Cape May.

Statue, Gettysburg

Fountains at Longwood Gardens

SIGHTS AT A GLANCE

SEE ALSO

KEY

— Highway
— Major road
— Other roads
-- Major rail
— Minor rail
— State boundary

Boy outside a candy and ice cream store in Strasburg

◁ Farmers using horse-drawn wagons and traditional implements in Lancaster County, Pennsylvania *(see p114)*

0 kilometers 25

0 miles 25

Glittering casinos and resorts light up Atlantic City

New York City

Pottsville
209

ountain

Allentown
78

Fleetwood
Laureldale
476
Quakertown

422
NEW HOPE
DOYLESTOWN 14
Lambertville
WASHINGTON CROSSING
HISTORIC PARK

LANDIS VALLEY
MUSEUM
176
Pottstown
Lansdale
TRENTON

ITITZ
Spring City
Norristown
Levittown
PENNSBURY MANOR

3
EPHRATA
Phoenixville
Abington

2
LANCASTER

1
INTERCOURSE
VALLEY FORGE
NATIONAL HISTORIC
PARK
Mount Holly
Browns
Mills

PARADISE
BRANDYWINE
BATTLEFIELD
STATE PARK
Philadelphia
Camden

STRASBURG

RD-IN-
AND
LONGWOOD
GARDENS
BRANDYWINE
RIVER MUSEUM
Cherry Hill
70

Oxford
WINTERTHUR
MUSEUM
HAGLEY MUSEUM
Lindenwold
206

Wilmington
295
Pitman
Pine
Barrens
New York
City

Newark
Carneys Point
Glassboro
NEW

Elkton
Pennsville
Elmer
JERSEY
9

ARYLAND
13
Salem
Buena
Egg Harbor City

Aberdeen
301
Vineland
40
Mays Landing
Brigantine

95
Middletown
49
Millville
Pleasantville

Edgewood
Bridgeton
Somers
Point
ATLANTIC
CITY

Smyrna
Maurice
Ocean City

Chestertown
Chester
DELAWARE
Port Norris
Woodbine

Dover
Delaware
Bay

Cape May
Court House
9
Avalon

Villas
North Wildwood

North Cape
May

CAPE MAY

Cape
May

Susquehanna

Delaware

GETTING AROUND

The SEPTA Regional Rail system provides excellent services
north to Doylestown and Trenton, and south toward Newark
and Wilmington, Delaware. New Jersey Transit from 30th Street
Station and bus lines offer services east to New Jersey Shore
points. Amtrak trains also departing from 30th Street Station
make stops at Harrisburg and Lancaster. A car is the best way
to explore the Pennsylvania Dutch Country and Gettysburg.
Take I-76 to points west, I-95 to points north and south, and
the Atlantic City Expressway to the New Jersey Shore.

Shoppers at Main Street, Lititz

For additional map symbols see back flap

Soldiers and Sailors Monument in Penn Square, Lancaster

Lancaster ❶

Lancaster County, PA. 👥 *55,000.*
🚉 🚌 ℹ *Pennsylvania Dutch Country Visitor Center: Route 30 at Greenfield Exit; 1-800-PADUTCH.*
www.padutchcountry.com

Founded by John Wright in 1730 and named after his birthplace in England, today Lancaster is the county seat. Its tree-shaded streets are still lined with 18th- and 19th-century buildings. In the heart of downtown is Penn Square with its centerpiece Soldiers and Sailors Monument, dedicated in 1874 to local men who fought in the American Civil War between 1861 and 1865. On the square's northwest corner, three adjoining buildings dating from the 1790s house the **Lancaster Heritage Center Museum**. Its collection includes striking colonial grandfather clocks. A Renaissance-style mural adorns the vaulted ceiling of one of the buildings.

At the **Lancaster Central Market**, next to the museum, vendors and Amish farmers sell cheeses, meats, flowers, fresh produce, and treats such as homemade cider. Nearby, in a Beaux Arts-style building modeled after New York's Penn Station, is the **Lancaster Quilt & Textile Museum** with a collection of 82 Amish and Mennonite quilts.

Located west of downtown is **Wheatland**, the estate of the 15th president of the US, James Buchanan, who served during the tumultuous years leading up to the Civil War. The house, named for the wheat fields it once overlooked, features most of Buchanan's original belongings, and has a beautiful 19th-century garden.

An old-fashioned pretzel

🏛 **Lancaster Heritage Center Museum**
5, W King St. *Tel (717) 299-6440.*
⏱ *9am–5pm Mon–Sat; first Fri of month: 5–9pm; Dec: noon–4pm Sun.* 📷 **www.**lancasterheritage.com

🏛 **Lancaster Quilt & Textile Museum**
37 N Market St. *Tel (717) 299-6440.*
⏱ *9am–5pm Mon–Sat; first Fri of month: 5–9pm; Dec: noon–4pm Sun.* 📷

🚏 **Wheatland**
1120 Marietta Ave. *Tel (717) 392-8721.* ⏱ *Apr–Oct: 10am–4:30pm Mon–Sat; noon–4pm Sun; Nov & Dec: 10am–4:30pm Fri & Sat.* 📷 *Thanksgiving, Dec 25, Jan–Mar.* 📷

Landis Valley Museum ❷

See pp116–17.

Lititz ❸

Lancaster County, PA. 👥 *9,000.*
ℹ *Lititz Welcome Center: 18 N Broad St, (717) 626-8981.* **www.**lititzpa.com

Named after a town in Bohemia, Lititz was founded by Moravians in 1756 and remained a closed settlement for nearly a century. The town boasts 18th-century buildings and a quaint Main Street, and features the Lititz Springs Park, which has a natural spring-fed creek. Moravian Church Square today includes the centerpiece church. Nearby is the **Lititz Historical Museum** with its star exhibit, the Johannes Mueller House, a restored 1792 Moravian stone house named for a local tanner and dyer. A room in the museum is dedicated to General John Sutter, founder of Sacramento and a Lititz resident. It was the discovery of gold on his land that led to the 1849 California Gold Rush.

The **Sturgis Pretzel House**, dating from 1861, offers visitors pretzel tours. The **Wilbur Chocolate Candy Store and Museum** displays 19th-century chocolate molds and recipe cards that highlight the company's history since 1884.

🏛 **Lititz Historical Museum**
137–145 East Main St. *Tel (717) 627-4636.* ⏱ *Memorial Day–Oct: 10am–4pm Mon–Sat; special weekends in May, Nov, & Dec.* 📷 📷

🚏 **Sturgis Pretzel House**
219 East Main St. *Tel (717) 626-4354.* ⏱ *9am–5pm Mon–Sat.* 📷 **www.**juliussturgis.com

🏛 **Wilbur Chocolate Candy Store and Museum**
48 N Broad St. *Tel (717) 626-3249.*
⏱ *10am–5pm Mon–Sat.*
www.wilburbuds.com

Lititz's historic Main Street shopping district

The Amish, Mennonites, and Brethren

The Mennonites and the Amish trace their roots to the Swiss Anabaptist ("New Birth") movement of 1525, an offshoot of the Protestant Reformation, whose creed rejected the formality of the established churches. Lured by the promise of religious freedom held out to them by William Penn, the Mennonites were the first to arrive in Germantown in the late 17th century. They were soon followed by the Amish

Detail from an Amish quilt

who settled in what is now Lancaster County in the early 18th century. However, not all Pennsylvania Dutch are Amish or Mennonites; Brethren and other sub-groups are also part of the community. The mostly German heritage of these groups has given rise to a popular myth about the name "Pennsylvania Dutch" – it is thought that it came from other early colonists mispronouncing "Pennsylvania Deutsch."

Amish farms *have changed little since the 17th century. Farming is usually done with horsedrawn equipment with bare metal wheels.*

AMISH

The Amish sect began in the 1690s when Jacob Amman, a Swiss bishop, split from the Mennonites. The conservative Old Order Amish disdain any device that would connect them to the larger world, including electricity, cars, modern farm tools, and telephones.

Amish families *dress in plain, dark attire, with women in white caps and men in straw hats.*

Buggies are used even today

MENNONITES

Taking their name from Menno Simons, a young Dutch priest who advocated adult baptism by faith in the 1530s, Mennonites are pacifists and believe in simple living. However, they do not segregate themselves from society, and in recent years, urbanization has lured many to the cities.

Mennonites in traditional dress

Old Order Brethren at a Pennsylvania Dutch Country covered bridge

BRETHREN

Alexander Mack founded this movement in 1708, breaking away from the established and reformed faiths of the time and following the German Pietists in espousing worship on a more personal level. The pacifist Brethren migrated to America in the late 1720s. They believe in adult baptism and adhere only to the teachings of the New Testament.

The Brethren church *is where the community worships and baptizes adults by "dunking" them thrice in the name of the Holy Trinity.*

Landis Valley Museum ❷

Wares at the Country Store

The descendents of German settlers, brothers George and Henry Landis, started the Landis Valley Museum in the 1920s. At that time, it included more than 75,000 objects from the 18th and 19th centuries, featuring the traditions and farming culture of the Pennsylvania German community. Now supported and run by the state Historical and Museum Commission, Landis Valley is a living history village of Pennsylvania German life and home to nearly 100,000 artifacts such as quilts, rugs, leather goods, carriages, kitchen utensils, baskets, and lace. More than 30 homes, barns, sheds, shops, and other structures highlight the trades and crafts of earlier generations, complemented by regular demonstrations by craftspeople.

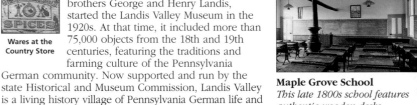

Maple Grove School
This late 1800s school features authentic wooden desks.

★ **Landis Collections Gallery**
Items like this silver lamp are displayed in the museum's historic collection, which dates from 1740 to 1940.

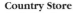

Country Store
A wide range of items, including farm tools, saddles, phonograph records, and glass-jarred licorice, stock the shelves of this reconstructed store.

STAR SIGHTS

★ Landis Collections Gallery

★ Transportation Building

★ Landis House and Stable

★ Gun Shop

Firehouse and Surveyor Shop
The larger firehouse, which has original pumpers inside, resembles a late 19th-century fire company.

★ Transportation Building

An assortment of late 19th-century sleighs is one of the displays in this building, which also houses horse-drawn buggies, carriages, wagons, and hand-drawn carts once used for light chores.

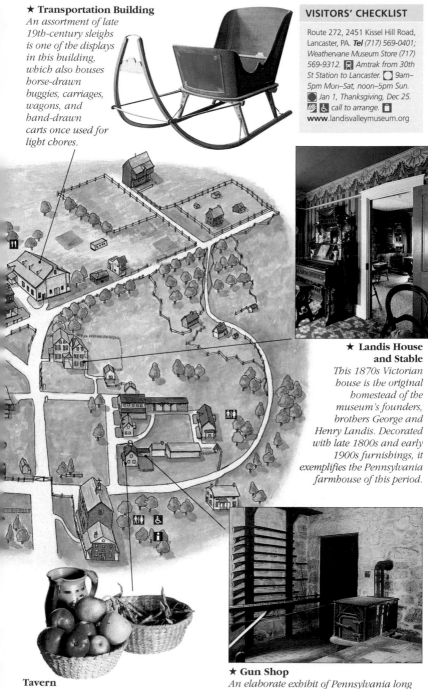

★ Landis House and Stable

This 1870s Victorian house is the original homestead of the museum's founders, brothers George and Henry Landis. Decorated with late 1800s and early 1900s furnishings, it exemplifies the Pennsylvania farmhouse of this period.

Tavern

The spacious brick-paved kitchen of the inn, with its enormous walk-in fireplace and displays of baskets, utensils, and stoneware jugs, reflects 18th-century cooking methods.

★ Gun Shop

An elaborate exhibit of Pennsylvania long rifles, powder horns, and gunsmithing tools sits within this stone structure. Early settlers used such shops to perfect the accuracy of their weapons.

Austere interior of the Saal, the meetinghouse in Ephrata Cloister

Ephrata ❹

Lancaster County, PA. 🏠 13,000. 🚌
🅸 77 Park Ave, Suite 1; (717) 738-9010. www.ephrata-area.org

This northern Lancaster County community was settled in 1732 by a German religious order led by Conrad Beissel, who founded one of America's earliest communal societies. The order built the medieval-style buildings that make up the **Ephrata Cloister**. Today, nine structures from the mid-1700s remain. The Sisters' House, next to the meetinghouse, has rows of windows for each small chamber where members slept on narrow benches. Other buildings include a schoolhouse, bakery, woodshop, and print shop. The visitor center displays artifacts, such as the Mennonites' 1,500-page *Martyrs' Mirror*. Just north of town, vendors at the Green Dragon Farmers' Market sell antiques, Pennsylvania Dutch treats, and crafts every Friday.

🏛 **Ephrata Cloister**
632 W Main St. *Tel* (717) 733-6600. ⬜ 9am–5pm Mon–Sat, noon–5pm Sun. 🖼
www.ephratacloister.org

Intercourse ❺

Lancaster County, PA. 🏠 900.
🚌 🅸 3551 Old Philadelphia Pike; (717) 768-3231. www.intercoursevillage.com

Theories abound on how the village acquired its interesting name, including it coming from the intersection of the two main roads, from an old racecourse, or even from Intercourse being a center for social interaction. Founded in 1754, the village is one of the main centers for Amish business. Key to its success are the extensive gift shops and stores that lure tourists by the busloads. For instance, Kitchen Kettle Village, a mini-shopping center, has over 30 restaurants and country shops selling everything from quilts and baskets to woodcraft. One store delights customers with homemade jellies and relishes bottled on the spot by Amish women. In the center of town, along Old Philadelphia Pike, is the **People's Place Quilt Museum**. Opened in 1988, the museum displays antique Mennonite and Amish quilts through rotating exhibitions.

Exhibit detail at the People's Place Quilt Museum

West of the town center is the **Amish Experience**, where visitors can learn about local culture by touring a modern Amish home and through the multimedia show, *Jacob's Choice*, which chronicles an Amish family's efforts to preserve its lifestyle.

🏛 **People's Place Quilt Museum**
3510 Old Philadelphia Pike.
Tel (800) 828-8218.
⬜ 9am–5pm Mon–Sat. 🖼
www.ppquiltmuseum.com

🏛 **Amish Experience**
Route 340 between Bird-In-Hand & Intercourse. *Tel* (717) 768-3600 ext 210. ⬜ mid-Apr–Jun: 8:30am–5pm Mon–Sat; Jul–Oct: 8:30am–8pm Mon–Sat, 10:30am–5pm Sun; Nov–Dec: 10am–5pm Mon–Sat; Jan–mid-Apr: 9:30am–5pm Sat & Sun (times subject to change – call for details). www.amishexperience.com

Bird-In-Hand ❻

Lancaster County, PA. 🏠 300. 🚌
🅸 2727 Old Philadelphia Pike; (800) 665-8780. www.bird-in-hand.com

This village is said to have received its unusual name from a historic 1734 inn (*see p141*) that once dangled a tavern sign depicting a man with a perched bird in his hand. The village contains a cluster of restaurants, stores, hotels, and quaint farmhouses.

The **Farmers' Market** bustles with stalls packed with foods ranging from farm vegetables to fresh bacon and sausage. Across the street, the **Americana Museum** displays antiques from 1890 through 1930, which depict important professions and trades, and include an early 20th-century toy store, apothecary, print shop, wheelwright shop, and milliner's. Set up in 1877, the Weavertown One-Room

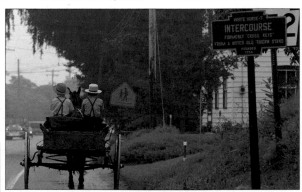

Amish boys ride a buggy into the village of Intercourse

School showcases a typical schoolhouse still attended by Amish children today.

Farmers' Market

Rte 340 & Maple Ave. ◻ *Apr–Jun & Nov: 8:30am–5:30pm Wed, Fri, & Sat; Jul–Oct: 8:30am–5:30pm Wed–Sat; Dec–Mar: 8:30am–5:30pm Fri & Sat.*

🏛 Americana Museum

2709 Old Philadelphia Pike. *Tel (717) 391-9780.* ◻ *Apr–Nov: 10am–5pm Tue–Sat; winter tours by request.* 🖼

Paradise ❼

Lancaster County, PA. 🔠 *1,000.*
🚉 ℹ *Pennsylvania Dutch Country Visitor Center: Route 30 at Greenfield Exit; (717) 299-8901.*
www.800padutch.com

The origins of this small village along Route 30 date from colonial times when the road served as a link between Lancaster and Philadelphia. Paradise grew as the number of inns and taverns increased along Route 30. One of them, the Historic Revere Tavern, was built in 1740 and is still a working restaurant *(see p153).* President James Buchanan purchased it in 1841 as a home for his brother, a reverend, whose wife was the sister of songsmith Stephen Foster, writer of such American favorites as "Oh! Susanna" and "My Olde Kentucky Home".

A short drive east is the one-of-a-kind **National Christmas Center**, where the spirit of Yuletide is always in the air. Spread over 20,000 sq ft (1,860 sq m) are life-sized scenes depicting Christmas feasts and snowy villages, toy train and nativity displays, and several versions of St. Nicholas from around the globe.

🏛 National Christmas Center

3427 Lincoln Hwy East.
Tel (717) 442-7950. ◻ *May 1–Jan 1: 10am–6pm daily; Mar & Apr: 10am–6pm Sat & Sun* ◼ *Jan–Feb, Thanksgiving, Dec 25.* **www.** nationalchristmascenter.com

An Amish house and buggy in Strasburg

Strasburg ❽

Lancaster County, PA. 🔠 *2,800.* ℹ *Pennsylvania Dutch Country Visitor Center: Route 30 at Greenfield; (717) 687-0405.* **www.**strasburgpa.com

Initially settled by French Huguenots in the early 1700s, Strasburg is named after the cathedral city of Strasbourg in France. The first structures, built in 1733, are now part of the historical district along with numerous colonial stone and log homes. The town developed as an educational and cultural center as followers of different faiths chose to settle here. But by the mid-19th century, it had become home to the railroads that are today its most popular attraction. Set up in 1832, the **Strasburg Railroad** offers 45-minute rides in refurbished railcars pulled by early 20th-century coal-fired, smoke-belching locomotives. Directly across the highway is the **Railroad Museum of Pennsylvania**, with spacious hangars housing one of the nation's largest collections of classic railroad cars, locomotives, and colorful cabooses. The **National Toy Train Museum** has exhibitions of collector-item locomotives and exquisite

Signage at the National Christmas Center

model train layouts. The **Choo Choo Barn**, meanwhile, has one of the most unique model railroads in the world, with 22 trains running through scenes of Lancaster County.

North of town is the **Amish Village** with an 1840s Amish house, smokehouse, blacksmith shop, and operational water wheel. The majestic Millennium Theater nearby is home to inspirational, Biblical-themed stage productions.

🚂 Strasburg Railroad

301 Gap Rd Ronks, Rte 741, E of Strasburg. *Tel (717) 687-7522.* ◻ *Feb–Dec; check website or call for times.* ◼ *Jan.* **www.** strasburgrailroad.com

🏛 Railroad Museum of Pennsylvania

300 Gap Rd. *Tel (717) 687-8628.* ◻ *Apr–Oct: 9am–5pm Mon–Sat, noon–5pm Sun; Nov–Mar: 9am–5pm Tue–Sat, noon–5pm Sun.* ◼ *Jan 1, Easter, Nov 11, Thanksgiving, Dec 24, 25, & 31.*

🏛 National Toy Train Museum

300 Paradise Lane, off Rte 741, E of Strasburg. *Tel (717) 687-8976.* ◻ *Apr–Dec: 10am–4:30pm Mon–Fri (also Sat & Sun in Dec).* ◼ *Jan–Mar.*

🏛 Choo Choo Barn

Rte 741, E of Strasburg. *Tel (717) 687-7911.* ◻ *Apr–Dec: 10am–4:30pm.* ◼ *Jan–Mar, Easter, Thanksgiving, Dec 25.* **www.** choochoobarn.com

🚂 Amish Village

Rte 896, N of Strasburg. *Tel (717) 687-8511.* ◻ *spring, summer & fall: 9am- 5pm Mon Sat, 10am 5pm Sun.* **www.**800padutch.com/ avillage.html

Gettysburg ❾

Lincoln's chair at Wills House

This south-central Pennsylvania town amidst gently sloping hills is home to the greatest military encounter ever fought in North America, the Battle of Gettysburg in 1863, during the Civil War (1861–65). Shaded streets are lined with well-preserved Civil War-era buildings, which served as makeshift hospitals during the conflict. Many of these have today been converted into museums, restaurants, and hotels. Shops sell Civil War souvenirs and artifacts, including authentic rifles and a seemingly unending supply of cannon balls and bullets unearthed from the battleground. Other attractions include museums with dioramas – some with waxwork figures – depicting events of the Gettysburg battle and the Civil War.

The *Gettysburg Cyclorama*, a 360-degree painting of Pickett's Charge

🏛 Gettysburg Museum and Visitor Center

1195 Baltimore Pike. **Tel** *(717) 334-6274.* ⬜ *8am–6pm daily (to 7pm Jun–Aug).* ⬤ *Jan 1, Thanksgiving, Dec 25.* 🖼 **www**.nps.gov/gett

The Gettysburg Museum and Visitor Center opened in 2008 at the Gettysburg National Military Park. The 139,000 sq ft (12,900 sq m), awe-inspiring facility houses a modern visitor center that serves to navigate visitors around the park. A 20-minute film, introducing the Battle of Gettysburg, is repeated here every 30 minutes throughout the day. The facility also houses the Museum of Civil War where wide-ranging military artifacts, including an impressive display of artillery shells and fuses, are on display. Also on view is the *Gettysburg Cyclorama*. First exhibited in Boston in 1883, this colossal panoramic painting depicts Pickett's Charge, the conflict's climactic moment *(see pp122–3).*

🍴 Dobbin House Tavern

89 Steinwehr Ave. **Tel** *(717) 334-2100.* ⬜ *11:30am onward.* **www**.dobbinhouse.com

Built in 1776, this stone house is Gettysburg's oldest standing structure. An upstairs museum displays a secret crawl space that once hid runaway slaves as part of the Underground Railroad *(see p60).* Now a restaurant, the building has original fireplaces, hand-carved woodwork, and a colonial wooden bar in the downstairs tavern *(see p152).*

🍴 Eisenhower National Historic Site

250 Eisenhower Farm Drive. **Tel** *(717) 338-9114.* ⬜ *9am–4pm.* ⬤ *Jan 1, Thanksgiving, Dec 25.* 🖼 🎟 *mandatory.* **www**.nps.gov/eise

Before being elected president in 1952, Dwight D. Eisenhower had served as Supreme Commander of the Allied Forces during World War II. While president, he and his wife Mamie owned this farm on the outskirts of Gettysburg and used it for weekend retreats. Inside are original furnishings and exhibits highlighting his career as general and president.

🍴 Farnsworth House Inn

401 Baltimore St. **Tel** *(717) 334-8838.* ⬜ *hours vary.* **www**.farnsworthhouseinn.com

Dating from 1810, this historic home sheltered Confederate sharpshooters, one of whom is thought to have shot Jennie Wade. Most impressive are the more than 100 bullet piercings still evident on the house's brick façade from Union soldiers returning fire. Now an inn *(see p152),* the house offers ghost tours and an interesting Mourning Theatre in the cellar with Civil War-related ghost tales told around a coffin by candlelight.

🍴 General Lee's Headquarters

401 Buford Ave. **Tel** *(717) 334-3141.* ⬜ *mid-Feb–Nov: 9am–5pm.* ⬤ *Dec–mid-Feb.*

Confederate General Robert E. Lee chose to spend the night of July 1, 1863, at this house so he could see the Union line with his fieldglasses. Inside are war artifacts and the original wooden table on which he dined.

General Lee's Headquarters, today a museum

Entrance to the Pennsylvania Memorial in Gettysburg

🏛 Shriver House Museum

309 Baltimore St. **Tel** *(717) 337-2800.*
⏱ *Apr–Nov: 10am–5pm Mon–Sat,
noon–5pm Sun; Dec–Mar: noon–5pm
Sat & Sun.* ⬤ *Jan.* 🖼 🎦
This 19th-century home
portrays the life of a family
under the three-day Confederate occupation. The third-
floor attic has original holes
in the brick wall where rebel
sharpshooters stood poised.
A small museum displays
artifacts, including three
unfired bullets discovered
during restoration.

🏛 Wills House and Lincoln Room Museum

12 Lincoln Square. **Tel** *(717) 334-
8188.* ⏱ *9am–5pm; extended hours
on some weekends.*
President Abraham Lincoln
slept in this corner house on
the town's center square the
night before he delivered the
Gettysburg Address. His bedroom, where he made final
revisions to his speech, is part
of the Lincoln Room Museum.
It houses copies of the letter
sent by attorney and home-
owner David Wills inviting
Lincoln to visit the town.

🎪 Jennie Wade House

528 Baltimore St. **Tel** *(717) 334-
4100.* ⏱ *Mar–Sep: 9am–5pm.* 🖼
www.jennie-wade-house.com
Twenty-year-old Jennie
Wade was the only
civilian killed during
the Battle of
Gettysburg. A
sharpshooter's bullet
pierced two doors
and struck her while
she baked bread
for Union soldiers.
The home contains
original furnishings,
and a statue of her
stands outside.

in various conflicts in
America's history, from the
Civil War to the Vietnam War.
More than 3,500 are Union
soldiers killed at the three-
day Battle of Gettysburg.
They are buried in a semi-
circle around the Soldiers'
National Monument,
which marks the
spot where
President Lincoln
delivered his
moving Gettysburg
Address. The
now-famous
address is com-
memorated by
the nearby
Lincoln Speech Memorial,
which contains an inscription
of his speech and his bust.

**Soldiers' National
Monument**

🎪 Lincoln Railroad Station

35 Carlisle St. ⏱ *10am–5pm;
extended hours in summer.*
This 1858 Italianate-styled
railroad depot is where
President Lincoln stepped off
the train from Washington, a
day before delivering the
Gettysburg Address. Inside
is an interpretive center,
with exhibits about the train
station and town history,
and information on sights,
attractions, and tours.

🪦 Soldiers' National Cemetery

Taneytown Rd, across Visitor Center.
www.nps.gov/gett/gncem.htm
This peaceful and shaded
cemetery contains the graves
of 6,000 US servicemen killed

LINCOLN'S GETTYSBURG ADDRESS

Four months after the battle, President
Abraham Lincoln visited Gettysburg to
dedicate a cemetery for Union soldiers.
Although not the main speaker, and
asked only to make "a few appropriate
remarks," Lincoln's 272-words, two-minute
speech on November 19, 1863 not only
gave new meaning to the war's losses,
but was an inspiration to preserve
a nation divided. His words
conferred significance on
the sacrifice of the thousands who
died during the battle, urging for
the "resolve that these dead
shall not have died in vain."

**Lincoln's bust at Soldiers'
National Cemetery**

A Tour of Gettysburg National Military Park

The Battle of Gettysburg was fought on the first three days of July 1863. Not only was it the turning point of the American Civil War between the North and South, it was also the war's largest battle, leaving more than 51,000 Union and Confederate soldiers killed, wounded, captured, or missing. Although the Union army won this critical battle, it took a further two years for them to decisively win the Civil War on April 26, 1865. This self-guided tour traces the course of the three-day battle.

Eternal Light Peace Memorial ②
From Oak Hill, Confederates attacked Union forces on the first day. This memorial to "Peace Eternal in a Nation United" was built in 1938.

McPherson's Ridge ①
This quiet farm with McPherson's barn is where the Battle of Gettysburg began early in the morning on July 1, 1863. Confederate infantry advanced eastward and engaged in heavy fire with Union Cavalry.

Oak Ridge ③
Union troops held this ridge but retreated to Cemetery Hill on July 1 as their defenses collapsed.

North Carolina Memorial ④
On the second day, the Confederates stood on Seminary Ridge. Union troops held Culp's and Cemetery Hills.

Virginia Memorial ⑤
This monument on Seminary Ridge overlooks the field where, on July 3, 12,000 Confederates launched their last major assault, known as "Pickett's Charge." In less than an hour, 10,000 of them were dead or wounded.

Pitzer Woods ⑥
Confederates occupied these woods on the second day. An observation tower offers grand views of the "Pickett's Charge" battlefield.

EISENHOWER NATIONAL HISTORIC SITE

0 meters 500
0 yards 500

BR 15

Emmitsburg

KEY

▬ Suggested route

═ Other roads

ℹ Visitor information

🅿 Parking

Warfield Ridge ⑦
On the battle's second day, Confederates charged Union troops at Devil's Den and Little and Big Round Tops.

High Water Mark ⑮
On the last day, Union troops held off "Pickett's Charge" here, forcing the Confederates to retreat. The spot is marked by memorials and old cannon.

TIPS FOR DRIVERS

Tour length: 18 miles (29 km).
Duration of tour: About 3 hours.
Distance from Philadelphia: 118 miles (189 km). This is usually a 2-hour drive.
Starting point: Gettysburg National Military Park Visitor Center.
Stop-off points: The tour has 16 stops, all of which have plaques explaining historical significance. Some stops have a scattering of monuments.
When to go: Mar–Dec.
Tourist information: Gettysburg National Military Park Visitor Center, 1195 Baltimore Pike.
Tel (717) 334-4274.
www.nps.gov/gett/

National Cemetery ⑯
This is the site of Lincoln's Gettysburg Address. 3,500 Civil War dead are buried here.

East Cemetery Hill ⑭
Confederates unsuccessfully attacked Union forces occupying the hill, ending the battle's second day.

Spangler's Spring ⑬
Confederates attacked the Union army at this spring below Culp's Hill, but were forced to retreat after seven hours of fighting. The spring has since been covered.

Pennsylvania Memorial ⑫
An ornate, stately memorial marks the Union position along Cemetery Ridge.

Plum Run ⑪
Union forces crossed this area as they retreated from Peach Orchard to Cemetery Ridge.

Peach Orchard ⑩
On the second day, Confederate soldiers overran this position despite heavy Union cannon fire.

The Wheatfield ⑨
Charges and countercharges here on the second day left over 4,000 men dead and wounded.

Little Round Top ⑧
At first undefended on the second day, this position was reinforced when an alert Union general called for help. Monuments, such as this one to the 155th Pennsylvania Volunteer Infantry, dot the hill.

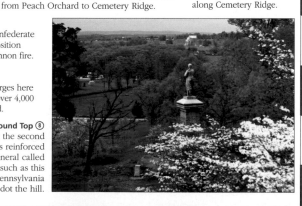

GETTYSBURG
York Street
East Middle Street
Slocum
Baltimore

The Golden Plough Tavern, one of York's historic establishments

York ⑩

York County, PA. 🏃 *40,500.* 🚇 🚌
ℹ️ *1425 Eden Rd, (717) 852-9675.*
www.yorkpa.org

The first Pennsylvania town west of the Susquehanna River, York was laid out in 1741, with inhabitants that were mainly tavern-keepers and craftspeople catering to pioneers heading west. Since then, manufacturing has been the town's economic strength.

East of York is the **Harley-Davidson Final Assembly Plant**, noisy, colorful, and the size of two football fields. Its giant presses mold steel while motorcycles fly overhead. A small museum depicts Harley Davidson's history from its 1903 inception as a motorized bike company to the present.

🏛 **Harley-Davidson Final Assembly Plant**
1425 Eden Rd. **Tel** *(717) 848-1177.*
⏲ *8am–4:30pm Mon–Fri.* 📷 *9am–2pm Mon–Fri; some Saturdays in summer; under 12s not allowed.*

Harrisburg ⑪

Dauphin County, PA. 🏃 *47,000.* 🚇
🚌 ℹ️ *Hershey Capital Region Visitors Bureau: (717) 231-7788.*
www.pacapitalregions.com

First settled in the early 1700s by Englishman John Harris, Harrisburg is situated along the Susquehanna River. The city was not planned until the 1780s and became the capital of Pennsylvania in 1812. Today, the state government is the biggest employer in the city, which has the impressive **State Capitol** as a focal point. The Renaissance-style building was dedicated in 1906 by President Theodore Roosevelt.

The **National Civil War Museum** tells the story of the war through permanent displays of artifacts, photographs, manuscripts, and documents from its 24,000-item collection. City Island, located in the middle of the Susquehanna, offers panoramic views of the city. It includes marinas, parks and nature areas, riverboat rides and dinner cruises, and a replica of John Harris's 18th-century trading post.

🏛 **State Capitol**
3rd & State Sts. **Tel** *(717) 787-6810.*
⏲ *8:30am–4:30pm Mon–Fri.* 📷
8:30am–4:30pm Mon–Fri, 9am, 11am,

1pm, 3pm Sat–Sun & hols. ⏲ *Jan 1, Easter, Thanksgiving, Dec 25.* 🚻

🏛 **National Civil War Museum**
Lincoln Circle (Reservoir Pk). **Tel** *(717) 260-1861.* ⏲ *10am–5pm Mon–Sat, noon–5pm Sun.* ⏲ *Mon, Jan–Mar.*
📷 🚻 **www**.
nationalcivilwarmuseum.org

Hershey ⑫

Dauphin County, PA. 🏃 *12,800.*
🚇 🚌 **www**.hersheypa.com

This factory town, now a tourist destination, revolves around chocolate, so much so that even its streetlights are shaped like silver-foil-wrapped Hershey Kisses. The town's main attraction is **Hershey Park**, an amusement park that has 80 rides on offer, and a fine, four-row carousel. There are also two resort hotels in the park. Nearby is Chocolate World, which features a 15-minute ride through animated tableaux that reveal Hershey's chocolate-making process. A free sample awaits at the end of the tour.

Hershey's Chocolate World signage

🎢 **Hershey Park**
100 W Hersheypark Drive.
Tel *1-800-HERSHEY.* ⏲ *May 21–Sep 1: 10am–8pm daily (for other times check website).* 📷 **www**.
hersheypark.com

State Capitol complex in Harrisburg, the seat of Pennsylvania's government

The towers and parapets of Mercer Castle, Doylestown

Reading ⑬

Berks County, PA. 🚶 80,000. 🚉 🚌
🛈 201 Washington St, (610) 375–
4085. www.readingberkspa.com

Once a center of industry,
Reading has reinvented itself
as a discount-store capital
(see p157), with more than
80 name-brand stores, from
Brooks Brothers to Mikasa
and Wedgewood. The
Reading Pagoda, on the outskirts of the town, is the main
attraction here. Built in the
early 1900s, it is modeled
after a Shogun structure.

The **Mid-Atlantic Air
Museum**, located at Reading
Regional Airport, includes a
selection of over 60 different
military and civilian aircraft.

🏛 **Mid-Atlantic Air Museum**
11 Museum Drive. **Tel** (610) 372-
7333. ◯ 9:30am–4pm.
www.maam.org

Doylestown ⑭

Bucks County, PA. 🚶 9,200. 🚉 🚌
🛈 Bucks County Visitors Center: 3207
Street Road, Bensalem, (800) 836-2825.

The origins of Doylestown
date to 1745, when William
Doyle built a tavern here. The
town was later developed as
a cultural and commercial
center, and today it is also
the Bucks County seat.

The biggest attractions in
town are the castle-like museums that tower over shaded
grassy areas close to the town
center. The **Mercer Museum**,

built by archaeologist Henry
Mercer in 1916, displays his
collection of folk art, wood
work, textiles, and furnishings. After his death in 1930,
his 44-room home, **Fonthill**,
was turned into a tile museum.

Named after a famous writer
from this area, the **James A.
Michener Art Museum**,
located in a 19th-century
county jail, has a world-class
collection of Pennsylvania
Impressionist paintings.

🏛 **Mercer Museum**
84 S Pine St. **Tel** (215) 345-0210.
◯ 10am–5pm Mon–Sat, noon–5pm
Sun, until 9pm Tue.

🏛 **Fonthill Museum**
E Court St and Rt 313. **Tel** (215) 348-
9461. 📷 mandatory; reservations
advised. www.fonthillmuseum.org

🏛 **James A. Michener Art
Museum**
138 S Pine St. **Tel** (215) 340-9800.
◯ 10am–4:30pm Tue–Fri, 10am–
5pm Sat & Sun. 📷
www.michenerartmuseum.org

New Hope ⑮

Bucks County, PA. 🚶 2000. 🛈 Visitor
Center: Main & Mechanic Sts, (215)
862-5030. www.newhopepa.com

This delightful waterfront
village and shoppers' paradise
teems with upscale boutiques
and restaurants. Tracing its
roots to the early 1700s, it
gained its name when
Benjamin Parry's gristmill,
which ground grain, burned
down in 1790. He rebuilt it
and named it "New Hope
Mills" with a promise
of prosperity for the town.

Today, that prosperity is
evident with more than 200 art
galleries, boutiques, and craft
and antiques shops, including
a branch of the **James A.
Michener Art Museum**. Train
rides aboard restored 1920
passenger cars, horse-drawn
carriages, and mule-drawn
barge trips down the scenic
19th-century canal add to the
town's ambience.

Parry, who also helped
finance the first bridge across
the Delaware, built a house in
1784 that was occupied by
successive generations of his
family until 1966. Today, the
Parry Mansion Museum
showcases its separate rooms,
decorated according to different periods of its history.

🏛 **Parry Mansion Museum**
45 S Main St. **Tel** (215) 862-5652.
◯ late Apr–early Dec: 1–5pm Sat &
Sun. 📷 by appointment. 📷

🏛 **James A. Michener Art
Museum – New Hope**
500 Union Square Dr, New Hope.
Tel (215) 862-7633. 📷 www.
michenerartmuseum.org

Storefronts line New Hope's old-world, picturesque streets

Delaware River at Washington Crossing Historic Park

Washington Crossing Historic Park ⑯

Washington Crossing, PA. **Tel** (215) 493-4076. 🔲 9am–5pm Tue–Sat, noon–5pm Sun. ⬤ public hols except Jul 4, Memorial Day, Labor Day, Dec 25. 🏳️

This waterfront park, set up in 1917 to commemorate Washington's historic crossing of the Delaware River, is divided into two sections. The McConkey's Ferry section, named after a local 18th-century inn, includes the riverbank from which Washington and his army departed in Durham boats. A monument marks this area outside the visitor center. Nearby is a 19th-century boathouse containing replicas of the boats, which are now used for the annual Christmas Day crossing reenactment.

About 4 miles (6 km) upstream is the Thompson's Mill section, which includes historic buildings, a gristmill, an observation tower, and a cemetery along the peaceful Delaware Canal containing the graves of Revolutionary War soldiers.

On the New Jersey side of the river, Washington Crossing State Park marks the site where Washington landed. This forested area includes historic homes, a visitor center and museum, and miles of hiking, riding, and biking trails.

Trenton ⑰

Mercer County, NJ. 🏛 85,000. 🚌 ℹ️ Lafayette at Barrack St, (609) 777-1770. **www**.trentonnj.com

The capital of New Jersey, Trenton's origin dates to 1679 when Quaker Mahlon Stacy built a gristmill along the Delaware. In 1714, his son sold land to merchant William Trent who laid out a new city called "Trent's Town" in 1721. Today, a big attraction is the Trenton Battle Monument. It pays tribute to the Battle of Trenton, in which General Washington and 2,400 men crossed the ice-clogged Delaware River on December 25, 1776, to launch an attack on British and Hessian soldiers. The latter were defeated and this battle was the turning point in the Revolutionary War. Prior to this, the Continental Army had suffered many defeats, and a win was badly needed

Plaque marking the river crossing

to boost morale in the fight for independence. The Old Barracks, dating to 1758, were occupied by Hessian soldiers during the encounter, and now house a museum.

🏛 **Old Barracks Museum**
Barrack St. **Tel** (609) 396-1776. 🔲 10am–5pm. ⬤ Jan 1, Easter, Thanksgiving, Dec 24–25. 🏳️

Pennsbury Manor ⑱

400 Pennsbury Memorial Rd, Morrisville, PA. **Tel** (215) 946-0400. 🔲 9am–5pm Tue–Sat, noon–5pm Sun. 🅿️ 🏳️ **www**.pennsbury manor.org

An elegant brick Georgian house 26 miles (42 km) north of Philadelphia, this manor is a re-creation of William Penn's country home and estate from the 1680s. The plantation sits on the site chosen by Penn, and this manor was built in 1939 on original foundations, where some 17th-century bricks are the only remnants of Penn's initial home. Inside, a hall served as a waiting room between the family's quarters and governor's parlor, while the second floor had three bedrooms and a nursery.

The estate today includes farm animals similar to those owned by Penn. Other recreated structures include a blacksmith shop, brew house, smokehouse, and horse shelter. The $3.5 million visitor center offers activities for schools, a gallery, office space, an auditorium and facilities for video conferencing.

Gardens at Pennsbury Manor, Penn's country estate

Atlantic City's glamorous resorts by night – lighting up the Jersey coast

Atlantic City ⓳

Atlantic County, NJ. 🏠 40,000. 🚌
🚆 ℹ *Atlantic City Convention &
Visitors Authority: 2314 Pacific Ave.*
Tel *(609) 348-7100, (888) 222-4748.*
www atlanticcitynj.com

Called the "Queen of the
Coast" by generations of
beachgoers, Atlantic City has
been a favored vacation spot
since the mid-1800s. The
first casino opened on
the famous
Boardwalk in
1978, and
since then
the town has
become one of
the most popular
destinations on the
eastern seaboard.
All gambling –
euphemistically referred to as
"gaming" – takes place in the
large, ostentatious casino
hotels that lie within a block
of the beach and Boardwalk,
which is lined with shops and
amusement arcades.
More than a dozen casino
resorts – with their towers
shooting up along the Boardwalk – make up the dazzling
city skyline. They include
Caesars, Bally's, Harrah's,
Showboat, Resorts, Tropicana,
and the properties owned by
billionaire developer Donald
Trump, such as the 51-story
Trump Taj Mahal *(see p139)*.
One of the flashiest hotels is
the Borgata Hotel Casino
and Spa, a $1-billion, 2,000-
room hotel. Many of these
resorts include spas, several
restaurants each, convention
facilities, nightclubs, and
concert halls featuring popular
comedy and musical acts.

**Playing cards used
in gaming**

Visitors not enchanted by the
casinos instead head for the
lively local attractions. Amusement parks with roller coasters
jut out over the ocean on the
Central Pier Arcade and
Speedway, and the famous
Steel Pier. Another attraction
is the Absecon Lighthouse,
the tallest lighthouse in New
Jersey, which offers splendid
views of the city and waterfront. Atlantic City also hosts
the prestigious annual
Miss America
Pageant, held
here since
1928.
Shopping
is also a big
draw, with the
arrival of Atlantic
City Outlet – The
Walk – housing
stores like Banana Republic,
Nautica, and Coach.
In nearby Margate City,
Lucy the Elephant stands tall
in celebration of American
marketing ingenuity. Built by
a real estate developer
in 1881 to draw pro-
spective buyers to his
holdings, "Lucy" has
served as a residence
and a tavern over the
years. Today, guided
tours take visitors into
the structure that has
become instantly recog-
nizable as part of the
Jersey shoreline.

🐘 **Lucy the Elephant**
3200 Atlantic Ave, Margate.
Tel *(609) 823-6473.* ⏱ *mid-
Jun–Labor Day: 10am–8pm
Mon–Sat, 10am–5pm Sun;
weekends in spring and fall;
Nov–Dec: hours vary.* 🖼
www lucytheelephant.org

Cape May ⓴

Cape May County, NJ. 🏠 4,000.
ℹ *Cape May Welcome Center: Elmira
& Lafayette Sts, (609) 884-5508.*

First explored by Cornelius
Mey for the Dutch West India
Company in 1621, Cape May
is one of the oldest resorts on
the Atlantic coast. Popular
with Philadelphia socialites
during the late 1800s, it has,
since then, continued to enjoy
a fine reputation among beach
lovers. The building boom of
the Victorian era characterizes
Cape May today. **Historic Cold
Spring Village** is a living
history museum showcasing
25 restored buildings, with
costumed actors portraying
19th-century lifestyles.

🏛 **Historic Cold Spring
Village**
720 US 9. **Tel** *(609) 898-2300.* ⏱ *mid-
Jun–Labor Day: 10am–4:30pm Tue–
Sun; only weekends Labor Day–mid-
Sep & Memorial Day–mid-Jun.* 🖼 &

**Brightly painted façade of a house at Cape
May, America's largest Victorian district**

Hagley Museum ㉑

200 Hagley Rd, Rte 141, Wilmington, DE. *Tel (302) 658-2400.* ☐ *Jan–mid-Mar: 9:30am– 4:30pm Sat & Sun, mid-Mar–Dec: 9:30am–4:30pm daily.* ● *Thanksgiving, Dec 25 & 31.* ☑ *Jan–mid-Mar: 1:30pm Mon–Fri.* ☐ 🌐 www.hagley.org

Not a museum in the conventional sense, this forested site along the rocky Brandywine River is where the DuPont Company was founded. In 1802, French immigrant Eleuthere Irenee du Pont built a factory to manufacture gunpowder and "black powder" used in explosives. The earliest buildings included the first du Pont family home, gardens, and company office. Through its 119-year-history, overseen by five generations of du Ponts, the mill expanded downriver, with waterwheels powering production facilities that sifted, mixed, and crushed raw materials into fine powder.

Today, only the façades of the original buildings remain. Some have working exhibitions, such as a rolling mill using safe charcoal. Staff members demonstrate the workings of a steam engine and the operations in a machine shop, but most impressive is the ignition of a powder sample. Some buildings house artifacts, original furniture, and rare du Pont cars, including a 1911 electric car and a 1928 Phaeton.

View of the Brandywine River at Hagley Museum

Interior of the conservatory at Longwood Gardens

Winterthur Museum ㉒

5105 Kennett Pike, Rte 52, Winterthur, DE. *Tel (302) 888-4600.* ☐ *10am–5pm Tue–Sun.* ● *Mon (except hols), Jan 1, Thanksgiving, Dec 25.* 🌐 ☑ ☐ www.winterthur.org

Once the home of Henry Francis du Pont, great-grandson of Eleuthere Irenee du Pont, this vast estate contains an extraordinary 175-room mansion. The original home, the core of the current mansion, dates to 1839. It was built by J.A. Bidermann and his wife, Evelina, Eleuthere du Pont's daughter. Henry Francis inherited the estate in 1926, expanding it during the two-decade-long conversion of his home into a museum. Today, it houses 85,000 items from the 17th to the 19th centuries, including paintings, textiles, furniture, ceramics, and Chinese porcelain. The main dining room features original silver tankards crafted by Paul Revere, and works of art by Gilbert Stuart and Benjamin West. The parlor features a unique oval Mont Morency staircase and is elegantly decorated with Chippendale furniture. The estate contains meadows, streams, and woods, including a tulip-poplar tree, which has been around when William Penn was alive.

Longwood Gardens ㉓

Rte 1, Kennett Square, PA. *Tel (800) 737-5500, (610) 388-1000.* ☐ *Apr–Oct: 9am–6pm; Nov–Mar: 9am–5pm.* ● *Mon (except hols), Jan 1, Thanksgiving, Dec 25.* 🌐 ♿ www.longwoodgardens.org

This well-manicured horticultural wonderland consists of colorful gardens, woodlands, lush meadows, greenhouses, and spectacular fountains amid idyllic bucolic scenery. Settler George Pierce acquired the land in 1700, and in 1798, his descendants established an arboretum that, by the mid-19th century was one the nation's finest.

Industrialist Pierre S. du Pont bought it in 1906 and it is his design that remains today. It includes over 11,000 plant varieties in both indoor and outdoor displays, whimsical topiaries, and a children's garden. The massive main greenhouse and conservatory are engineering marvels that shelter an array of exotic plant life. But the most breathtaking sights are the fabulous fountains with choreographed eruptions highlighted at night by colored lights, which create dazzling displays that are often the backdrop of musical events.

Brandywine Battlefield State Park ❷

878 Baltimore Pike, Rte 1, Chadds Ford, PA. *Tel (610) 459-3342.* ⬜ *9am–5pm Tue–Sat, noon–5pm Sun.* ⬛ *Mon.* 🈂 🅿

The Battle of Brandywine, fought on these rolling hills on September 11, 1777, was the biggest engagement of the American Revolution. General Washington stationed his troops atop this high ground at Chadds Ford along the Brandywine River in an attempt to stop the advancing British. The Americans were outmaneuvered as the British crossed the Brandywine River at an unguarded ford to the north of Washington's troops, forcing them to retreat.

Today, the battlefield is a state park with a visitor center and two historic houses, both restored to the way they were in 1777. The Benjamin Ring House was owned by a Quaker farmer and served as Washington's headquarters on the eve of the battle. The French patriot and American Revolution hero, Marquis de La Fayette, stayed in the farmhouse of Quaker Gideon Gilpin. The visitor center includes a small museum.

Revolutionary War hero La Fayette's quarters at Brandywine Park

Brandywine River Museum ❷

100 Creek Rd, Rte 1, Chadds Ford, PA. *Tel (610) 388-2700.* ⬜ *9:30am–4:30pm.* ⬛ *Dec 25.* 🈂 *Apr–mid-Nov: timed tours of N.C. Wyeth House & Studio, and Kuerner Farm Wed–Sun.* 🈂 🚻 🅿 www.brandywine museum.org

Located in a Civil War-era gristmill along Brandywine River, this museum is best known for housing artworks by three generations of the Wyeths – N.C., Andrew, and Jamie. Galleries showcase landscapes inspired by the Brandywine River Valley, and paintings and illustrations by the Wyeths and other artists. N.C. Wyeth (1882–1945) was a famous illustrator of the early 20th century, completing more than 1,000 illustrations, including some for classics such as *Treasure Island and Robin Hood.* N.C.'s son Andrew is known for mastering drybrush watercolor and egg tempura mediums. His son Jamie painted portraits of figures such as President John F. Kennedy and artist Andy Warhol.

Tours are organized to the N.C. Wyeth House and Studio, and the Kuerner Farm, which inspired Andrew for over 70 years. A farmhouse and barn display his works related to the farm.

National Memorial Arch at Valley Forge

George Washington's restored headquarters at Valley Forge

Valley Forge National Historic Park ❷

Rte 23 & North Gulph Rd, Valley Forge, PA. *Tel (610) 783-1077* ⬜ *Visitor Center: 9am–5pm.* ⬛ *Jan 1, Thanksgiving, Dec 25.* 🈂 🅿 www.nps.gov/vafo

George Washington and his soldiers spent the harsh winter of 1777–78 at Valley Forge, retreating to these hills after losing to British forces at Brandywine and Germantown *(see p107).* No battles were fought here, but nearly 2,000 soldiers died of typhus, typhoid, pneumonia, and dysentery. Today, reconstructed cabins, statues, and cannon are scattered through the park. Key exhibits are the National Memorial Arch, designed by Paul Cret, and built in 1917 in the memory of those who died in the winter of 1777–78, and stone farmhouses that once served as officers' quarters. The park has miles of fields and woods crisscrossed by hiking paths, and a visitor center with artifacts such as muskets and powder horns.

The American Revolution Center is the country's first museum dedicated to that conflict. Built within a quarry bluff, the vast space will showcase the largest collection of Revolutionary artifacts, information, and experiences ever assembled.

Cloth Angels
Handmade by
an Amish girl
12.00 plus tx.

TRAVELERS' NEEDS

WHERE TO STAY

The Philadelphia area offers a wide selection of hotel rooms to fit every style and budget. More expensive hotels include towers overlooking scenic Center City and riverfront views, boutique hotels, upscale chain hotels, and smaller but luxurious bed-and-breakfasts – some with colonial themes. The more budget-conscious traveler will find a wide range of comfortable chain hotels, motels, inns, and bed-and-breakfasts within the city and beyond. Hotel rates are quite reasonable, though they tend to be higher in the more popular business district and tourist areas.

Doorman at Westin

LOCATIONS

The Center City district has the highest concentration of hotel rooms in the Philadelphia metropolitan area with over 10,000 rooms available. Business travelers prefer to stay in one of the many Center City properties, which include high-end names, such as the Four Seasons Hotel and the Ritz Carlton. In particular, hotels are clustered near Logan Square and on Market, Chestnut, and Walnut Streets, with many in and around Rittenhouse Square, the Pennsylvania Convention Center, and along the Avenue of the Arts in the theater district.

A few hotels can be found in Old City and Society Hill, while some are also located along the Delaware River waterfront. Quality hotels are also concentrated in University City, along City Line Avenue on the city's north-western edge, at the airport, and in the suburbs of Valley Forge and King of Prussia.

FACILITIES AND AMENITIES

All hotels in Philadelphia have standard air conditioning, cable TV, and other conveniences. Upscale properties and some chain hotels have in-room business services and centers, including computer and fax facilities, though only a few smaller hotels or bed-and-breakfasts offer Internet access to guests.

Chain hotels, in particular, offer fitness facilities and some of the larger hotels have pools. Sometimes, hotels make arrangements with nearby health clubs for the use of their facilities by hotel guests. Additional charges may apply for certain amenities, and some may be costly. It is best to call and clarify when booking accommodation.

RESERVATIONS

Most larger chain hotels have toll-free reservation numbers, or visitors can make reservations through their Internet sites, with some offering discounts for online bookings. Prices quoted are often for double occupancy and do not include taxes or parking charges. Online hotel reservation service companies offer reduced rates for rooms, but often add hidden fees and taxes. A good resource is the website of the **Greater Philadelphia Tourism and Marketing Corporation**, with current hotel packages that may include tours, show performance tickets, and other offers.

HIDDEN COSTS

If you are traveling solo, always make sure you are quoted the rate for one person, as hotels usually quote room rates assuming double occupancy. Room taxes in Philadelphia amount to around 14 percent, while parking rates range anywhere from $10 to $30 per day. Rooms with a view can also cost more – the splendid panoramas of the waterfront, skyline, and neighborhoods can be seen from the higher floors of many hotels in the city.

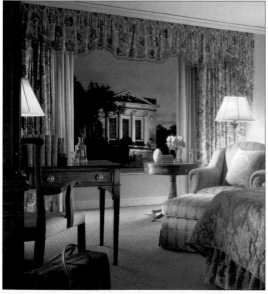

View of the First Bank of the US from a Ritz Carlton room *(see p136)*

◁ Jars of traditional Amish jams, jellies, preserves, and pickles at Reading Terminal Market

Entrance to the Radisson Plaza-Warwick Hotel Philadelphia *(see p136)*

DISCOUNTS

Discounts are often available when booking packages. The "Philly's More Fun When You Sleep Over" promotion runs at different times in the year and offers free parking, gifts, and other discounts on two weekend hotel nights for two. It is also available through the website of the **Greater Philadelphia Tourism and Marketing Corporation**.

BED-AND-BREAKFASTS

Accommodations at places offering bed-and-breakfast (B&Bs) are found within quiet and shaded neighborhoods, with some housed in quaint 18th- and 19th-century buildings and Victorian homes. Prices vary depending on services, amenities, and location. B&Bs include breakfast, but tend not to have restaurants, business facilities or exercise areas. Most B&Bs in the city are located in the neighborhoods of University City,

Chestnut Hill, Center City, and near City Line Avenue. To find out more and make reservations, contact **A Bed and Breakfast Connection of Philadelphia**.

HOSTELS

Younger travelers and students often stay in hostels, which offer much cheaper accommodation than hotel rooms. Some good hostels are: the **Bank Street Hostel**, in a renovated 19th-century building, has modern amenities and is located near Independence Mall; and the **Hosteling International Chamounix Mansion**, which is situated in one of Fairmount Park's historic homes.

TRAVELING WITH CHILDREN

With Philadelphia's many historic attractions and science-oriented museums, children are warmly welcomed at most city hotels. Younger children can usually stay for free in their parents' rooms, but it is best to check when making reservations. Ask about family rates and suites that might better accommodate kids. Hotels often supply cots at an additional cost. Family hotel packages are available through the **Greater Philadelphia Tourism and Marketing Corporation** website. These may include accommodations, meals, tickets for different historic tours, or free child meals and free parking.

DISABLED TRAVELERS

Most of the larger hotels accommodate wheelchairs, while smaller establishments, such as B&Bs, may not have full amenities for the disabled as they are housed in 18th- and 19th-century homes. For more information, contact the hotels or call the **Mayor's Commission on People with Disabilities**.

Bedroom at Rittenhouse 1715, a boutique hotel *(see p136)*

Choosing a Hotel

Hotels have been selected across a wide price range for facilities, good value, and location. All rooms have private bath, TV, air conditioning, and have disabled access unless otherwise indicated. Most have Internet access, and in some cases, fitness facilities may be offsite. The hotels are listed by area. For map references, *see pp194–97.*

PRICE CATEGORIES
The price ranges are for a standard double room per night, including tax, during the high season. Breakfast is not included, unless specified.

$ $60–$105
$$ $106–$145
$$$ $146–$185
$$$$ $186–$240
$$$$$ Over $240

OLD CITY

Comfort Inn Downtown/Historic Area $$
100 N Columbus Blvd, Philadelphia **Tel** *(215) 627-7900* **Fax** *(215) 238-0809* **Rooms** *185*   **Map** *4 E2*

This budget-priced, high-rise hotel has no frills but is in a great location within walking distance of historic sites. It offers clean, comfortable rooms, as well as a free Continental breakfast. In addition, children under 18 stay free with parents. It offers easy access to the I-95 and good views of the Delaware River. **www.choicehotels.com**

The Thomas Bond House $$
129 S 2nd St, Philadelphia **Tel** *(215) 923-8523* **Fax** *(215) 923-8504* **Rooms** *12*   **Map** *4 E3*

Once the home of prominent colonial physician, Thomas Bond, this historic inn dates back to 1769. Rooms are decorated with period furniture that create an ambience of colonial warmth and quiet luxury. Guests can make use of fitness facilities at an establishment close to the inn. **www.winston-salem-inn.com/philadelphia**

Best Western Independence Park Hotel $$$
235 Chestnut St, Philadelphia **Tel** *(215) 922-4443* **Fax** *(215) 922-4487* **Rooms** *36*   **Map** *4 E3*

Small, historic hotel dating back to 1856 with exquisitely decorated rooms, located within the heart of Old City and just a few blocks from Independence Mall and Penn's Landing. The hotel offers complimentary breafast and free wired or wireless high-speed Internet access. **www.independenceparkinn.com**

Holiday Inn Historic District $$$
400 Arch St, Philadelphia **Tel** *(215) 923-8660* **Fax** *(215) 829-1796* **Rooms** *364*   **Map** *4 E2*

Comfortable chain hotel with reasonably priced rooms. Its excellent and convenient location – one block from Independence Mall and within walking distance of the Market Street shopping area – make it a popular destination for tourists. Children love the rooftop pool during the warmer months. **www.holiday-inn.com/phlhistoric**

Morris House Hotel $$$
225 S 8th St, Philadelphia **Tel** *(215) 922-2446* **Fax** *(215) 922-2466* **Rooms** *15*   **Map** *3 C3*

This 1787 home is now a luxury boutique hotel and is one of the city's best hotels to experience colonial ambience. It has the coziness of a B&B and unique features such as a private garden, colonial-style reading room, two dining rooms with fireplaces, and rooms with hardwood floors. **www.morrishousehotel.com**

Omni Hotel $$$$
401 Chestnut St, Philadelphia **Tel** *(215) 925-0000* **Fax** *(215) 925-1263* **Rooms** *150*   **Map** *4 D3*

This four-star, four-diamond hotel has large-sized rooms with marble bathrooms. It is just a few blocks from key restaurants and nightlife spots, and within walking distance of shopping stores and Jewelers' Row. The rooms offer views of the Independence Mall area. **www.omnihotels.com**

Penn's View Hotel $$$$
14 N Front & Market Sts, Philadelphia **Tel** *(215) 922-7600* **Fax** *(215) 922-7642* **Rooms** *52*   **Map** *4 E3*

Cozy and family owned, this European-style hotel features murals and marble throughout the property. Its superb Italian restaurant and the unique "Il Bar" offers over 120 wines by the glass *(see p147)*. Situated across from Penn's Landing, it is just a block away from excellent restaurants and nightlife. **www.pennsviewhotel.com**

SOCIETY HILL AND PENN'S LANDING

Sheraton Society Hill $$$
1 Dock St, Philadelphia **Tel** *(215) 238-6000* **Fax** *(215) 238-6652* **Rooms** *365*   **Map** *4 E4*

The Sheraton Society Hill is another excellent hotel for the business traveler. There is a 24-hour business center, computer rentals, and a secretarial service. Situated on cobblestoned Dock Street, the hotel is also ideal for tourists as it is just a block or two from Penn's Landing. **www.sheraton.com/societyhill**

Key to Symbols *see back cover flap*

Hyatt Regency Philadelphia at Penn's Landing

🖼 P 🍴 ≋ 🏃 📺 🛗   ⑤⑤⑤⑤

201 S Columbus Blvd, Philadelphia **Tel** *(215) 928-1234* **Fax** *(215) 521-6543* **Rooms** *350*   *Map 4 F3*

Opened in 2000, this upscale property on Penn's Landing is Philadelphia's only waterfront hotel. Twenty-two stories overlook the Delaware River, and also offer superb views of Society Hill and Center City. Elegant rooms with a full range of amenities make it ideal for the business traveler. **www.pennslanding.hyatt.com**

CENTER CITY

Rodeway Inn

🖼 P ≋ 📺 🛗   ⑤

1208 Walnut St, Philadelphia **Tel** *(215) 546-7000* **Fax** *(215) 546-7573* **Rooms** *32*   *Map 3 B3*

This small, family-owned Victorian inn offers all the comfort and friendliness of a B&B. Located one block from the Forrest Theatre, it is within walking distance of Market Street and the city's historic sights. Guests can use the pool and fitness facilities at nearby establishments. **www.rodeway.com/hotel/pa271**

Alexander Inn

🖼 P 🍴 📺 🛗   ⑤⑤

12th & Spruce Sts, Philadelphia **Tel** *(215) 923-3535* **Fax** *(215) 923-1004* **Rooms** *48*   *Map 3 B3*

This boutique hotel has modern decor that adds a touch of European charm. It has an excellent Center City location, just a couple of blocks from the theater district. The restaurant only serves a breakfast buffet, and the business center allows guests to access emails. **www.alexanderinn.com**

Hampton Inn Convention Center

🖼 P ≋ 📺 🛗   ⑤⑤

1301 Race St, Philadelphia **Tel** *(215) 665-9100* **Fax** *(215) 665-9200* **Rooms** *250*   *Map 3 B1*

Located right next to the Convention Center, this property is ideal for people attending conventions. It is situated a few blocks from Chinatown and the Market Street shopping area and within walking distance of historic sights. The clean rooms have modern amenities, including high-speed Internet access. **www.hamptoninn.com**

Hilton Garden Inn Philadelphia Center City

🖼 P 🍴 ≋ 📺 🛗   ⑤⑤

1100 Arch St, Philadelphia **Tel** *(215) 923-0100* **Fax** *(215) 925-0800* **Rooms** *279*   *Map 3 C2*

This popular and fashionable chain hotel has newly renovated rooms and is located near the Pennsylvania Convention Center, a block or two from Chinatown. All rooms are outfitted with modern amenities, such as microwaves and refrigerators. The rooftop restaurant and lounge offer city views. **www.philadelphiacentercity.stayhgi.com**

Holiday Inn Express Midtown

🖼 P ≋ 🛗   ⑤⑤

1305 Walnut St, Philadelphia **Tel** *(215) 735-9300* **Fax** *(215) 732-2593* **Rooms** *168*   *Map 3 B3*

A comfortable budget chain hotel, this Holiday Inn has a convenient location just a few blocks from the theater district and the Market Street shopping area. Complimentary Continental breakfast is served and the hotel gives passes for a nearby fitness center to those guests who wish to keep in shape. **www.himidtown.com**

La Reserve

🏃 📺 🛗   ⑤⑤

1804 Pine St, Philadelphia **Tel** *(215) 735-1137* **Fax** *(215) 735-0582* **Rooms** *7*   *Map 2 D5*

A luxurious and cozy B&B in a refurbished Philadelphia townhouse, La Reserve has elegant rooms with antiques and beautiful lamps. The establishment has an all-you-can-eat gourmet breakfast and free wireless Internet access. Parking is available at nearby lots. **www.lareservebandb.com**

Travelodge

🖼 P   ⑤⑤

1227 Race St, Philadelphia **Tel** *(215) 564-2888* **Fax** *(215) 564-2700* **Rooms** *50*   *Map 3 B1*

This budget chain hotel has clean rooms and serves a complimentary Continental breakfast. Located directly across from the Pennsylvania Convention Center and just one block from Chinatown, it is within walking distance of historic sights and the Market Street shopping district. **www.travelodge.com**

Courtyard by Marriott Philadelphia Downtown

🖼 P 🍴 ≋ 🏃 📺 🛗   ⑤⑤⑤

21 N Juniper St, Philadelphia **Tel** *(215) 496-3200* **Fax** *(215) 496-3696* **Rooms** *498*   *Map 2 F4*

This is a comfortable Marriott-brand hotel housed in the historic, former City Hall Annex building. Located across the street from the Masonic Temple and the Pennsylvania Academy of the Fine Arts, it is just a few blocks from the Convention Center. Lobby and lounge areas are expansive. **www.philadelphiadowntowncourtyard.com**

Doubletree Hotel Philadelphia

🖼 P 🍴 ≋ 🏃 📺 🛗   ⑤⑤⑤

237 S Broad St, Philadelphia **Tel** *(215) 893-1600* **Fax** *(215) 893-1664* **Rooms** *434*   *Map 2 F5*

A high-rise hotel in the heart of Philadelphia on the Avenue of the Arts, this property is across from the Kimmel Center, the Academy of Music, and the Merriam Theater. The lobby has a comfortable lounge area and sports bar and bistro, and the roof garden sports a jogging track. **www.philadelphia.doubletree.com**

Latham Hotel

🖼 P 🍴 📺 🛗   ⑤⑤⑤

135 S 17th St, Philadelphia **Tel** *(215) 563-7474* **Fax** *(215) 563-4034* **Rooms** *139*   *Map 2 D4*

This small, European-style boutique hotel is in the heart of the fashionable Rittenhouse Row shopping district. Rooms are decorated in Victorian style. It offers all modern amenities, including free wireless Internet access in all rooms. It also boasts a hip bar and restaurant *(see p148)*. **www.lathamhotel.com**

The Independent Hotel

🔲 🎁 ⑤⑤⑤

1234 Locust St, Philadelphia **Tel** *(215) 772-1440* **Fax** *(215) 772-1022* **Rooms** *24*   **Map** *3 B3*

This sophisticated boutique hotel is housed in a restored Georgian Revival building in Center City's hip, midtown village district. The rooms are stylish and well equipped; single and double rooms have queen size beds while the executive room beds are king size. A complimentary breakfast is served in the hotel's fireside lounge. **www.theindependenthotel.com**

Crowne Plaza Philadelphia Center City

🔲 **P** 🎁 ≋ 🖭 🛁 ⑤⑤⑤⑤

1800 Market St, Philadelphia **Tel** *(215) 561-7500* **Fax** *(215) 561-2556* **Rooms** *445*   **Map** *2 E4*

Located within the city's cluster of skyscrapers, this chain hotel is ideal for business travelers. It offers modern, comfortable rooms. Just a few blocks from Rittenhouse Square with its many fine restaurants and boutiques, it is within walking distance of the theater and museum districts. **www.crowneplaza.com/philadelphia-centercity**

Loews Philadelphia

🔲 **P** 🎁 ≋ 🛉 🖭 🛁 ⑤⑤⑤⑤

1200 Market St, Philadelphia **Tel** *(215) 627-1200* **Fax** *(215) 231-7205* **Rooms** *583*   **Map** *3 B2*

This high-rise luxury hotel is housed in the landmark PSFS building, a 1932 former bank office. It has been renovated with elegant decor and Art Deco accents, including exotic woods and carved glass. Rooms offer astounding views. A spa and fitness center encompass the entire fifth floor of the hotel. **www.loewshotels.com**

Park Hyatt Philadelphia at the Bellevue

🔲 **P** 🎁 🖭 🛁 ⑤⑤⑤⑤

Broad & Walnut Sts, Philadelphia **Tel** *(215) 893-1234* **Fax** *(215) 732-8518* **Rooms** *172*   **Map** *2 E5*

A residential-style hotel with international flair, the Hyatt is perched on the upper floors of the 100-year-old Bellevue Building, which was once nicknamed the "Grand Dame of Broad Street." Marble staircases and chandeliers highlight the old world elegance. The property has upscale shops on its premises. **www.parkphiladelphia.hyatt.com**

Philadelphia Marriott Downtown

🔲 **P** 🎁 ≋ 🛉 🖭 🛁 ⑤⑤⑤⑤

1201 Market St, Philadelphia **Tel** *(215) 625-2900* **Fax** *(215) 625-6000* **Rooms** *1,410*   **Map** *3 B2*

A world-class convention hotel connected to the Convention Center and Reading Terminal Market, the Philadelphia Downtown Marriott offers upgraded amenities on concierge-level floors. Located in the heart of the Market Street shopping area and within walking distance of historic sights and the theater district. **www.philadelphiamarriott.com**

Radisson Plaza-Warwick Hotel Philadelphia

🔲 **P** 🎁 🛉 🖭 🛁 ⑤⑤⑤⑤

1701 Locust St, Philadelphia **Tel** *(215) 735-6000* **Fax** *(215) 790-7788* **Rooms** *301*   **Map** *2 E5*

One block from fashionable Rittenhouse Square, this is a prestigious hotel whose guests have included celebrities and presidents. Built in 1926 in English Renaissance style, it has a majestic two-story lobby with a sweeping staircase, and an upscale steakhouse, The Prime Rib *(see p149)*. **www.radisson.com/philadelphiapa**

Sofitel Philadelphia

🔲 **P** 🎁 🖭 🛁 ⑤⑤⑤⑤

120 S 17th St, Philadelphia **Tel** *(215) 569-8300* **Fax** *(215) 569-1492* **Rooms** *306*   **Map** *2 E4*

An elegant, four-diamond hotel with a distinctive French flair in design and embellishments, the Sofitel houses a chic French restaurant, and the lobby has a bar with dramatic floor-to-ceiling windows. The spacious rooms have elegant and modern decor. Rittenhouse Row shopping areas and restaurants are only a block away. **www.sofitel.com**

The Westin Philadelphia

🔲 **P** 🎁 🛉 🖭 🛁 ⑤⑤⑤⑤

99 S 17th St, Philadelphia **Tel** *(215) 563-1600* **Fax** *(215) 564-9559* **Rooms** *290*   **Map** *2 E4*

This is an elegant chain hotel with luxuriously decorated lobby, lounge areas, and restaurants. The hotel is connected to Liberty Place, which has trendy shops and boutiques. It has a great location just a few blocks from the Rittenhouse Row shopping hub, and the theater and museum districts. **www.westin.com/philadelphia**

One Rittenhouse Square

🔲 ⑤⑤⑤⑤⑤

135 S 18th St, Philadelphia **Tel** *(215) 825-7000* **Fax** *(215) 563-8486* **Rooms** *80*   **Map** *2 D5*

This luxury development, overlooking Rittenhouse Square, is one of a new generation of extended stay hotel residences that offer the comfort of a furnished apartment with the amenities of a hotel. Accommodations comprise contemporary studios, one and two bedroom apartments, and penthouse suites. Minimum one week stay. **www.hotelaka.com**

Rittenhouse 1715

🔲 🛁 ⑤⑤⑤⑤⑤

1715 Rittenhouse Sq, Philadelphia **Tel** *(215) 546-6500* **Fax** *(215) 546-8787* **Rooms** *23*   **Map** *2 D5*

This 16-room boutique hotel offers posh accommodation in a refurbished 1900s Philadelphia carriage house. It boasts a private, elegant, and luxurious lobby, serves a complimentary Continental breakfast in a Parisian-like break-fast room, and has a 24-hour concierge service. Parking is available at nearby lots. **www.rittenhouse1715.com**

The Rittenhouse Hotel

🔲 **P** 🎁 🛉 🖭 🛁 ⑤⑤⑤⑤⑤

210 W Rittenhouse Sq, Philadelphia **Tel** *(215) 546-9000* **Fax** *(215) 732-3364* **Rooms** *98*   **Map** *2 D5*

This top-of-the-line luxury hotel is one of the city's finest and boasts two award-winning restaurants, the Lacroix and the Smith & Wollensky steakhouse *(see p149)*. A five-diamond property with lavishly decorated rooms and marble bathrooms, the hotel also has an upscale spa and salon. **www.rittenhousehotel.com**

The Ritz Carlton Philadelphia

🔲 **P** 🎁 🛉 🖭 🛁 ⑤⑤⑤⑤⑤

10 S Broad St, Philadelphia **Tel** *(215) 523-8000* **Fax** *(215) 568-0942* **Rooms** *303*   **Map** *2 F4*

This exquisite, five-diamond luxury hotel sits directly across from City Hall in the former Girard/Mellon Bank Building. It has an impressive columned façade entrance and the lobby is situated in the expansive rotunda. The rooms are lavishly decorated and have superb city views. **www.ritzcarlton.com**

Key to Price Guide *see p134* **Key to Symbols** *see back cover flap*

LOGAN SQUARE AND THE MUSEUM DISTRICT

Best Western Center City Hotel
$$$

501 N 22nd St, Philadelphia **Tel** *(215) 568-8300* **Fax** *(215) 557-0259* **Rooms** *183*   **Map** *2 D1*

A newly renovated four-story budget hotel, this Best Western has the advantage of a good location within walking distance of the museum district. Some rooms offer excellent views of the Philadelphia skyline. Children who are 18 and younger can stay free with a paying adult. **www.bestwestern.com/centercityhotel**

Embassy Suites Hotel Philadelphia Center City
$$$

1776 Benjamin Franklin Pkwy, Philadelphia **Tel** *(215) 561-1776* **Fax** *(215) 561-1850* **Rooms** *288*   **Map** *2 E3*

Popular hotel in a landmark cylindrical building opposite Logan Square. This chain features only suites – every room has an adjacent living room and a balcony. Situated in the museum district and close to the Museum of Art and Rittenhouse Square. The fitness room has a jogging track. **www.embassysuites.com**

Sheraton Philadelphia City Center Hotel
$$$

17th & Race Sts, Philadelphia **Tel** *(215) 448-2000* **Fax** *(215) 448-2853* **Rooms** *758*   **Map** *2 E3*

This upscale, high-rise hotel is ideal for both the business and vacation traveler. Located four blocks from the Convention Center, it has a fabulous seafood restaurant and an impressive modern design with a four-story high lobby atrium. The comfortable and gracious rooms have all the modern amenities. **www.sheraton.com**

The Windsor Suites
$$$$

1700 Benjamin Franklin Pkwy, Philadelphia **Tel** *(215) 981-5678* **Fax** *(215) 981-5609* **Rooms** *267*   **Map** *2 E3*

Specialty hotel that offers furnished suites and unfurnished apartments. All rooms have complimentary high-speed Internet access and kitchens. Some suites have living rooms, separate sleeping areas, and private balconies. The hotel has two restaurants on its premises. **www.windsorsuites.com**

Four Seasons Hotel
$$$$$

1 Logan Sq, Philadelphia **Tel** *(215) 963-1500* **Fax** *(215) 963-9507* **Rooms** *364*   **Map** *2 E3*

One of Philadelphia's most elegant hotels, the Four Seasons is luxuriously decorated with Federal-style furnishings. It features one of the city's best restaurants *(see p150)*, as well as a courtyard café with decorative water fountains. It is located close to the financial, commercial, and museum districts. **www.fourseasons.com/philadelphia**

FARTHER AFIELD

Best Western Hotel Philadelphia Northeast
$

11580 Roosevelt Blvd, Philadelphia, PA, 19116 **Tel** *(215) 464-9500* **Fax** *(215) 464-8511* **Rooms** *100*

This reliable and comfortable chain hotel has well-decorated rooms with modern amenities. The hotel is within walking distance of several restaurants, while the Franklin Mills Outlet Mall and the Philadelphia Park Race Track are a short drive away. Convenient access to major interstates and turnpikes. **www.philadelphia-phl.com**

Holiday Inn Philadelphia – Cherry Hill
$

2175 W Marlton Pike, Cherry Hill, NJ, 08002 **Tel** *(856) 663-5300* **Fax** *(856) 662-2913* **Rooms** *186*

In the heart of southern New Jersey, this Holiday Inn is a popular, mid-range chain hotel that caters to both business and leisure travelers. The in-house restaurant is the Red Hot & Blue, a Memphis-style barbecue restaurant. Close to attractions along the Camden Waterfront and 6 miles (10 km) from Center City. **www.holidaycherryhill.com**

Howard Johnson Inn and Conference Center
$

2389 Rt 70 West, Cherry Hill, NJ, 08002 **Tel** *(856) 317-1900* **Fax** *(856) 317-0800* **Rooms** *90*

This budget hotel is located within 5 miles (8 km) of Center City in Philadelphia. It is also well-placed to visit other sights, such as the Adventure Aquarium and the Camden Waterfront. The hotel offers a complimentary Continental breakfast and there is an Indian restaurant on the premises. **www.hojo.com**

Mount Laurel Marriott
$

915 Rt 73, Mount Laurel, NJ, 08054 **Tel** *(856) 234-7300* **Fax** *(856) 802-3912* **Rooms** *283*

This pleasant suburban hotel is excellent for both business travelers and tourists. The hotel features a new premier steakhouse and a heated pool. Concierge-level rooms have upgraded amenities and balconies. There is also a game room for children and tennis courts. **www.mtlaurelmarriott.com**

Ramada Inn Philadelphia Airport
$

76 Industrial Hwy, Essington, PA, 19029 **Tel** *(610) 521-9600* **Fax** *(610) 521-9388* **Rooms** *292*

Located 3 miles (5 km) south of Philadelphia Airport, this comfortable hotel has a complimentary, 24-hour shuttle service to the airport. Each room has its own balcony. Special discounts are available for groups of ten or more people. **www.phillyramadainn.com**

Chestnut Hill Hotel
8229 Germantown Ave, Philadelphia, PA, 19118 **Tel** *(215) 242-5905* **Fax** *(215) 242-8778* **Rooms** *36*

Built in 1891, this historic hotel is situated along the cobblestoned streets of Germantown Avenue. Although furnished with 18th-century decor, it offers all modern amenities. Within walking distance of Fairmount Park's Wissahickon Gorge and a short drive from historic Germantown. **www.chestnuthillhotel.com**

Clarion Hotel & Conference Center
1450 Rt 70 E and I-295, Cherry Hill, NJ, 08034 **Tel** *(856) 428-2300* **Fax** *(856) 354-7662* **Rooms** *204*

Across the Delaware River, this hotel and conference center is ideal for both the business and leisure traveler. An in-house café serves breakfast, entrées, and pastries, and a neighborhood-like pub and restaurant is next door. The hotel is a short drive from the Camden Waterfront and central Philadelphia. **www.clarionofcherryhill.com**

Conwell Inn at Temple University
1331 W Berks St, Philadelphia, PA, 19122 **Tel** *(215) 235-6200* **Fax** *(215) 235-6235* **Rooms** *22*

A small hotel, Conwell Inn lies within the heart of the Temple University campus. A deluxe historic landmark hotel, it has cozy and comfortable rooms and suites that have been decorated very tastefully. The hotel provides a complimentary European breakfast. **www.conwellinn.com**

Hampton Inn Philadelphia Airport
8600 Bartram Ave, Philadelphia, PA, 19158 **Tel** *(215) 966-1300* **Fax** *(215) 966-1313* **Rooms** *152*

The Hampton Inn is a quality budget hotel with clean and comfortable rooms. The newly renovated hotel offers a shuttle service to the airport, which is about 2 miles (3 km) away. A short drive away are professional sports stadiums and south Philadelphia sights, including the Italian Market. **www.hamptoninn.com**

Fairfield Inn Philadelphia Airport
8800 Bartram Ave, Philadelphia, PA, 19153 **Tel** *(215) 365-2254* **Fax** *(215) 365-2254* **Rooms** *109*

Located just half a mile away from the airport, this comfortable, high-end budget property by Marriott offers full amenities and conveniences at superior value for the dollar. Complimentary Continental breakfast. 3 miles (5 km) from professional sports venues in south Philadelphia. **www.marriott.com**

Quality Inn & Conference Center
531 Rt 38 W, Maple Shade, NJ, 08052 **Tel** *(856) 235-6400* **Fax** *(856) 727-1027* **Rooms** *109*

This three-diamond hotel and conference center is ideal for both the business and leisure traveler and features Jacuzzi suites. The bar by the poolside is open only on the weekends. About 10 miles (16 km) from central Philadelphia, it is also close to a number of entertainment areas. **www.qualityinn.com/hotel/nj129**

Cornerstone Bed & Breakfast
3300 Baring St, Philadelphia, PA, 19104 **Tel** *(215) 387-6065* **Fax** *(215) 387-0590* **Rooms** *6*   **Map** *1 A2*

This intimate urban inn sits in a restored 1870s church-stone mansion, and has a wrap-around porch and stained glass windows. Its lavishly decorated rooms and lounge areas have original wood floors and high ceilings. The inn is situated close to the Philadelphia Zoo and the Museum of Art. **www.cornerstonebandb.com**

Embassy Suites Hotel – Philadelphia International Airport
9000 Bartram Ave, Philadelphia, PA, 19153 **Tel** *(215) 365-4500* **Fax** *(215) 365-4803* **Rooms** *263*

This recently renovated three-diamond, modern chain hotel is an all-suites establishment. It has a unique tropical atrium lobby, which is filled with ducks and fishponds. The hotel offers a complimentary cook-to-order breakfast. Just one mile (1.6 km) from the Philadelphia Airport. Free airport shuttle. **www.philadelphiaairport.embsuites.com**

Hilton Philadelphia Airport
4509 Island Ave, Philadelphia, PA, 19153 **Tel** *(215) 365-4150* **Fax** *(215) 937-6382* **Rooms** *331*

The Hilton chain offers comfort and a touch of elegance with this full-service hotel, located just one mile (1.6 km) from the airport. The Landing Restaurant and Grill is highly recommended, as are its bar and indoor pool. A complimentary 24-hour airport shuttle service is offered. Close to the city's sports stadiums. **www.hilton.com**

Crowne Plaza Hotel Philadelphia – Cherry Hill
2349 W Marlton Pike, Cherry Hill, NJ, 08002 **Tel** *(856) 665-6666* **Fax** *(856) 662-1414* **Rooms** *408*

Located in suburban Cherry Hill, this upscale and full-service Hilton property features modern rooms with full amenities, dark oak furniture, and marble countertops. It is convenient for visiting the Adventure Aquarium and the Camden Waterfront, while the Atlantic City beaches and casinos are just an hour away. **www.crowneplaza.com/cherryhillnj**

Hilton Philadelphia City Avenue
4200 City Ave, Philadelphia, PA, 19131 **Tel** *(215) 879-4000* **Fax** *(215) 879-9020* **Rooms** *209*

An upscale chain hotel on the outskirts of the city, this Hilton hotel is a short drive from Fairmount Park and the Barnes Foundation. It has comfortable and elegantly furnished rooms. Guests can indulge in plenty of shopping and culinary delights in the shops and restaurants on City Avenue. **www.philadelphiacityavenue.hilton.com**

Holiday Inn Philadelphia Stadium
900 Packer Ave, Philadelphia, PA, 19148 **Tel** *(215) 755-9500* **Fax** *(215) 339-0842* **Rooms** *238*

This newly renovated property is a hotel ideal for fans taking in a game at one of nearby professional sports venues in south Philadelphia. Comfortable rooms with a full range of amenities for leisure and business travelers as well. There is a sports bar and restaurant on the premises. **www.ichotelsgroup.com**

Key to Price Guide *see p134* **Key to Symbols** *see back cover flap*

Sheraton University City Hotel

3549 Chestnut St, Philadelphia, PA, 19104 **Tel** *(215) 387-8000* **Fax** *(215) 387-7920* **Rooms** *316*

This is a large and efficient full-service chain hotel on the University of Pennsylvania campus. Rooms have modern decor with plush beds and oversized chairs. Ideal for visiting Philadelphia Zoo and the Museum of Archaeology and Anthropology. The lobby features complimentary, wireless Internet access. **www.philadelphiasheraton.com**

The Inn at Penn

3600 Sansom St, Philadelphia, PA, 19104 **Tel** *(215) 222-0200* **Fax** *(215) 222-4600* **Rooms** *238*

Just across the Schuylkill River from Center City, this upscale Hilton hotel sits in the heart of the University of Pennsylvania campus. Also close to the Drexel University, Philadelphia Zoo, 30th Street Amtrak Station, and the University of Pennsylvania's Museum of Archaeology and Anthropology. **www.theinnatpenn.com**

Renaissance Hotel Philadelphia Airport

500 Stevens Dr, Philadelphia, PA, 19113 **Tel** *(610) 521-5900* **Fax** *(610) 521-8954* **Rooms** *350*

This four-diamond, modern, and upscale chain hotel is on I-95, close to the airport. It is tastefully decorated with the Renaissance's signature European flair. There is an expansive lobby atrium and the rooms have high-speed Internet access. It is in a convenient location for a quick drive into the city on the interstate. **www.renaissancehotels.com**

Philadelphia Airport Marriott

Arrivals Rd, Philadelphia, PA, 19153 **Tel** *(215) 492-9000* **Fax** *(215) 492-4799* **Rooms** *419*

This upscale and full-service Marriott Hotel is the only one in Philadelphia connected to the airport via a skybridge to Terminal B. Nearby is the convenient R1 commuter train linking the airport with Center City. Terrific in-hotel dining and lounge at Riverbend Bar and Grille. **www.philadelphiaairportmarriott.com**

BEYOND PHILADELPHIA

ATLANTIC CITY Bally's Atlantic City Hotel & Casino

1900 Pacific Ave, Atlantic City, NJ, 08401 **Tel** *(609) 340-2000* **Fax** *(609) 340-4713* **Rooms** *1,246*

One of the few remnants of historic Atlantic City, the 1860s Dennis Hotel has been restored as part of this mega-resort complex, which also includes a modern 45-story tower. Fans of the board game Monopoly will know that the hotel stands on the city's most valuable corner. The hotel's casino features a Wild West theme. **www.harrahs.com**

ATLANTIC CITY Caesars Atlantic City Hotel Casino

2100 Pacific Ave, Atlantic City, NJ, 08401 **Tel** *(609) 348-4411* **Fax** *(609) 343-2405* **Rooms** *1,144*

A premier destination on the New Jersey shore, Caesars is a luxurious hotel and casino on the Boardwalk with an "Ancient Rome" theme. The hotel's lobby is done up to look like a Roman temple, and there are 11 restaurants and three lounges. The 1,100-seat Circus Maximus Theater offers the best in entertainment. **www.harrahs.com**

ATLANTIC CITY Trump Taj Mahal Hotel Casino and Resort

1000 Boardwalk at Virginia Ave, Atlantic City, NJ, 08401 **Tel** *(609) 449-1000* **Rooms** *1,250*

One of Atlantic City's landmark casinos, this luxury five-diamond resort has all the opulence that lives up to the Trump name. A 51-story tower hovers over the Boardwalk, and the themed hotel and casino has nine in-house restaurants *(see p152)* and a 5,000-seat arena for concerts and sports events. **www.trumptaj.com**

BRANDYWINE VALLEY Brandywine River Hotel

Rts 1 & 100, Chadds Ford, PA, 19317 **Tel** *(610) 388-1200* **Rooms** *40*

A Victorian-style country B&B, the Brandywine River Hotel has elegantly decorated rooms with fireplaces and Jacuzzis. It is a short drive from Longwood Gardens, Brandywine Battlefield, Brandywine River Museum, Chadds Ford, and Winterthur. The hotel is surrounded by several award-winning restaurants. **www.brandywineriverhotel.com**

CAPE MAY The Chalfonte Hotel

301 Howard St, Cape May, NJ, 08204 **Tel** *(609) 884-8409* **Fax** *(609) 884-4588* **Rooms** *70*

This whitewashed Victorian-era hotel was built in 1874 and offers old-fashioned charm with rocking chairs on the wrap-around front porch. Chalfonte has always been unconventional – rooms have no televisions or phones, and the hotel is just two blocks from the beach. **www.chalfonte.com**

CAPE MAY Queen Victoria Bed and Breakfast

102 Ocean St, Cape May, NJ, 08204 **Tel** *(609) 884-8720* **Rooms** *32*

Built in the 1870s and fully restored in 1995, this mansard-roofed Victorian inn is located in the heart of Cape May, just a block from the beach, antiques shops, gourmet dining, and historic tours. Bicycles to tour the area are available for free, and the hotel provides a complimentary European breakfast buffet. **www.queenvictoria.com**

DELAWARE Hotel du Pont

11th & Market Sts, Wilmington, DE, 19801 **Tel** *(302) 594-3100* **Fax** *(302) 594-3108* **Rooms** *218*

Dating back to 1913, this four-diamond, four-star hotel is the ultimate in luxury in Delaware. Each room is lavishly furnished with mahogany furniture and brass bathroom fixtures. Close to most of the region's attractions, including the Brandywine River Museum, Winterthur, Hagley Museum, and Longwood Gardens. **www.hoteldupont.com**

DOYLESTOWN 1814 House Inn Bed & Breakfast   🅿 📶   ⑤⑤⑤
50 S Main St, Doylestown, PA, 18901 **Tel** *(215) 340-1814* **Fax** *(215) 340-2234* **Rooms** *7*

This historic inn is within walking distance of the Mercer Museum and the James A. Michener Art Museum. Many rooms overlook Doylestown Historical Society Park. The rooms are decorated with 19th-century furnishings, but have all modern conveniences. A full country breakfast is offered on weekends. **www.1814houseinn.com**

GETTYSBURG Quality Inn at General Lee's Headquarters   🅿 📶 📶 🅰 📶 📶   ⑤
401 Buford Ave, Gettysburg, PA, 17325 **Tel** *(717) 334-3141* **Fax** *(717) 334-1813* **Rooms** *45*

Quaint inn with renovated rooms next to Confederate General Robert E. Lee's former headquarters. The three-diamond inn has spacious, bright, and clean rooms with antique furniture. Two-story suites are also available. Free Continental breakfast and admission to General Lee's Headquarters Museum. **www.thegettysburgaddress.com**

GETTYSBURG Farnsworth House Inn   🅿 📶   ⑤⑤
401 Baltimore St, Gettysburg, PA, 17325 **Tel** *(717) 334-8838* **Fax** *(717) 334-5862* **Rooms** *16*

This B&B is housed in one of Gettysburg's most historic buildings, with walls that still have bullet holes from the Civil War, and a small open-air garden. The lavish rooms have period decor, and the B&B conducts ghost tours of some of the "haunted" rooms. It also has quaint dining rooms *(see p152)*. **www.farnsworthhouseinn.com**

GETTYSBURG Gettystown Inn   🅿 📶 📶   ⑤⑤
89 Steinwehr Ave, Gettysburg, PA, 17325 **Tel** *(717) 334-2100* **Fax** *(717) 334-6905* **Rooms** *9*

Victorian B&B consisting of three separate Civil War-era houses near where President Lincoln delivered his famous Gettysburg Address *(see p121)*. Rooms are lavishly decorated with 19th-century antiques and furnishings. A complimentary breakfast is served at the adjacent Dobbin House Tavern *(see p152)*. **www.dobbinhouse.com**

GETTYSBURG The Brafferton Inn   🅿   ⑤⑤⑤
44 York St, Gettysburg, PA, 17325 **Tel** *(717) 337-3423, (866) 337-3423* **Rooms** *17*

This elegant and lovely B&B is located in a 1786 fieldstone house – the oldest residence in Gettysburg. All rooms are furnished with 18th- and 19th-century family antiques, elaborate stencils, and family portraits. A two-night stay is the minimum on weekends from April to November. **www.brafferton.com**

GETTYSBURG Hilton Garden Inn Gettysburg   📶 🅿 📶 📶 🅰 📶 📶   ⑤⑤⑤
1061 York St, Gettysburg, PA, 17325 **Tel** *(717) 334-2040* **Fax** *(717) 334-2073* **Rooms** *88*

A pleasant hotel focused on both business and leisure travelers. All the rooms are beautifully appointed, with a refrigerator, microwave, and complimentary Internet access. The hotel is located a short distance away from the historic battlefield, museums, and the town center. **www.hiltongardeninn.com**

HARRISBURG Hilton Harrisburg   📶 🅿 📶 📶 📶 📶   ⑤⑤⑤
1 N 2nd St, Harrisburg, PA, 17101 **Tel** *(717) 233-6000* **Fax** *(717) 233-6830* **Rooms** *341*

This upscale, full-service Hilton hotel is just three blocks from the State Capitol. It has elegant rooms; "Tower Level" guest rooms are accorded enhanced amenities, including a complimentary Continental breakfast and evening hors d'ouevres. The hotel has four restaurants on its premises. **www.harrisburg.hilton.com**

HERSHEY Hampton Inn & Suites Hershey   📶 🅿 📶 📶 📶   ⑤⑤⑤⑤
749 East Chocolate Ave, Hershey, PA, 17033 **Tel** *(717) 533-8400* **Fax** *(717) 520-1892* **Rooms** *110*

A comfortable chain hotel in downtown Hershey, the Hampton Inn & Suites is only 1 mile (1.6 km) from the renowned attractions of the area, including Hershey Chocolate World and Hershey Park. The hotel offers a complimentary Continental breakfast and high-speed Internet access. **www.hamptoninn.com**

HERSHEY The Hotel Hershey   📶 🅿 📶 📶 📶 📶 📶   ⑤⑤⑤⑤⑤
100 Hotel Rd, Hershey, PA, 17033 **Tel** *(717) 533-2171* **Fax** *(717) 534-8887* **Rooms** *232*

This grand hotel with its majestic gardens and fountains sits atop a hill overlooking the town. Luxurious and lavishly decorated rooms and common areas have old-world charm, and historic photographs and original artworks line the walls. Turndown service at night with Hershey's "Kisses" chocolates. **www.thehotelhershey.com**

PENNSYLVANIA DUTCH COUNTRY General Sutter Inn   🅿 📶   ⑤
14 E Main St, Lititz, PA, 17543 **Tel** *(717) 626-2115* **Fax** *(717) 626-0992* **Rooms** *15*

The General Sutter Inn is one of the oldest in Pennsylvania, dating back to 1764. Spacious rooms and suites are decorated with antiques in Victorian style. It is home to two fine restaurants and a lively bar, and has a delightful courtyard that is used for outdoor dining and cocktails. **www.generalsutterinn.com**

PENNSYLVANIA DUTCH COUNTRY Revere Inn & Suites   📶 🅿 📶 📶 📶 📶   ⑤
3063 Lincoln Hwy, Paradise, PA, 17562 **Tel** *(717) 687-8601* **Fax** *(717) 687-6141* **Rooms** *95*

This unique hotel has comfortable and tastefully decorated rooms and suites in three different buildings, including the 18th-century Revere House. All rooms have modern amenities and the historic Revere Tavern restaurant is situated on the property. Located on Route 30 in the heart of the Pennsylvania Dutch Country. **www.revereinn.com**

PENNSYLVANIA DUTCH COUNTRY Bird-In-Hand Family Inn   📶 🅿 📶 📶 🅰 📶   ⑤⑤
2740 Old Philadelphia Pike, Bird-In-Hand, PA, 17505 **Tel** *(717) 768-8271* **Fax** *(717) 768-1117* **Rooms** *125*

This large, three-diamond property is an ideal getaway for a family holiday. Facilities such as tennis courts, mini-golf, a playground, game room, and even a petting zoo keep the kids busy. It has a family restaurant with an all-you-can-eat buffet. **www.bird-in-hand.com/familyinn**

Key to Price Guide *see p134* **Key to Symbols** *see back cover flap*

PENNSYLVANIA DUTCH COUNTRY Bird-In-Hand Village Inn & Suites   🅿 ⬚   ⑤⑤

2695 Old Philadelphia Pike, Bird-In-Hand, PA, 17505 Tel (717) 293-8369 Fax (717) 768-1117 Rooms 24

This 1734 inn is responsible for the unique naming of this small town. Four well-preserved historic buildings house rooms and suites. The complimentary Continental breakfast includes local freshly-baked treats. Guests can take a 2-hour complimentary bus tour of the area. **www.bird-in-hand.com/villageinn**

PENNSYLVANIA DUTCH COUNTRY Fulton Steamboat Inn   🖥 🅿 ⑪ ⬚ ♿ 🎦 🛢   ⑤⑤

Rt 30 at Rt 896, Strasburg, PA, 17579 Tel (717) 299-9999 Fax (717) 299-9992 Rooms 97

This unique hotel is shaped like a 19th-century steamboat in honor of inventor Robert Fulton, who was born nearby in 1765. Family-oriented, with three "decks" of spacious guest rooms and "cabins" with bunk beds for kids, the inn is not far from the Strasburg Railroad and the Amish Village. Two-night minimum stay. **www.fultonsteamboatinn.com**

PENNSYLVANIA DUTCH COUNTRY Lodging at Kitchen Kettle Village   🅿 ⑪   ⑤⑤

Rt 340, Intercourse, PA, 17534 Tel (717) 768-8261 Rooms 11

Located among Pennsylvania Dutch Country farms, 11 tastefully decorated rooms and suites are tucked amidst the specialty shops at Kitchen Kettle Village, which comprises 32 shops, restaurants, and lodging. The rooms are comfortable and offer all modern amenities. **www.kitchenkettle.com**

PENNSYLVANIA DUTCH COUNTRY Strasburg Village Inn   🅿   ⑤⑤

1 W Main St, Strasburg, PA, 17579 Tel (717) 687-0900 Fax (717) 687-3650 Rooms 10

Dating back to the late 1780s, this historic inn is situated on one corner of Strasburg's center square. Ten rooms in "Williamsburg" style are warmly furnished in Victorian-style decor with canopy beds and antiques. The inn sits next door to the old-style Strasburg Creamery, an ice cream and sandwich shop. **www.strasburg.com**

PENNSYLVANIA DUTCH COUNTRY Amishview Inns & Suites   🖥 🅿 ⑪ ⬚ ♿ 🎦 🛢   ⑤⑤⑤

Rt 340, 3125 Old Philadelphia Pike, Bird-In-Hand, PA, 17505 Tel (717) 768-1102 Rooms 50

This recently constructed country inn has scenic views of cornfields and silos. It is located halfway between Intercourse and Bird-In-Hand on the Plain and Fancy Farm, which is also home to Lancaster's first family-style restaurant *(see p153)*. Adjacent to the Amish Experience Theater and the Amish Homestead. **www.amishviewinn.com**

PENNSYLVANIA DUTCH COUNTRY Historic Strasburg Inn   🅿 ⑪ ⬚ ♿ 🎦 🛢   ⑤⑤⑤

One Historic Dr, Strasburg, PA, 17579 Tel (717) 687-7691 Fax (717) 687-5290 Rooms 102

The Historic Strasburg Inn sits on 18 acres (7 ha) of beautifully landscaped grounds with views of Amish farmland and is just a short walk from popular shops and restaurants. The accommodation ranges from traditional doubles to multi-room family options to luxury jacuzzi suites. **www.historicinnofstrasburg.com**

PENNSYLVANIA DUTCH COUNTRY Intercourse Village Bed & Breakfast Suites 🅿   ⑤⑤⑤

Rt 340, Main Street, Intercourse, PA, 17534 Tel (717) 768-1162 Rooms 12

This 1909, Victorian-style B&B is a four-diamond facility with traditional fireplaces in suites with beamed ceilings and private baths with Jacuzzis. Enjoy candlelit gourmet breakfasts in the ornate dining room. The B&B is located close to antiques and craft shops in the heart of Intercourse's main shopping street. **www.amishcountryinns.com**

TRENTON Trenton Marriott at Lafayette Yard   🖥 🅿 ⑪ 🎦 🛢   ⑤⑤

1 W Lafayette St, Trenton, NJ, 08608 Tel (609) 421-4000 Fax (609) 421-4002 Rooms 197

An upscale and modern three-diamond hotel in downtown Trenton, the hotel has elegant guest rooms. It is adjacent to the Trenton War Memorial, and is just one block from the tourist information center and Old Barracks Museum. A short drive away are Washington Crossing State Park and New Hope. **www.marriott.com**

VALLEY FORGE Dolce Valley Forge   ⑪ ⬚ 🎦   ⑤⑤

215 West Dekalb Pike, King of Prussia, PA, 19406 Tel (610) 337-1200 Fax (610) 337-1959 Rooms 348

This hotel has had a $17 million facelift and provides lodging just minutes from Valley Forge National Historic Park. Each guest room artfully combines traditional touches with modern facilities and amenities. The hotel's executive and luxury suites are ideal for extended stays. **www.dolce-valley-forge-hotel.com**

VALLEY FORGE Crowne Plaza Valley Forge   🖥 🅿 ⑪ ⬚ 🎦 🛢   ⑤⑤⑤

260 Mall Blvd, King of Prussia, PA, 19406 Tel (610) 265-7500 Fax (610) 265-4076 Rooms 225

Opened in 2004, this upscale hotel is walking distance from the colossal King of Prussia Mall. The property has tastefully decorated rooms with many amenities, including Jacuzzis. It also offers complete business facilities. The hotel is 2 miles (3 km) from the Valley Forge National Historic Park. **www.cpvalleyforge.com**

VALLEY FORGE Homewood Suites Valley Forge   🖥 🅿 ⬚ ♿ 🎦 🛢   ⑤⑤⑤

681 Shannondell Blvd, Audubon, PA, 19403 Tel (610) 539-7300 Fax (610) 539-2970 Rooms 123

This spacious, all-suite hotel is located near Valley Forge National Historic Park and the King of Prussia Mall. Suites are available for short and extended stays; all have fully equipped kitchens and free Internet access. Breakfast (daily) and light evening meals (Monday through Thursday) are complimentary. **www.homewoodsuitesvalleyforge.com**

VALLEY FORGE Wayne Hotel   🖥 🅿 ⑪   ⑤⑤⑤

139 E Lancaster Ave, Wayne, PA, 19087 Tel (610) 687-5000 Fax (610) 687-8387 Rooms 40

Dating back to 1906, this century-old hotel along Philadelphia's fashionable Main Line has been restored to its former Victorian elegance. Tudor Revival-style architecture adds to the old-world charm. It is a just a few miles from the King of Prussia Mall. Fitness facilities and pool can be used at nearby establishments. **www.waynehotel.com**

RESTAURANTS AND CAFES

Though the city is perhaps traditionally best known for the Philadelphia cheesesteak, its culinary repertoire has expanded widely and is today home to some of the country's top-rated restaurants. In addition to superb American fare, some of the city's best dining rooms specialize in international cuisine, including French, Italian, Thai,

Typical Dutch Country pretzel

Moroccan, Chinese, and more. Excellent bistros, seafood restaurants, and steakhouses that feature cooking styles from Southern home cooking and colonial fare to Pennsylvania Dutch can be found in Center City. Modest restaurants and eateries, many serving traditional cheesesteak sandwiches, can be found in every city neighborhood and beyond.

Park-side alfresco dining at Rouge in Rittenhouse Square *(see p149)*

PHILLY FARE

For breakfast, the locals love to order grilled pork rolls along with their eggs and hash brown potatoes. At noon, cheesesteaks and lunchmeat-filled "hoagies" or "grinders" are favorites, and these can be found at the many food courts, pizzerias, and sandwich shops dotted around the city. Hoagies are Italian rolls filled with fresh meats and cheeses, as well as lettuce, tomatoes, and onions, topped off with a dash of oregano. Philly cheesesteaks consist of finely-sliced grilled beef along with onions, which are topped off with thick cheese sauce served up in a foot-long roll.

In Pennsylvania Dutch Country, meals are influenced by the traditional cooking of the Amish and Mennonites *(see p115)*. Family-style restaurants usually offer a good selection of this distinctive food, while staple and favorite treats are readily available at local farmers' markets scattered throughout the area *(see p144)*.

RESTAURANTS, BISTROS, AND CAFES

Many of Philadelphia's best restaurants are in Center City. Fine dining rooms can also be found in Center City hotels and near the theater district, home to the Kimmel Center and other performing arts venues. In Old City, head to the area around

Market and Chestnut Streets, between Front and 4th Streets, where some popular establishments can be found. Chinatown is home to several excellent restaurants, while some of the best family-owned trattorias are located in the Italian Market in south Philadelphia.

Numerous restaurants in the city's popular outdoor areas, such as Rittenhouse Square, Manayunk, and Chestnut Hill are stylish with upscale bistros and cafés. There are more than 200 restaurants here offering outdoor dining. Many are small, cozy establishments serving cocktails and trendsetting dishes in an ambience reminiscent of a Parisian café. Several restaurants and comfortable neighborhood bars are also located along Fairmount Avenue, close to the Museum of Art.

Cuba Libre in Old City recreates 1940s Havana *(see p146)*

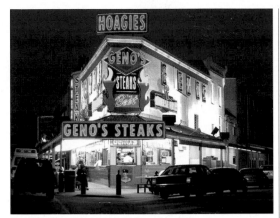

Geno's Steaks on Philadelphia's 9th Street *(see p150)*

HOURS AND PRICES

Luncheonettes and coffee shops open early for breakfast and may stay open through lunch only, catering to office workers. Finer restaurants open for lunch and dinner, with lunch served from 11:30am to 2:30pm or 3pm, and dinner from 5:30pm until 10pm or 10:30pm, and often later on weekends. Late-night restaurants that are also nightclubs stay open until 2am, but may stop serving food earlier.

Breakfast at diners and eateries can cost anywhere from $5 to $10 with a tip, while hotel buffet breakfasts can cost from $10 to $20. Full Sunday brunches at upscale restaurants and hotels can range from around $20 to $30 or more per person.

A typical lunch ranges from on-the-go sandwiches and sodas, from $5 to $9, to sit-down meals at restaurants that will cost $8 to $15 with a tip. Dinner is usually the big meal of the day. Starters and salads cost $5 to $10. Entrées can run $12 to $28, and up to $40 or more at high-end steakhouses and restaurants. Desserts and wine by the glass usually cost $5 to $12.

Some ethnic restaurants offer great quality food at less expensive costs. Greek, Chinese, Indian, Mexican, and Middle Eastern restaurants serve very generous portions at reasonable prices, with meals costing up to $15 or more per person.

EATERIES AND FAST FOOD

Good pizza, salads, hoagies, and Italian hot sandwiches are an inexpensive alternative found in the city's many pizzerias. Eateries in food courts serve balanced and tasty meals for $5 or more. Similar prices are charged at fast food restaurants that serve hamburgers, tacos, and fried chicken.

ALCOHOL AND SMOKING

Many restaurants serve wine by the glass or bottle. Eateries and fast food restaurants do not serve alcohol, while patrons of some establishments have the option to "bring your own bottle" (of wine). Restaurants and bars stop serving alcohol by 2am. The legal drinking age in Pennsylvania is 21, restaurant staff and shop owners may ask to see proof of age when purchasing alcohol. Restau-

rants and bars in Philadelphia are now all non-smoking establishments. However, smoking may be permitted at outdoor café-style eating places.

RESERVATIONS AND DRESS

Reservations for dining at upscale restaurants are recommended, and are often required on weekend nights. Nonetheless, some popular spots may not reserve tables, and use waiting lists. Even if you have reservations, you might have to wait for up to an hour on busy days.

Casual wear is accepted at most city restaurants, although there are some trendy and fine-dining establishments that expect patrons to wear smart-casual styles or business attire, so it is best to check when making reservations.

TIPPING

At most restaurants, your waitperson will bring you your bill, which can be paid through cash, credit cards, or traveler's checks. A 15 percent tip is standard, with up to 20 percent or more for excellent service.

CHILDREN

Well-behaved children are usually welcome in restaurants. It is not recommended, however, to bring young children to establishments that have late-night crowds and a large bar area, as patrons aged 21 or younger may not be allowed inside.

Le Bec-Fin, a celebrated French restaurant *(see p149)*

Flavors of the Pennsylvania Dutch Country

Philadelphians savor the broad range of American and ethnic tastes from the many cultures that call the city home. Nearby Pennsylvania Dutch Country has its own unique flavors, comprising basic, hearty foods prepared from simple recipes. Amish and Mennonite cooks take advantage of the plentiful harvests to prepare dishes often characterized as good home cooking. To preserve the excess from the harvests, fresh country produce is both canned and jarred in homes and small shops, with much of it turned into tangy relishes and sweet jams. Such treats are available at various farmers' markets.

Corn-on-the-cob

Fresh produce at a farmer's market in Lancaster County

BOUNTIFUL HARVESTS

Amish and Mennonite food-stems from the cultural tastes that the settlers brought from their home countries of Germany and Switzerland – recipes later adapted to the available crops that could be cultivated in the New World. Throughout the generations, the Amish have continued to nurture their gardens and fields through traditional methods with horse-drawn farming equipment. They grow all manner of fresh vegetables including corn, string beans, carrots, beets, onions, tomatoes, peppers, lettuce, potatoes, sweet potatoes, cauliflower, and more. Fruits include apples, cherries, plums, peaches, and sweet watermelon, with many used as ingredients for the delicious desserts that have made the Pennsylvania Dutch Country famous.

MEATS AND DELIS

Amish delis and restaurants-feature a wide variety of cheeses, meats, and poultry, including fresh country sausages, sweet bologna, bacon, ham, dried beef and jerky, and smoked turkey. Cuts of fresh beef, pork, and chicken are favorites among the locals, who serve them up as part of tasty recipes such as scrapple, a dish that is made of pork, onions, cornmeal, and spices.

Whoopie pie

Molasses cookies

Mincemeat cookies

Apple pie

Shoofly pie

A selection of Pennsylvania Dutch Country cakes and desserts

LOCAL DISHES AND SPECIALITIES

Pennsylvania Dutch restaurants are known for their family-style buffets with meat dishes such as golden fried chicken, roast beef, chicken pot pie, and spicy sausage. Staples include mashed potatoes, home-made noodles and breads, and a choice of vegetables. Popular jellies and relishes include smooth apple butter, and Chow Chow, a mixture of sweet pickled vegeta-bles. Amish recipes are handed down from mother to daughter to granddaughter, making for unique tastes. Dishes include Amish bean soup, corn fritters, spare ribs and sauerkraut, baking powder biscuits, cornmeal mush, and "Schnitz and Knepp," made with dried apples and ham. Popular desserts include Whoopie pie – chocolate cake surrounding white icing – and Shoofly pie, which has a coffeecake-like topping with a thick molasses bottom.

Fresh green apples

Chicken pot pie *comprises tender chicken pieces with vegetables and noodles, cooked in a pot of broth.*

Choosing a Restaurant

The restaurants in this guide have been selected for value, quality of food, atmosphere, and location. They are listed by area, starting with Philadelphia's Old City and moving on to restaurants farther away and beyond the city. All restaurants are non-smoking. For map references, *see pp194–97*.

PRICE CATEGORIES
The price ranges represent a three-course evening meal for one, a glass of house wine, tax, and service charges.

$ $25
$$ $26–$35
$$$ $36–$50
$$$$ $51–$70
$$$$$ Over $70

OLD CITY

Ariana Restaurant $
134 Chestnut St, Philadelphia, PA, 19106 **Tel** *(215) 922-1535*   **Map** *4 E3*

This small and cozy restaurant serves authentic Afghan cuisine featuring Kabuli *pulao* (rice with vegetables and meat), marinated lamb kebabs, and dishes scented with spices such as cinnamon and cumin. The decor includes ethnic photographs, creating a unique atmosphere. There is bay window seating for groups in traditional Afghan style.

Aromatic House of Kebob $
113 Chestnut St, Philadelphia, PA, 19106 **Tel** *(215) 923-4510*   **Map** *4 E3*

A family-owned eatery in historic Old City, this restaurant features a comfortable café-like setting. It specializes in traditional Persian cooking, but also offers other popular fare such as *souvlaki* and *gyros* (Greek meat dishes) and kebabs. The restaurant usually stays open for patrons visiting the Old City in the late hours.

The Bourse $
111 S Independence Mall East, Philadelphia, PA, 19106 **Tel** *(215) 625-0300*   **Map** *4 D3*

The lobby of the Bourse, a historic 19th-century commodities exchange building *(see p156)*, is home to a food court and several souvenir shops. Its many eateries offer Chinese food, pizzas, cheesesteaks, sandwiches, burgers, and more. The food court is an ideal lunch venue for sightseers in Independence National Historic Park.

Mexican Post Restaurant and Bar $
104 Chestnut St, Philadelphia, PA, 19106 **Tel** *(215) 923 5233*   **Map** *4 E3*

This informal and friendly restaurant serves a wide range of popular Mexican dishes. It features an extensive menu of taco salads, sizzling fajitas, burritos, salads, soups, and chicken and fish specialties, in addition to combination meals. The lively bar serves eight flavors of margaritas. A second Mexican Post is located in Center City *(see p148)*.

Café Spice $$
35 S 2nd St, Philadelphia, PA, 19106 **Tel** *(215) 627-6273*   **Map** *4 E3*

A trendy, vibrant bistro which gives a contemporary edge to traditional fare from all over India, such as kebabs and chicken tikka. Spacious interiors with modern decor and warm colors add to the chic and elegant atmosphere. The bar offers an extensive martini list. A DJ spins on weekends.

Continental Restaurant and Martini Bar $$
138 Market St, Philadelphia, PA, 19106 **Tel** *(215) 923-6069*   **Map** *4 E3*

With its imaginative interior, the Continental is one of the hippest and most popular after-dark spots in the Old City's lively nightlife district. It serves contemporary cuisine with a pan-Asian flair, and has extensive martini, champagne, and wine lists. Latin and lounge music is played. Weekday lunch, weekend brunch, and daily dinner service.

Kabul Afghan Cuisine Restaurant $$
106 Chestnut St, Philadelphia, PA, 19106 **Tel** *(215) 922-3676*   **Map** *4 E3*

This popular ethnic restaurant near the heart of Old City has traditional Afghan decor and a warm and welcoming atmosphere. The menu is replete with meat kebab and vegetarian specialties cooked with exotic Afghan spices. Call in advance to dine in traditional Afghan style on a platform with rugs and pillows. No lunch service.

Karma Restaurant and Bar $$
114 Chestnut St, Philadelphia, PA, 19106 **Tel** *(215) 925-1444*   **Map** *4 E3*

An upscale and cheerful Indian restaurant decorated with contemporary art. It serves up traditional dishes from all over India, with baked salmon and chicken tikka masala among other specialties. The lunch buffet provides a taste of the chef's award-winning dishes. The restaurant also has banquet facilities and a full bar.

Amada $$$
217 Chestnut St, Philadelphia, PA, 19106 **Tel** *(215) 625-2450*   **Map** *4 E3*

A Spanish restaurant serving authentic tapas based on the earthy Mediterranean flavors that have long been the passion of founder and executive chef Jose Garces. The impressive menu of inspired creations gives guests the opportunity to mix and share multiple dishes. Signature tapas include octopus, garlic shrimps, and tortilla.

Key to Symbols *see back cover flap*

Brasil's Restaurant and Nightspot
| 🦽 ♫ ❯ 🍸 | $$$ |

112 Chestnut St, Philadelphia, PA, 19106 **Tel** *(215) 413-1700* | **Map** *4 E3*

Try out this restaurant and nightclub in Old City for Brazilian cuisine and Latin-style dancing. The food includes hearty meat and seafood dishes with exciting South American and tropical accents. The nightclub offers dancing lessons and bands playing Brazilian, South American, and Caribbean music. Closed Sunday–Tuesday.

City Tavern
| 🏃 🦽 🍸 | $$$ |

138 S 2nd St, Philadelphia, PA, 19106 **Tel** *(215) 413-1443* | **Map** *4 E3*

Authentic colonial-style cuisine, such as West Indies pepperpot soup, is served at this historically accurate reconstruction of the original 1773 tavern. Colonial ales brewed according to George Washington's and Thomas Jefferson's original recipes are also served. Three floors with colonial decor and staff in period costume.

Cuba Libre Restaurant and Rum Bar
| 🏃 🦽 ❯ 🍸 | $$$ |

10 S 2nd St, Philadelphia, PA, 19106 **Tel** *(215) 627-0666* | **Map** *4 E3*

Trendy and happening, this restaurant's spacious atrium reaches out onto the sidewalk for alfresco dining in warmer months. Bright colors and balconies evoke memories of 1940s Havana. Two bars and four dining rooms serve up contemporary Cuban and inventive Latin cuisine. Brunch is on offer on the weekend.

DiNardo's Famous Crabs
| 🏃 🦽 🍸 | $$$ |

312 Race St, Philadelphia, PA, 19106 **Tel** *(215) 925-5115* | **Map** *4 E2*

A favorite since 1976, this seafood restaurant serves up excellent crabs in a casual and friendly atmosphere. Specialties include steamed Louisiana crabs served "hot and dirty" Baltimore-style, jumbo shrimp, stuffed flounder, and more. Located one block from St. George's Church and Fireman's Hall. No lunch service on Sunday.

Eulogy Belgian Tavern
| 🏃 🦽 ❯ 🍸 | $$$ |

136 Chestnut St, Philadelphia, PA, 19106 **Tel** *(215) 413-1918* | **Map** *4 E3*

This cozy pub and restaurant features an enormous selection of 185 international and Belgian beers. Traditional Belgian fare, including fish, meatballs, fries, and mussels, is prepared in five different sauces. The restaurant has limited wheelchair access and does not allow children after 8pm.

Philadelphia Fish & Company
| 🏃 🦽 🍸 | $$$ |

207 Chestnut St, Philadelphia, PA, 19106 **Tel** *(215) 625-8605* | **Map** *4 E3*

This popular restaurant has an outdoor deck, and has a continually evolving menu that showcases fish, meat, and fowl dishes in dazzling sauces. The eatery is upbeat, modern interiors with rich mahogany trim and furnishings in a Zinfandel red and pale meadow green color scheme. Children allowed only on request.

The Plough & The Stars
| 🏃 🦽 ♫ 🍸 | $$$ |

207 Chestnut St, Philadelphia, PA, 19106 **Tel** *(215) 735-0300* | **Map** *4 E3*

This trendy Irish pub is housed in the Corn Exchange Building. The restaurant plays traditional Irish music on Sundays and has plenty of Guinness on tap. The fare, however, is not necessarily traditional but instead gourmet and creative. The pub has some outdoor seating in the warmer months.

Serrano-Tin Angel
| 🦽 ♫ ❯ 🍸 | $$$ |

20 S 2nd St, Philadelphia, PA, 19106 **Tel** *(215) 928-0770* | **Map** *4 E3*

This stylish restaurant sits in a 1820s townhouse-like building with the popular folk music café, Tin Angel, on the second level. It offers international cooking, with specialties such as Malaysian pork chop, vegetable *kung pao*, and calamari. No lunch service.

Spasso Italian Grille
| 🏃 ❯ 🍸 | $$$ |

34 S Front St, Philadelphia, PA, 19106 **Tel** *(215) 592-7661* | **Map** *4 E3*

This old world-style trattoria is located across from Penn's Landing and features traditional Italian cuisine with dishes from both southern and northern Italy. Popular dishes include home-made pastas, fresh seafood, veal, and chicken. The restaurant sports a warm and casual atmosphere. No lunch service on the weekend.

Fork
| 🏃 🦽 ❯ 🍸 | $$$$ |

306 Market St, Philadelphia, PA, 19106 **Tel** *(215) 625-9425* | **Map** *4 E3*

Located in the heart of the Old City nightlife district, Fork offers a mix of casual sophistication and an urban, upscale style. It serves new American, bistro-style cuisine with an international flavor. Decor includes delicately painted velvet curtains and chandeliers. It also has a unique center bar. No lunch service on Saturday.

Patou
| 🏃 🦽 ❯ 🍸 | $$$$ |

312 Market St, Philadelphia, PA, 19106 **Tel** *(215) 928-2987* | **Map** *4 E3*

Cool Mediterranean colors add to the ambience of this spacious, modern French bar and restaurant that features an open-air kitchen. Côte d'Azur-influenced seafood dishes dominate the menu, with a mix of traditional French cooking accented with a contemporary flair. No lunch service on weekdays. Brunch only on Sunday. Closed Monday.

Ristorante Panorama and Il Bar
| 🏃 🦽 🍸 | $$$$ |

Front and Market Sts, Philadelphia, PA, 19106 **Tel** *(215) 922-7800* | **Map** *4 E3*

This is an exquisite family-owned hotel *(see p134)* and restaurant near Penn's Landing. The bustling trattoria decorated with Florentine tiles and hand-painted murals features Italian food – home-made pastas and the finest cuts of veal. The unique "Il Bar" features the world's largest wine dispensing system and offers 120 wines by the glass.

Key to Price Guide *see p145* **Key to Symbols** *see back cover flap*

Swanky Bubbles Restaurant and Champagne Bar $$$$

10 S Front St, Philadelphia, PA, 19106 **Tel** *(215) 928-1200*   **Map** *4 E3*

An eclectic and premier champagne bar and restaurant serving sushi and pan-Asian cuisine with French and Spanish influences. Located opposite Penn's Landing, it features an extensive selection of champagnes and sparkling wines, some of which are sold by the glass. Dinner is served from 5pm until 1am. No lunch service.

Tangerine $$$$

232 Market St, Philadelphia, PA, 19106 **Tel** *(215) 627-5116*   **Map** *4 E3*

Moroccan chic is the style of this excellent restaurant designed by Stephen Starr. The cuisine is a blend of traditional European and North African styles; specialties include pistachio crusted duck breast and lamb and honey tangine. The drinks menu is equally eclectic, and the desserts are definitely worth saving room for.

Buddakan $$$$$

325 Chestnut St, Philadelphia, PA, 19106 **Tel** *(215) 574-9440*   **Map** *4 E3*

Tables are set amidst a gilded Buddha in one of the city's most happening and elegant restaurants. Modern Asian cuisine is served in a lively atmosphere. Most popular are communal tables where guests participate in a family-style, pass-the-plate dining experience. Wear smart casual to dressy clothes.

Morimoto $$$$$

723 Chestnut St, Philadelphia, PA, 19106 **Tel** *(215) 413-9070*   **Map** *4 D3*

This renowned restaurant's dining room is elegant and upscale with modern decor. One of the best fusion restaurants in Philadelphia, it brings contemporary Japanese cuisine to the table through Chef Morimoto's blending of traditional Japanese cooking with Western flair.

SOCIETY HILL AND PENN'S LANDING

Jim's Steaks $

400 South St, Philadelphia, PA, 19147 **Tel** *(215) 928-1911*   **Map** *4 D4*

With its distinctive Art Deco storefront, Jim's is undoubtedly one of Philadelphia's busiest and most popular eateries. Long lines often stretch onto hip South Street as visitors and locals alike flock here for authentic Philly cheesesteaks with mounds of onions and dripping hot cheese. It also serves excellent hoagies.

South Street Souvlaki $

509 S St, Philadelphia, PA, 19147 **Tel** *(215) 925-3026*   **Map** *4 D4*

One of the town's oldest and most popular Greek restaurants, this South Street icon recently celebrated its 25th anniversary. Specialties include classic Greek and Mediterranean cuisine, including lamb, seafood, and vegetarian dishes. Pleasant dining room and streetfront takeout window as well.

Jon's Bar and Grille $$

606 S 3rd St, Philadelphia, PA, 19147 **Tel** *(215) 592-1390*   **Map** *4 D4*

A hip restaurant with an upstairs deck and patio seating along busy South Street. The building that houses this eatery was the birthplace of actor Larry Fine of *Three Stooges* fame. Though most popular for burgers and Philly cheesesteaks, the menu also offers a wide range of home-made soups, steaks, and fish.

Marrakesh $$

517 Leithgow St, Philadelphia, PA, 19147 **Tel** *(215) 925-5929*   **Map** *4 D5*

At Marrakesh you can sit on cushioned pillows and enjoy an authentic seven-course Moroccan feast beginning with a hand-washing ritual and ending with a tea ceremony. The restaurant has a number of private dining rooms for hire, and belly dancers are available upon request.

Bistro Romano $$$

120 Lombard St, Philadelphia, PA, 19147 **Tel** *(215) 925-8880*   **Map** *4 E4*

Once an 18th-century granary, the main dining room of this classic Italian restaurant was part of the Underground Railroad *(see p60)*. Authentic, regional Italian dishes and the popular Caesar salad are prepared tableside. It has a piano bar and displays include 18th-century artifacts. Children allowed on request. No lunch service.

Bridget Foy's $$$

200 South St, Philadelphia, PA, 19147 **Tel** *(215) 922-1813*   **Map** *4 E5*

An American grill in the South Street district, it faces New Market and Head House Square. The menu offers American cuisine, with old standards such as steaks, fresh fish, burgers, and sandwiches. An outdoor café makes this great spot to break for lunch on bustling South Street.

Dark Horse Pub $$$

421 S 2nd St, Philadelphia, PA, 19147 **Tel** *(215) 928-9307*   **Map** *4 E4*

A popular watering hole that doubles up as a restaurant. This colonial inn-style restaurant serves hearty pub fare, including steak and mushroom pie, as well as gourmet cuisine. It has five bars with a range of beers and wines. No lunch service on Monday.

Downey's $$$

526 S Front St, Philadelphia, PA, 19147 **Tel** *(215) 625-9500*

Map 4 E5

Blessed with its great location at South and Front Streets, Downey's – a "drinking house and dining saloon" – has been a neighborhood mainstay since 1976. Pub decor includes antiques and Irish memorabilia, while the menu features hearty Irish stews and American fare. It is also a vibrant night spot.

Sfizzio Restaurant $$$

237 St. James Place, Philadelphia, PA, 19106 **Tel** *(215) 925-1802*

Map 4 E4

This trendy restaurant sits nestled under the Society Hill Towers and serves fresh Italian fare with an accent on Naples and southern Italy. Specialties include Pasta Positano and *langostino* pastas. Features a mosaic decor with postmodernist touches. Some tables have views of the landmark Merchants' Exchange Building.

Chart House $$$$

555 S Columbus Blvd at Penn's Landing, Philadelphia, PA, 19147 **Tel** *(215) 625-8383*

Map 4 E5

Seafood appetizers, entrées, and chowders dominate the menu of this contemporary restaurant and Philadelphia institution. Opened in 1961 on a prime waterfront location on the Delaware, it offers stunning river views. This is a great place for a Sunday brunch of shrimp, crab, tuna, and mussels.

Moshulu $$$$$

401 S Columbus Blvd, Philadelphia, PA, 19106 **Tel** *(215) 923-2500*

Map 4 F4

Lovely fine-dining restaurant aboard a restored, century-old sailing ship moored off Penn's Landing. The four-masted vessel is ablaze with lights at night, and offers excellent river and skyline views from indoor dining rooms and from atop the deck in warmer months. Bar and deck menu also available.

CENTER CITY

Cosi $

1128 Walnut St, Philadelphia, PA, 19107 **Tel** *(215) 413-1608*

Map 3 B3

Comfortable and casual, this café-style restaurant has heart-warming soups, tangy salads, baked breads and sandwiches, pasta dishes, pizzas, and more. There are several Cosis, and this branch is situated a few blocks from the theater district and across from the Forrest Theatre.

Mexican Post Center City $

1601 Cherry St, Philadelphia, PA, 19102 **Tel** *(215) 568-2667*

Map 2 E3

This local mini-chain has spruced up its image for its sleek Center City location – a second Mexican Post is situated in Old City *(see p145)*. Authentic Mexican fare is on offer, including fresh guacamole and salsa, and with more than 100 tequilas this is also a great place to drink. In summer the restaurant is home to the city's largest outdoor dining patio.

Penang $

117 N 10th St, Philadelphia, PA, 19107 **Tel** *(215) 413-2531, (215) 413-2532*

Map 3 C2

This trendy, storefront restaurant in the heart of Chinatown is always buzzing with activity. It has a predominantly Malaysian cuisine featuring spicy curry and seafood dishes, along with some Thai, Indian, and Indonesian specialties as well. Also serves beer and wine.

El Vez $$

121 S 13th St, Philadelphia, PA, 19103 **Tel** *(215) 928-9800*

Map 2 F3

DIne on delicious, modern versions of traditional Mexican classics at this fashionable Center City restaurant. The made-to-order guacamole and the Mahi-Mahi tacos are highly recommended. There is also an extensive selection of drinks, including wonderful pomegranate margaritas.

Imperial Inn $$

142 N 10th St, Philadelphia, PA, 19107 **Tel** *(215) 627-2299, (215) 627-5588*

Map 3 C2

Despite its modest decor, the locals will tell you the Imperial Inn is one of Chinatown's best. Opened in 1973, this casual dining restaurant has consistently been serving traditional, quality Chinese food, including dim sum dishes, as well as wines and liquors. An excellent option for those looking for great Chinese food at good prices.

The Black Sheep Pub and Restaurant $$$

17th & Latimer Sts, Philadelphia, PA, 19103 **Tel** *(215) 545-9473*

Map 2 E5

Dine on hearty Irish stews and other favorites, including shepherd's pie, sandwiches, crab cakes, and more. Just one block from Rittenhouse Square, this pub and restaurant offers a relaxed atmosphere and has friendly staff. There are three floors with antique bars, and a drink selection from around the world. Wheelchair access limited to first level.

Brasserie Perrier $$$

1619 Walnut St, Philadelphia, PA, 19103 **Tel** *(215) 568-3000*

Map 2 E4

Chef Georges Perrier's second venture in Philadelphia after Le Bec-Fin, this is a trendy restaurant along Rittenhouse Row. Its menu features modern French cuisine with Italian and Asian influences. Art Deco interiors with silver leaf ceilings and light cherry wood. Definitely more affordable than Le Bec-Fin. No lunch service on Sunday.

Key to Price Guide *see p145* **Key to Symbols** *see back cover flap*

McCormick and Schmick's Seafood Restaurant $$$

1 S Broad St, Philadelphia, PA, 19102 **Tel** *(215) 568-6888*   **Map** *2 F4*

This upbeat and lively restaurant is an upscale fish house, located just across from historic City Hall. Features over 40 varieties of fresh fish that are flown in daily from both the Atlantic and Pacific Oceans. The two-story restaurant has a dark wood-paneled dining room accented by stained glass ceilings and mosaic floor.

Pietro's Coal Oven Pizzeria $$$

1714 Walnut St, Philadelphia, PA, 19103 **Tel** *(215) 735-8090*   **Map** *2 E5*

This lively restaurant offers thin-crust pizzas baked in a coal oven, served with a choice of 17 gourmet toppings, and other Italian specialties such as home-made pasta entrées in family-sized portions. There is outdoor seating along Walnut Street in warmer months.

Rouge $$$

205 S 18th St, Philadelphia, PA, 19103 **Tel** *(215) 732-6622*   **Map** *2 D5*

A hip bistro and popular late night spot in the swanky Rittenhouse Square area. They have wines of exquisite vintage and a trendsetting menu that is a cross between Continental, American, and French fare with contemporary seafood, poultry, and beef dishes. The biggest draw is the location, with outdoor seating facing the square.

Roy's $$$

124 S 15th St, Philadelphia, PA, 19102 **Tel** *(215) 988-1814*   **Map** *2 E4*

This restaurant features unique Hawaiian fusion cuisine. Chef-owner Roy Yamaguchi's specialties are created with local ingredients accented with European sauces and bold Asian spices. Just one block from Rittenhouse Row, the restaurant is housed in a refurbished bank building. No lunch service.

Alma de Cuba $$$

1023 Walnut St, Philadelphia, PA, 19103 **Tel** *(215) 988-1799*   **Map** *2 E5*

This cutting-edge restaurant, bar, and lounge brings modern Cuban cuisine to Philadelphia. Festive Cuban cocktails such as Mojitos and Daiquiris perfectly compliment the flavors, brilliant colors, and textures of the spectacular cuisine. Dishes include red bean soup with pumpkin and chorizo, and octopus *Escabeche* (pickled).

Devon Seafood Grill $$$$

225 S 18th St, Philadelphia, PA, 19103 **Tel** *(215) 546-5940*   **Map** *2 D5*

A much-visited and comfortable restaurant, the Devon Seafood Grill serves fresh fish specialties, including Maryland crab cakes, pan-roasted Alaskan halibut, live Maine lobsters, Block Island swordfish, and more. The dining room is elegant. It is particularly popular in the warmer months with sidewalk seating facing Rittenhouse Square.

Parc $$$$

227 S 18th St, Philadelphia, PA, 19103 **Tel** *(215) 545-2262*   **Map** *2 D5*

This stylish addition to Rittenhouse Square pays tribute to French café culture. Ideal for a light snack or a more leisurely meal, this French bistro offers many classics such as onion soup and escargots, as well as meat and fish platters and a choice of baguettes. Inside are red leather banquettes backed with panels of frosted glass for privacy.

Susanna Foo Chinese Cuisine $$$$

1512 Walnut St, Philadelphia, PA, 19102 **Tel** *(215) 545-2666*   **Map** *2 E5*

Not traditional Chinese by any means, this is one of the city's most popular fine-dining restaurants along ritzy Rittenhouse Row. Owner and chef Susanna Foo adds a French influence to classical Chinese dishes, creating more flavorful sauces. No lunch service on the weekend. Reservations are advised.

The Prime Rib $$$$

1701 Locust St, Philadelphia, PA, 19103 **Tel** *(215) 772-1701*   **Map** *2 E5*

This upscale steakhouse is one of Philadelphia's best. Housed in the prestigious Radisson-brand Warwick Hotel *(see p136)*, its decor is reminiscent of a 1940s Manhattan supper club. Its specialties include aged prime rib, blue-ribbon steaks, extra thick chops, and fresh seafood. Children are allowed only on request. Formal dress required. No lunch service.

Lacroix at the Rittenhouse $$$$$

210 W Rittenhouse Square, Philadelphia, PA, 19103 **Tel** *(215) 790-2533*   **Map** *2 D5*

Elegant restaurant on the second floor of the Rittenhouse Hotel *(see p136)* with stunning views of Rittenhouse Square. Decorated with minimalist and Asian theme, it serves French-American cuisine with options of three, four, or five courses, and diners can also create their own menus. Dessert complimentary as a gift from the chef.

Le Bec-Fin $$$$$

1523 Walnut St, Philadelphia, PA, 19102 **Tel** *(215) 567-1000*   **Map** *2 E5*

Philadelphia's best and one of the country's top French restaurants run by chef-owner Georges Perrier. Mirrored walls and silk panels add to the elegant dining experience with exquisite dishes like *escargot* in champagne and hazelnut garlic butter sauce, served by an army of waiting staff. There is an extensive wine cellar with 700 wines. Formal dress required.

Smith & Wollensky $$$$$

210 W Rittenhouse Square, Philadelphia, PA, 19103 **Tel** *(215) 545-1700*   **Map** *2 D5*

One of the top steakhouses Philadelphia has to offer. *The New York Times* referred to this high end restaurant chain as "a steakhouse to end all arguments." Patrons are treated to up to 18 and 28-ounce cuts, good chops, salads, seafood, and an excellent wine list too. Located in the posh Rittenhouse Hotel *(see p136)*.

LOGAN SQUARE AND THE MUSEUM DISTRICT

Illuminare

$$

2321 Fairmount Ave, Philadelphia, PA, 19130 **Tel** (215) 765-0202 **Map** 2 D1

From brick oven pizza to veal chops and filet mignon, this upscale restaurant serves wide-ranging Italian cuisine, which also includes fresh pastas and seafood. Housed in a renovated rowhouse, it has elegant decor that showcases stunning handcrafted woodwork, tile-work, and stained glass.

The Bishop's Collar

$$$

2349 Fairmount Ave, Philadelphia, PA, 19130 **Tel** (215) 765-1616 **Map** 2 D1

This friendly corner watering hole and restaurant serves creative pub fare, along with a wide-ranging selection of beers and ales. Tables are set up outdoors in the warmer months. Situated a couple of blocks from the Philadelphia Museum of Art and the Kelly Drive walking path along Boathouse Row.

Gloria's Gourmet Seafood

$$$

2120 Fairmount Ave, Philadelphia, PA, 19130 **Tel** (215) 235-3082 **Map** 2 D1

An elegant seafood restaurant and upbeat nightclub with some of Philadelphia's best jazz music. Menu features fresh fish, crab, and lobster specialties, as well as Southern-style and soul food dishes. A few blocks from the Philadelphia Museum of Art and across from the Eastern State Penitentiary. Children are not allowed after 7pm.

Jack's Firehouse

$$$

2130 Fairmount Ave, Philadelphia, PA, 19130 **Tel** (215) 232-9000 **Map** 2 D1

This unique restaurant sits within a former firehouse building that still retains its original interiors – complete with a firemen's sliding pole and an expansive arched doorway. Popular chef-owner Jack McDavid uses fresh local ingredients for "down home" American fare, often accenting Southern cooking styles. Live music on the first Friday of each month.

London Grill

$$$

2301 Fairmount Ave, Philadelphia, PA, 19130 **Tel** (215) 978-4545 **Map** 2 D1

Trendy and comfortable, this corner restaurant combines the coziness of a neighborhood pub with the elegance of fine dining. The menu changes daily, and dishes such as roasted chicken with garlic mashed potato cake, broccoli rosemary jus, and honey glazed grilled salmon are on offer. No lunch service on Saturday.

Rembrandt's

$$$

741 N 23rd St, Philadelphia, PA, 19130 **Tel** (215) 763-2228, (800) 736-2726 **Map** 2 D1

Located near the Philadelphia Museum of Art, this elegant restaurant is known for its fine dining, accented by fabulous views of the city skyline. Specialties include creative seafood, meat, pasta, and vegetarian dishes. It also has a full tavern menu and eight draught beers on tap.

Water Works Restaurant and Lounge

$$$

640 Water Works Drive, Philadelphia, PA, 19130 **Tel** (215) 448-2700 **Map** 1 B1

Built in 1812, the Fairmount Water Works building is now a national historic landmark overlooking the Schuylkill River. The restaurant's superb location and innovative American fusion cuisine makes for a fine dining experience and reservations are recommended. Wines are available by the glass.

Zorba's Tavern

$$$

2230 Fairmount Ave, Philadelphia, PA, 19130 **Tel** (215) 978-5990 **Map** 2 D1

Discover sumptuous Greek food at this family-owned restaurant. Paintings depicting old-world Greece add a special ambience to the authentic cuisine. It offers a full menu with lamb and seafood specialties, and all the traditional dishes. Located within walking distance of the Philadelphia Museum of Art and Boathouse Row. Closed Monday.

Fountain Restaurant

$$$$$

1 Logan Square, Philadelphia, PA, 19103 **Tel** (215) 963-1500 **Map** 2 E2

Living up to the reputation of the posh Four Seasons Hotel (see p137), this restaurant has been repeatedly rated as one of the city's best restaurants, serving Continental cuisine with delicate international influences. Elegant dining room with rich fabrics and warm woods. The restaurant offers splendid views of the Swann Fountain. Formal dress required.

FARTHER AFIELD

Geno's Steaks

$

1219 S 9th St, Philadelphia, PA, 19147 **Tel** (215) 389-0659

Geno's is one of Philadelphia's cheesesteak giants on the outskirts of the Italian Market. Founded in 1966 opposite Pat's King of Steaks, it serves delicious, piping hot cheesesteak sandwiches 24 hours a day, seven days a week from a bright, neon-lit corner storefront.

Key to Price Guide see p145 **Key to Symbols** see back cover flap

Pat's King of Steaks

1301 S 9th St, Philadelphia, PA, 19147 **Tel** *(215) 468-1546*

Founded in and family-owned since 1930, Pat's is known as the originator of the Philly cheesesteak with its sliced rib-eye steak, onions, cheese, and fresh Italian bread. In fact, locals will tell you it makes the city's best. Outside vendor windows and outside seating only. It is located at the Italian Market. Open 24 hours a day.

Chickie's and Pete's Café

1526 Packer Ave, Philadelphia, PA, 19145 **Tel** *(215) 218-0500*

This casual, south Philadelphia hotspot near the city's sports venues is always busy when the home teams play. Sightings of local personalities is common. The menu features crab fries, sandwiches, and cheesesteaks. Children have to be accompanied by adults after 10pm. A DJ plays recorded music.

Manayunk Brewery and Restaurant

4120 Main St, Manayunk, Philadelphia, PA, 19127 **Tel** *(215) 482-8220*

Housed in a former Manayunk textile mill, this upbeat restaurant with an in-house brewery serves classic American and Continental fare – grilled meats and seafood, pastas, and pizza. It has a rotisserie and sushi bar too, and a range of beverages. There is a large outdoor dining area that overlooks the Schuylkill River.

Zocalo Restaurant

3604 Lancaster Ave, Philadelphia, PA, 19104 **Tel** *(215) 895-0139*

Located in University City, this hip, bistro-like restaurant serves traditional, mouthwatering Mexican favorites enhanced by contemporary tastes. The drinks menu features margaritas, beers, and wine, which is sold by the glass. Outdoor dining is an option in the warmer months.

Derek's

4411 Main St, Manayunk, Philadelphia, PA, 19127 **Tel** *(215) 483-9400*

A special occasion restaurant, casual café, and vodka bar can all be found at Derek's. The menu is sophisticated American, with a range of dishes from fresh salads to steakhouse cuts of meat. The bar serves home-made vodka infusions in a variety of sweet flavours. The entire establishment is smoke free, including the bar areas.

Ralph's Italian Restaurant

760 S 9th St, Philadelphia, PA, 19147 **Tel** *(215) 627-6011*

Cozy, comfortable, and classy restaurant at the Italian Market. Owned and operated by four generations of the same family since 1900, this neighborhood restaurant is one of the city's most popular Italian eateries. It serves up classic red sauce and pastas, veal, poultry, seafood, and meat dishes, including the likes of Pork Chops Pizzaiola.

White Dog Café

3420 Sansom St, Philadelphia, PA, 19104 **Tel** *(215) 386-9224*

An eclectic University City cafe housed in three adjacent Victorian brownstones. On the menu is an unusual blend of contemporary American cuisine that uses fresh ingredients from local, self-reliant farmers. Music is played in the smoke-free piano parlor. The bar offers happy hours from 10pm to midnight Sunday through Thursday.

Zesty's

4382 Main St, Manayunk, Philadelphia, PA, 19127 **Tel** *(215) 483-6226, (800) 816-3463*

This upbeat restaurant offers a unique Greek and Roman menu prepared the old-fashioned way. Serves regional Mediterranean fish not found elsewhere in the city, such as pageot, sargo, and royal dorado from Greece. Calamari, lamb, veal, and lots of traditional dishes too. The wine list includes Greek wines.

General Lafayette Inn and Brewery

646 Germantown Pike, Lafayette Hill, PA, 19444 **Tel** *(610) 941-0600, (800) 251-0181*

A short drive from Chestnut Hill, this fine-dining American-fare restaurant is housed in a well-preserved 1732 country inn. Six working fireplaces and Baroque music add to the colonial ambience. An added attraction is the upstairs "haunted" dining room. Expect generous portions of delicious Southern and Native American dishes.

Hikaru

4348 Main St, Manayunk, Philadelphia, PA, 19127 **Tel** *(215) 487-3500*

A sushi bar is the highlight of this classy restaurant with a view of the Manayunk Bridge. Teppanyaki (tableside cooking) offers a host of specialties in addition to sashimi, sukiyaki, teriyaki, tempura, and more. Has one of the most extensive sushi menus in the Delaware Valley. Hikaru has another restaurant on South Street.

BEYOND PHILADELPHIA

ATLANTIC CITY Atlantic City Bar and Grill

1219 Pacific Ave, Atlantic City, NJ, 08401 **Tel** *(609) 348-8080, (609) 449-1991*

This family-owned restaurant opened more than 25 years ago and has become a favorite among locals, tourists, and even visiting celebrities and sports figures. Steaks, crabs, shrimp cocktail, lobsters, mussels, home-made pastas, pizzas, and sandwiches all feature on the menu. The spacious dining room has sports programming and is open until 4:30am.

ATLANTIC CITY Hard Rock Café $\$\$$

1000 Boardwalk at Virginia Ave, Atlantic City, NJ, 08401 **Tel** *(609) 441-0007*

Right on the Boardwalk, this chain restaurant is known for its rock 'n' roll memorabilia, signed guitars, and an all-American cuisine. Pastas, steaks, burgers, and smokehouse dishes are the most popular. Housed within the colossal Trump Taj Mahal Hotel Casino and Resort *(see p139)*, it offers seating on the Boardwalk in the warmer months.

ATLANTIC CITY Primavera $\$\$\$\$\$$

Caesars Casino, 2100 Pacific Ave, Atlantic City, NJ, 08401 **Tel** *(609) 348-4411, (800) 223-7272*

Fine dining with a range of northern Italian specialties and an extensive wine list in one of Atlantic City's best-known casino hotels, Caesars *(see p139)*. Try out the appetizer of oversized prawns with lemon-caper sauce. Intimate tables amidst artworks and murals of Venice enhance the ambience. Service is formal and reservations are required.

ATLANTIC CITY Suilan by Susanna Foo $\$\$\$\$\$$

One Borgata Way, Atlantic City, NJ, 08401 **Tel** *(609) 317-1000*

Prominent Philadelphia restauranteur Susanna Foo has brought her signature Chinese-fusion cooking style to Atlantic City's newest casino, The Borgata's. Elegant decor creates a modern and bold ambience. Traditional Chinese dishes are prepared with French accents and a European flair. Closed Tuesday and Wednesday.

BRANDYWINE VALLEY Buckley's Tavern $\$\$$

5812 Kennett Pike, Centreville, DE, 19807 **Tel** *(302) 656-9776*

A favorite meeting place for locals in the Brandywine Valley, this tavern serves a variety of fine food, from the likes of Maryland crab cakes to Vietnamese shrimp salad. There is a popular outdoor dining patio. It is close to Longwood Gardens, Winterthur, and other attractions such as the Brandywine River Museum and Brandywine Battlefield.

BRANDYWINE VALLEY Chadds Ford Tavern and Restaurant $\$\$$

US Rt 1 (1 mile south of Rt 202), Chadds Ford, PA, 19317 **Tel** *(610) 459-8453*

Family-owned and operated since 1968, this quaint country restaurant offers a menu ranging from home-made pub fare to fine food dishes. Housed in an 1830s tavern, the dining room is lit with hurricane candles and Tiffany lamps. Sample the crab cakes, a best-selling entrée. Reservations are recommended.

CAPE MAY Cabanas on the Beach $\$\$$

429 Beach Ave, Cape May, NJ, 08204 **Tel** *(609) 884-4800*

Enjoy great sandwiches, seafood, and more at this casual and easy-going beach bar that serves good food. Other attractions include a children's menu, open-air dining, and live blues and reggae entertainment acts. Oysters, shrimps, lots of shellfish specialties, crab, chicken, and prime ribs, are all on the menu.

CAPE MAY The Lobster House $\$\$$

Fisherman's Wharf, Cape May Harbor, Cape May, NJ, 08204 **Tel** *(609) 884-8296*

Feast on the region's freshest seafood in a picturesque dining room overlooking Cape May harbor, with many of the ingredients arriving in the kitchen via the restaurant's own boat. Cocktails can be enjoyed at dockside tables or on the deck of the 146-ft (50-m) *Schooner America*.

DOYLESTOWN Paganini Ristorante $\$\$\$$

81 West State St, Doylestown, PA, 18901 **Tel** *(215) 348-5922*

A local favorite for fine Italian cuisine, this restaurant is in the heart of downtown Doylestown. It has several small dining rooms where patrons can ask for custom cooking such as fresh pastas and a variety of sauces. No dinner service on Saturday and no lunch service on Sunday.

GETTYSBURG Dobbin House Tavern $\$\$\$$

89 Steinwehr Ave, Gettysburg, PA, 17325 **Tel** *(717) 334-2100*

This cozy and quaint colonial tavern and restaurant *(see p140)* date to 1776. Full of antiques, it has costumed servers and a historic ambience. The menu consists of old-fashioned hearty dishes such as charbroiled meats and fowl. It is located across from where Abraham Lincoln delivered the Gettysburg Address *(see p121)*.

GETTYSBURG Farnsworth House Inn $\$\$\$$

401 Baltimore Ave, Gettysburg, PA, 17325 **Tel** *(717) 334-8838*

Quaint dining rooms housed in a historic 1810 Gettysburg in *(see p140)*, where over 100 bullet holes from the Civil War can still be seen. Period specialties include game pie, pumpkin fritters, peanut soup, and sweet potato pudding. It features dinner theater every Friday and Saturday evening from December through February.

GETTYSBURG Herr Tavern and Public House $\$\$\$$

900 Chambersburg Rd, Gettysburg, PA, 17325 **Tel** *(717) 334-4332*

Once used as the first Confederate hospital during the Battle of Gettysburg, this 1815 country inn is now a B&B with five elegantly decorated dining rooms. The menu offers carefully prepared meat and seafood entrées served with tasteful garnishes and sauces. Reservations are required on weekends. No lunch service on Sunday.

HARRISBURG Appalachian Brewing Company $\$$

50 N Cameron St, Harrisburg, PA, 17010 **Tel** *(717) 221-1080*

The first brewpub in Pennsylvania's state capital is located in an impressive, historic three-story brick-and-timber building. Along with a large selection of handcrafted ales and lagers there is also an innovative menu, with plenty of tasty choices to complement your drinks.

Key to Price Guide *see p145* **Key to Symbols** *see back cover flap*

HERSHEY Lebbie Lebkicher's at Hershey Lodge

West Chocolate Ave and University Dr, Hershey, PA, 17033 **Tel** *(717) 533-3311, (800) 437-7439*

This casual and friendly restaurant, located in the Hershey Lodge, offers full hot and cold buffets ranging from salads and soups to seafood and prime rib selections. A special buffet is set up for children with pizzas, chicken nuggets, macaroni and cheese, and other kid favorites. Near Hershey Park and other attractions.

KING OF PRUSSIA California Café Bar & Grill

The Plaza at King of Prussia Mall, 160 N Gulph Road, King of Prussia, PA, 19406 **Tel** *(610) 354-8686*

Buttercup yellow walls and funky sea-green architectural details set the tone for this cool California-style restaurant, part of a countrywide dining chain. Eclectic and themed menu offering "savory" American fare, all of which is prepared with fresh, regional foods of the season. An upbeat dining experience while at the King of Prussia Mall.

NEW HOPE Logan Inn Restaurant

10 W Ferry St, New Hope, PA, 18938 **Tel** *(215) 862-2300*

A fine-dining restaurant in a historic inn dating back to 1727, Logan Inn is one of the five oldest in the US. Located in the heart of New Hope, it features a lovely dining room and a porch that offers views of the bustling town center. Carefully prepared duck, seafood, beef, and pasta specialties available.

NEW HOPE Odette's Restaurant

274 South River Road, New Hope, PA, 18938 **Tel** *(215) 862-3000*

Just a few steps south of quaint New Hope center, Odette's is housed in a 200 year-old inn and features fine dining. Creative Continental cuisine, featuring a variety of beef, veal, fowl, seafood, and pasta specialties, is served in elegantly decorated dining rooms with views of the Delaware River. The piano bar is open late. Closed Tuesday.

PENNSYLVANIA DUTCH COUNTRY Plain and Fancy Farm Restaurant

3121 Old Philadelphia Pike, Bird-in-Hand, PA, 17505 **Tel** *(717) 768-4400*

Everyday is like grandmother's home cooking at this popular family-style restaurant near the Amishview Inns *(see p141)* in the Pennsylvania Dutch Country. Friendly pass-the-platter dining features roast beef, golden fried chicken, baked Lancaster County sausage, mashed potatoes, shoofly pie, apple dumplings, and more.

PENNSYLVANIA DUTCH COUNTRY The Family Cupboard Restaurant

3370 Harvest Dr, Intercourse, PA, 17534 **Tel** *(717) 768-4510*

Amish and Mennonite home cooking does not get much better than this. Daily specials and full lunch and dinner buffets feature made-from-scratch pies and dishes from fresh farm vegetables such as green beans and carrots, mashed potatoes, and ham, chicken, and beef. Great for family dining.

PENNSYLVANIA DUTCH COUNTRY Kling House Restaurant

Rt 340, Intercourse, PA, 17534 **Tel** *(717) 768-8261*

This popular restaurant offers unique Pennsylvania Dutch Country and American fare with home-made jellies and relishes made at the adjoining Kitchen Kettle Village. House specials include portabella mushroom focaccia and grilled pita-pizza, among others. Closed Sunday.

PENNSYLVANIA DUTCH COUNTRY Miller's Smorgasbord

2811 Lincoln Hwy East (Rt 30), Ronks, PA, 17572 **Tel** *(717) 687-6621*

Sample a wide range of Pennsylvania Dutch treats and eat as much as you want at this buffet-style eatery – a tradition since 1929. Chilled steamed shrimp and carved top sirloin, turkey, chicken pot pie, and fresh bakery desserts are favorites. No lunch service. Breakfast is served only on Sunday mornings starting at 8am. Located on busy Route 30.

PENNSYLVANIA DUTCH COUNTRY 1764 Restaurant

14 E Main St, Lititz, PA, 17543 **Tel** *(717) 626-2115*

An elegant dining room with colonial decor adds to the charm of this restaurant within the landmark 18th-century General Sutter Inn. Black Angus beef, oversized chops, seafood, fowl, and pasta highlight the menu's fine food selections. Breakfast specialties include farm fresh eggs and grilled cinnamon buns.

PENNSYLVANIA DUTCH COUNTRY Historic Revere Tavern

3063 Lincoln Hwy E, Paradise, PA, 17562 **Tel** *(717) 687-8601*

Built in 1740, this tavern was once owned by the 15th US president, James Buchanan. Casual dining in a colonial atmosphere with fireplaces. Seafood, steaks, and unique snapper turtle soup highlight the menu. Along busy Route 30 in the Pennsylvania Dutch Country. No lunch service on Sunday and Monday.

PENNSYLVANIA DUTCH COUNTRY Doneckers Restaurant

333 N State St, Ephrata, PA, 17522 **Tel** *(717) 738-9501*

This elegant French restaurant is housed within a community of fine fashion and art stores in the Pennsylvania Dutch Country. Exceptional nouveau French-American cuisine made from farm fresh ingredients and an excellent wine list with more than 500 international wines. Closed Sunday and Wednesday.

WASHINGTON CROSSING Washington Crossing Inn

1295 Washington Memorial Rd, Washington Crossing, PA, 18977 **Tel** *(215) 493-3634*

Dating to 1817, this restaurant sits near where General Washington crossed the Delaware River in 1776. New-style American cuisine is served in a colonial ambience. Chops, steaks, and seafood are very well prepared. Lunch menu includes radicchio and arugala salad, grilled rib-eye steak, and smoked turkey breast arugala.

SHOPS AND MARKETS

The Philadelphia area is a stronghold for shopping with stores and outlets ranging from specialty boutiques, grand shopping centers, and malls to discount retailers and factory stores. Key shopping areas mentioned on the following pages include Center City's boutiques and shops on Market and Walnut Streets, and the shops and galleries in Old City and in the chic district

Precious gems at Jewelers' Row

of South Street. Situated in downtown Philadelphia are Antique Row and Jewelers' Row, while a variety of upscale and trendy shops are the highlights on the main streets of Manayunk and Chestnut Hill. The King of Prussia Mall is one of the nation's largest retail shopping complexes, while the cities of Reading and Lancaster have perhaps the largest number of factory outlet stores in the country.

SHOPPING HOURS

Most retailers in central Philadelphia are open seven days a week, from 10am to 6pm on Mondays through Saturdays with some varying hours, and from noon until 5pm or 6pm on Sundays. Many Center City stores are open for an extra hour or two on Wednesday nights and sometimes on Friday nights.

Outside the city, individual retail stores usually have similar hours from 10am to 6pm. Malls, however, are often open until 9pm or 9:30pm Monday through Saturday, and noon until 6pm or 7pm on Sundays. Some specialty stores have reduced hours on weekends, or may close one or two days during the week.

The popular VF Outlet Village in Reading, Pennsylvania

Storefronts on a street in Chestnut Hill, Philadelphia

TAXES

There is no sales tax on clothing and shoes in Pennsylvania. For all other items, there is a 6 percent state sales tax and an additional 1 percent tax within Philadelphia, adding up to a 7 percent sales tax when shopping in the city. However, no sales tax is levied if your purchases are shipped to an address outside Pennsylvania, but additional shipping fees may apply. Foreign visitors may have to pay duties on larger purchases they wish to take home.

SALES

Finding a sale in the US is as easy as picking up a local newspaper – especially on weekends. Most large retailers compete on a daily basis, with many regularly slashing prices. Smaller stores may have clearance racks with reduced items, while sales are often more limited in trendy shops and

high-end boutiques. The nation's "biggest shopping day of the year" occurs on the day after Thanksgiving and is called "Black Friday," when prices are cut by 70 percent or more. Similar sales take place after Christmas.

PAYMENT

Except for the smallest stores, major credit cards are accepted at most shops, boutiques, and retail outlets. In fact, department stores usually issue their own credit cards for return shoppers, though these are often issued at higher interest rates. In the US, the major credit cards accepted are Visa, Master Card, American Express, Discover Card, and Diners Club.

Cash is always accepted, and identification is necessary when using traveler's checks. Personal checks are discouraged, unless drawn from a local or well-known US bank. Stores do not accept foreign currency.

RETURNING MERCHANDISE

Most shops and stores will-willingly issue refunds and credits for returns, providing the merchandise is in good condition and not used or damaged. Sales receipts must accompany goods. Time limits for returns vary from store to store, with most allowing between ten to 30 days. Be aware, however, that certain items purchased during special sales or promotions are non-returnable, and that some stores will issue in-store-credit returns only and not cash.

DEPARTMENT STORES

There is no shortage of world-class department stores in the Philadelphia area, with most concentrated in the **King of Prussia Mall** *(see p156)*, Center City, and a few other area malls.

The historic Wanamaker Building *(see p70)* at 13th and Market Streets was named after Pennsylvanian John Wanamaker, a businessman

A couple enjoying shopping

who is considered to be the father of the department store. This Italian Renaissance-style building has housed many of the best department stores since its completion in 1910.

Today, **Macy's** Center City occupies this impressive space. This flagship store features high-end designers and affordable brand names. It also has a full-service Visitors' Center where shoppers can make dinner reservations and get information on the city's attractions. Another upmarket retail giant to open its doors in Center City is **Barney's** and in the King of Prussia Mall, the high-end department store **Neiman Marcus** offers the ultimate shopping experience with some of the best names in fashion in women's apparel, accessories, shoes, and jewelry. The same is true for children's and men's clothing. The store also offers quality bed and bath items, novelty rugs, and furniture.

Nordstrom, another leading fashion specialty store, offers high-quality gifts, apparel, shoes, and beauty products from several hundred brand names. High

fashion, stylish accessories, and the latest fragrances can be found at **Bloomingdale's**, which also stocks a wide range of house gifts, luggage, and more. **JCPenney** has a broad range of apparel, shoes, and gifts for men, women, and children. **Sears** is also one of the nation's best-known department stores, known for its large appliances, tools, lawn and garden gear, automobile repair services, and household services. The King of Prussia Mall also has another branch of Macy's.

DIRECTORY

CENTER CITY

Barney's
10 Rittenhouse Sq. **Map** 2 D5.
www.barneys.com

Macy's
1330 13th & Market Sts.
Map 3 B2. **Tel** (215) 214-9000.
www.macys.com

KING OF PRUSSIA MALL

Bloomingdale's
Tel (610) 337-6300.
www.bloomingdales.com

JCPenney
Tel (610) 992-1096.
www.jcpenney.com

King of Prussia
Rt 202 & Mall Blvd, King of Prussia
Tel (610) 337-1210.
www.kingofprussia.com

Lord and Taylor
Tel (610) 992-0333.
www.lordandtaylor.com

Macy's
Tel (610) 337-9350.
www.macys.com

Neiman Marcus
Tel (610) 354-0500.
www.neimanmarcus.com

Nordstrom
Tel (610) 265-6111.
www.nordstrom.com

Sears
Tel (610) 962-6489.
www.sears.com

Interior of King of Prussia Mall, a retail shopping complex

Interior of Shops at Liberty Place, a shopping mall in Center City

MALLS

There are several indoor malls in and around Philadelphia, allowing people to enjoy and indulge in year-round shopping, dining, and entertainment.

The Gallery at Market East, the city's largest mall, is located in Center City along Market Street between 8th and 12th Streets. The four-level mall connects with both the Pennsylvania Convention Center and Market East Station. It houses another 130 shops and eateries, and more than 30 pushcarts stocked with merchandise ranging from sunglasses and artworks to household wares and all manner of eclectic items.

The **King of Prussia Mall**, located in a suburb to the northwest of the city, is accessible via the Schulykill Expressway and is a 30-minute drive from Center City. With seven department stores (see p155) and vast parking lots and garages, it is one of the nation's largest retail shopping complexes comprising two separate sections: The Plaza and The Court. Expansive buildings with elaborate glass-ceiling atriums house more than 360 specialty

shops, and an array of 40 restaurants and eateries. Nearby, Mall Boulevard has a good selection of retail and wholesale stores, and a multi-screen movie complex. North of the city, along Route 1 in Bensalem, is the **Neshaminy Mall**, which includes 125 stores, restaurants, and a colossal 24-screen cinema complex.

SPECIALTY SHOPPING CENTERS

Groups of specialty shops are housed in large central Philadelphia buildings, offering visitors and office workers easy access to shopping – especially during the lunch hour or after work.

With offices and the luxury Park Hyatt hotel above it, the century-old **Bellevue Building** in Center City has a host of upscale boutiques, world-class restaurants, a spa, a food court with the classic American steakhouse, The Palm, and more to offer. Also in Center City, the **Shops at Liberty Place** features 60 shops that sell fine apparel, shoes, jewelry, specialty foods, and beauty products.

Shop sign at Manayunk

An impressive glass dome sits atop a circular rotunda – all part of the complex that makes up Liberty Place (see p79).

The Bourse Food Court and Specialty Shops is in the heart of Independence Mall, directly across from the Liberty Bell Center. The Bourse offers tourists in Old City a break from sightseeing itineraries with gift and souvenir shops and a food court.

SHOPPING DISTRICTS

Clusters of shops and restaurants in popular neighborhoods are known as shopping districts. One of Center City's most chic areas, **Rittenhouse Row**, includes upscale establishments along Walnut Street leading up to Rittenhouse Square (see p78). Several restaurants have storefronts facing the square, with outdoor seating in summer.

Anchored by New Market and Head House Square, **South Street** (see p67) offers a diversity of stores, shops, restaurants, eateries, and bars. Many of these cater to the avant-garde and eclectic trends of the younger crowds that often cram the area along South Street from Front to 11th Streets. **Main Street Manayunk** (see p95) is very popular on weekends for its many restaurants, pubs, and nightlife. Clothes and shoe shops, salons, antique shops, and a host of

Shops and boutique windows at Main Street Manayunk

boutiques and galleries also line Main Street. In **Chestnut Hill** *(see p94)*, more than 100 boutiques, galleries, antiques stores, restaurants, and cafés take up nearly a dozen blocks along Germantown Avenue. **Jewelers' Row** and **Antique Row** span several blocks in Center City.

MARKETS

The city's central farmers' market is the popular **Reading Terminal Market** *(see p73)*, where vendors sell farm-fresh produce, meats, poultry and seafood, flowers, pastries, and baked goods. Amish specialties and ethnic dishes representing the city's diverse population are particularly popular.

The nation's oldest and largest outdoor market, the **Italian Market** *(see p97)*, features several blocks of vendors who sell seafood, fresh produce, meats, Italian specialties, and desserts. The area is home to some of the city's best Italian restaurants.

To savor some delicious, home-style cooking of the Pennsylvania Dutch Country,

Vendors at the Italian Market, one of the city's oldest outdoor markets

take some time to drive out to the small villages of Bird-In-Hand and Intercourse. **The Amish Barn Restaurant and Gift Shop**, for instance, offers authentic local food as well as handicrafts and souvenirs.

DISCOUNT AND OUTLET MALLS

Located in an area northeast of Philadelphia is the **Franklin Mills Mall**, home to more than 200 retail and factory stores such as Last Call, Neiman Marcus, Ann Taylor, and Factory Store. Its outlets include those for Casual Corner, Saks Fifth

Avenue, Polo Ralph Lauren, JCPenney, and many others.

A complex of restored old factory buildings, **VF Outlet Village** in Reading is one of the county's largest groupings of factory store outlets. Several multistory buildings house discounted clothing, shoes, and household wares from Vanity Fair, Wrangler, Lee, Liz Claiborne, London Fog, Tommy Hilfiger, and Reebok.

Atlantic City Outlets, The Walk, in New Jersey, has merchandise from manufacturers, including Van Heusen, Guess, Geoffrey Beene, Casual Corner, and Brooks Brothers, at reduced prices.

DIRECTORY

Fashion and Accessories

Center City is Philadelphia's main shopping district with more than 2,100 retail stores. Many offer the finest in clothes, shoes, accessories, and jewelry. Key fashion shops and boutiques are located along Walnut Street on Rittenhouse Row. Designer clothing stores are also found at the Gallery at Market East mall, as well as within the small shopping centers at the Bellevue Building and Liberty Place. When looking for the latest in high fashion, do not forget the department stores and specialty stores at the King of Prussia Mall.

Entrance to the upmarket shops in Liberty Place

WOMEN'S FASHION

With so many stores and boutiques to choose from, women will be delighted with a shopping spree in Center City. Located just one block from Rittenhouse Square on Walnut Street, **Jones New York** offers a range of fine apparel. Nearby, the **Knit Wit** boutique carries a variety of elegant black cocktail dresses as well as cruise-wear. **Ann Taylor**, on the same block, has upbeat and high-fashion designs for both business and pleasure. **Ann Taylor Loft**, **Express**, and lingerie store **Victoria's Secret** are also at Liberty Place.

The number of women's apparel stores in the King of Prussia Mall is extensive and you will need plenty of time to get round them all. In addition to Victoria's Secret and Ann Taylor, there are upscale stores from top international designers, the latest classic and trendy fashions from **New York and Company** and **Lane Bryant**, and the risqué designs of **Frederick's of Hollywood**.

Main Street Manayunk features several women's clothing boutiques. **Showing with Style** offers fashionable maternity clothes, while Nicole Miller and **Paula Hian Designs** stock upscale evening wear for women.

MEN'S FASHION

Men looking for the perfect suit or designer clothing will not leave the city empty handed. **Boyds Philadelphia** has been around for over 60 years and is one of Center City's premier stores. One of the most elegant shops at the Bellevue, **Polo Ralph Lauren** has a full line of clothing from the world-renowned designer. Men will also find a variety of stores at the Shops at Liberty Place, including **Jos. A. Bank**, **Les Richard's Mensware**, and **Andrew's Ties**.

In the King of Prussia Mall, **Hugo Boss Store** features the label's clothing, sportswear, and accessories. Other popular men's stores include **Bachrach**, which is one of the nation's largest privately owned retailers, and **Talbots Mens** with its line of casual wear and outerwear.

Window shopping at one of Center City's numerous upscale boutiques

MEN'S AND WOMEN'S FASHION

With shops in the Bellevue Building and Manayunk, **Nicole Miller** features men's and women's formalwear, as well as accessories. A line of both casual and dressy apparel can be found at **J. Crew** and **Express** at the Shops at Liberty Place, while casual wear is the highlight of **Old Navy** and **Gap** at the Gallery at Market East. **Guess** features more trendsetting clothing at the same mall. At King of Prussia, **Brooks Brothers** sells traditional, fine-quality apparel. **Eddie Bauer** features winter clothes, while **Banana Republic** offers casual jeans and dressy jackets. Other popular outlets include **Abercrombie & Fitch**, and the hip styles of **Diesel**.

Casual sneakers

SHOES AND ACCESSORIES

Featuring a line of fur, shearling, leather, and cloth, **Jacques Ferber** on Walnut Street offers unique outerwear. **Touches**, in Center City, has many one-of-a-kind varieties of jewelry, picture frames, and scarves.

For men's shoes, **Sherman Brothers** offers a wide selection of top brands and hard-to-find sizes. Both men's and women's choices for shoes abound in the King of Prussia Mall, with stores including **Bakers**, **Kenneth Cole**, **Rockport**, **Timberland**, **Bostonian**, and **Johnston Murphy**.

JEWELRY

Philadelphia's Jewelers' Row was established in 1851, and is the nation's oldest and one of the largest diamond districts. Stores on the row include a seemingly unlimited selection of diamonds, rubies, sapphires, and emeralds. Owned by the same family for four generations, **Barsky Diamonds** specializes in diamonds. **Safian and Rudolph Jewelers**, in business for over 50 years, deals in precious stones, while **Tiffany and Company**, in Center City, has offered the finest in jewelry, crystal, and accessories for more than 150 years. Other prominent Center City jewelers include **Govberg Jewelers** and **LAGOS The Store**.

DIRECTORY

WOMEN'S FASHION

Ann Taylor
1713 Walnut St.
Map 2 E5.
Tel (215) 977-9336.
King of Prussia Mall.
Tel (610) 354-9380.

Ann Taylor Loft
Liberty Place. **Map** 2 E4.
Tel (215) 557-9181.
King of Prussia Mall.
Tel (610) 337-1550.

Daffy's
1700 Chestnut St.
Map 2 E4
Tel (215) 963-9996.

Frederick's of Hollywood
King of Prussia Mall.
Tel (610) 265-1499.

Jones New York
1711 Walnut St.
Map 2 E5.
Tel (215) 864–0110.

Knit Wit
1718 Walnut St.
Map 2 E5.
Tel (215) 564-4760.

Lane Bryant
King of Prussia Mall.
Tel (610) 265-6106.

New York and Company
King of Prussia Mall.
Tel (610) 354-0560.

Paula Hian Designs
106 Gay St, Manayunk.
Tel (215) 487-3067.

Showing with Style
4321 Main St, Manayunk.
Tel (267) 297-7035.

Victoria's Secret
Liberty Place. **Map** 2 E4.
Tel (215) 564-1142.
King of Prussia Mall.
Tel (610) 337-0788.

MEN'S FASHION

Andrew's Ties
1625 Chestnut St. **Map** 2 E4. *Tel (215) 988-1260.*

Bachrach
King of Prussia Mall.
Tel (610) 265-0159.

Hugo Boss Store
King of Prussia Mall.
Tel (610) 992-1400.

Boyds Philadelphia
1818 Chestnut St.
Map 2 D4.
Tel (215) 564-9000.

Jos. A. Bank
Liberty Place. **Map** 2 E4.
Tel (215) 563-5990.
King of Prussia Mall.
Tel (610) 337-2131.

Les Richard's Mensware
1625 Chestnut St. **Map** 2 E4. *Tel (215) 751-1155.*

Polo Ralph Lauren
200 S Broad St. **Map** 2 F5.
Tel (215) 985-2800.

Senor
4390 Main St, Manayunk.
Tel (215) 487-3667.

Talbots Mens
King of Prussia Mall.
Tel (610) 962-0881.

MEN'S AND WOMEN'S FASHION

Abercrombie & Fitch
King of Prussia Mall.
Tel (610) 265-5650.

Banana Republic
1401 Walnut St. **Map** 2 F5
Tel (215) 751-0292.
King of Prussia Mall.
Tel (610) 768-9007.

Brooks Brothers
1513 Walnut St. **Map** 2 E5
Tel (215) 564-4100.
King of Prussia Mall.
Tel (610) 337-9888.

Diesel
King of Prussia Mall.
Tel (610) 768-5855.

Express
Liberty Place. **Map** 2 E4.
Tel (215) 851-0699.
King of Prussia Mall.
Tel (610) 337-8912.

Gap
The Gallery at Market East, Market St between 9th & 11th Sts. **Map** 3 C2.
Tel (215) 925-9770.

Guess
The Gallery at Market East, Market St between 9th & 11th Sts. **Map** 3 C2.
Tel (215) 627-3573.

J. Crew
Liberty Place. **Map** 2 E4.
Tel (215) 940-2711.

Nicole Miller
200 S Broad St. **Map** 2 F5.
Tel (215) 546-5007.
4249 Main Street, Manayunk.
Tel (215) 930-0307.

Old Navy
The Gallery at Market East, Market St between 9th & 11th Sts. **Map** 3 C2.
Tel (215) 413-7012.

SHOES AND ACCESSORIES

Bostonian
King of Prussia Mall.
Tel (610) 265-4323.

Jacques Ferber
1708 Walnut St.
Map 2 E5.
Tel (215) 735-4173.

Johnston Murphy
King of Prussia Mall.
Tel (610) 265-0165.

Kenneth Cole
1420 Walnut St.
Map 2 E5.
Tel (215) 790-1690.
King of Prussia Mall.
Tel (610) 337-2650.

Nine West
Liberty Place.
Map 2 E4
Tel (215) 851-8570.

Rockport
King of Prussia Mall.
Tel (610) 265-5800.

Sherman Brothers Shoes
1520 Sansom St.
Map 2 E4.
Tel (215) 561-4550.

Timberland
King of Prussia Mall.
Tel (610) 265-2193.

JEWELRY

Barsky Diamonds
724 Sansom St.
Map 4 D3.
Tel (215) 925-8639.

Govberg Jewelers
1818 Chestnut St.
Map 2 E5.
Tel (215) 546-6505.

LAGOS The Store
1735 Walnut St.
Map 2 E4.
Tel (215) 567-0770.

Safian & Rudolph Jewelers
701 Sansom St.
Map 4 D3.
Tel (215) 627-1834.

Tiffany and Company
1414 Walnut St.
Map 2 E5.
Tel (215) 735-1919.

Specialty Shops

With shopping districts, upscale shops, and one-of-a-kind stores, central Philadelphia has a wide range of merchandise that would satisfy even the hard-to-please shopper. Many specialty shops and gift stores specialize in finding the perfect gift or souvenir. Antique Row has numerous stores along an eight-block stretch in Center City, while in Old City sits a large cluster of art galleries. Other key shopping areas with unique crafts, books, and flower stores include Manayunk and Chestnut Hill. The colossal King of Prussia Mall has a seemingly unending choice of everything, from home furnishings and electronics to sporting goods.

Shops located in the Chestnut Hill market area

ANTIQUES

Spread over eight blocks on Pine Street between 7th and 11th Streets, Antique Row *(see p157)* features boutiques and shops offering a selection of fine furniture, period antiques, collectibles, estate jewelry, and vintage clothing. One such store is **M. Finkel & Daughter**, which sells period furniture, 17th- to 19th-century needlework, and decorative accessories. The nearby **Classic Antiques** offers a large selection of country French furniture, mirrors, and accessories as well as 18th- and 19th-century European antiques. The **South Street Antiques Market** is the city's only indoor antiques market with 27 dealers selling pieces from vintage Victorian to modern, including estate jewelry, furniture, pottery, and accessories.

ART GALLERIES

The Old City Arts Association has 50 members, including art galleries, which are open until 9pm on the first Friday of every month – an event

that is appropriately called "First Friday." The **Berman Gallery** and the **Moderne Gallery** feature contemporary furniture, pottery, fine arts, and metalwork. The **Artists' House Gallery** offers works rendered by local artists and available for sale at affordable prices.

Located on Antique Row, **Seraphin Gallery** has art from international contemporary painters, sculptors, and photographers, including 18th- through 20th-century works by artists from America and Europe. In Center City, **Newman Galleries** specializes in 19th-century American and European paintings, and early 20th-century American art from the New Hope School.

The Clay Studio recently celebrated 30 years in Old City. This studio exhibits works by emerging and established artists and also offers a range of classes.

BOOKS

An excellent choice for mainstream books and magazines is **Barnes & Noble** at Rittenhouse Square. Similar in scope are **Borders** in Chestnut Hill, and at the King of Prussia Mall, and **B. Dalton Bookseller**, which has a store in Gallery at Market East mall.

For hard-to-find books, the **Philadelphia Rare Books and Manuscript Company** features early printed books dating from the 16th century, and manuscripts, old bibles, and other books from around the world that cover a wide realm of topics. Opened in 1936, **Robin's Bookstore** is the oldest independent bookstore in the city with a vast collection of African-American books, literature, poetry, New Age, and children's books.

FOOD AND COOKERY

Within the Italian Market are specialty food stores. Family owned for more than 50 years, **DiBruno Bros. House of Cheese** sells more than 400 types of cheese and gourmet foods. **Termini Brothers Gold Medal Pastry Bakery** is a local favorite with handmade Italian confections made from recipes that date to the 1800s. Serving chefs and home cooks since 1906, **Fante's Kitchen Wares Shop** offers an extensive selection of cooking wares and utensils.

Gourmet cheese

GIFTS, CRAFTS, AND SOUVENIRS

As a result of its varied traditions and its status as one of America's oldest cities, Philadelphia offers a range of gifts and mementos. **Xenos Candy'n Gifts** has classic souvenirs showcasing Old City sights, including replicas of Liberty Bell, flags, and other collectables. Similar items are found in **The Bourse** nearby, while the **Pennsylvania General Store** has locally-made foods and crafts. **Scarlett Alley** offers art, furnishings, jewelry, leather goods, books, and children's items. **Sweet Violet** features fine gifts for personal care as well as for homes. Fine-rolled, handmade cigars can be bought at the **Black Cat Cigar Company** and **Holt's Cigar Company** in Center City.

FLORISTS

A wide-ranging choice of flowers is available from Philadelphia's florists. Some, such as **Nature's Gallery Florist** in Center City, are also able to assist with the floral side of party planning. **Ten Pennies Florist**, a staple in Philadelphia for more than 20 years, offers exquisite arrangements for any occasion.

Music CDs

MUSIC

For the latest in music CDs and recordings, Borders and **Tower Records** in Center City have extensive music selections featuring rock, pop, hip-hop, jazz, folk, classical, and more. Visit **Repo Records** on South Street to thumb through a wide range of import singles, and rows of used records and CDs.

SPORTING GOODS

The nation's largest family-owned sports goods chain, **Modell's Sporting Goods**, has stores in Center City and King of Prussia Mall, and also sells home-team apparel and footwear. For camping gear, kayaks, and other outdoor items, shop at **Eastern Mountain Sports**, also at King of Prussia Mall.

DIRECTORY

ANTIQUES

Classic Antiques
922 Pine St. **Map** 3 C4.
Tel (215) 629-0211.

M. Finkel & Daughter
936 Pine St. **Map** 3 C4.
Tel (215) 627-7797.

South Street Antiques Market
615 S 6th St. **Map** 3 D5.
Tel (215) 592-0256.

ART GALLERIES

Artists' House Gallery
57 N 2nd St. **Map** 4 E2.
Tel (215) 923-8440.

Berman Gallery
136 N 2nd St. **Map** 4 E2.
Tel (215) 733-0707.

The Clay Gallery
139 N Second St.
Map 4 E2.
Tel (215) 925-3453.

Moderne Gallery
111 N 3rd St. **Map** 4 E2.
Tel (215) 923-8536.

Newman Galleries
1425 Walnut St. **Map** 2 E5.
Tel (215) 563-1779.

Seraphin Gallery
1108 Pine St. **Map** *3* B4.
Tel (215) 923-7000.

BOOKS

B. Dalton Bookseller
The Gallery at Market East, Market St. **Map** 3 C2.
Tel (215) 592-8700.

Barnes & Noble
1805 Walnut St.
Map 2 D4.
Tel (215) 665-0716.

Borders
1 S Broad St. **Map** 3 B2.
Tel (215) 568-7400.
8701 Germantown Ave, Chestnut Hill.
Tel (215) 248-1213.
King of Prussia Mall.
Tel (610) 337-9009.

Philadelphia Rare Books and Manuscript Company
Tel (215) 744-6734.

Robin's Bookstore
108 S 13th St. **Map** 3 B3.
Tel (215) 547-2415.

FOOD AND COOKERY

DiBruno Bros. House of Cheese
Italian Market, 930 S 9th St. **Map** 3 C5.
Tel (215) 922-2876.
109 S 18th St. **Map** 2 E4.
Tel (215) 665-9220.

Fante's Kitchen Wares Shop
Italian Market, 1006 S 9th St. **Map** 3 C5.
Tel (215) 922-5557.

Termini Brothers Gold Medal Pastry Bakery
1523 S 8th St.
Tel (215) 334-1816.

GIFTS, CRAFTS, AND SOUVENIRS

Black Cat Cigar Company
1518 Sansom Street.
Map 2 E4.
Tel (800) 220-9850.

The Bourse
5th between Market & Chestnut Sts. **Map** 4 D3.
Tel (215) 625-0300.

Holt's Cigar Company
1522 Walnut St.
Map 2 E5.
Tel (215) 732-8500.

Pennsylvania General Store
Reading Terminal Market.
Map 3 C2
Tel (215) 592-0455.

Scarlett Alley
241 Race St. **Map** 4E2.
Tel (215) 592-7898.

Sweet Violet
4361 Main St, Manayunk.
Tel (215) 483-2826

Xenos Candy n Gifts
231 Chestnut St.
Map 4 F3.
Tel (215) 922-1445.

FLORISTS

Nature's Gallery Florist
Map 2 D4.
Tel (215) 563-5554.

Ten Pennies Florist
1921 S Broad St.
Map 3 C2.
Tel (215) 336-3557.

MUSIC

Repo Records
538 South St. **Map** 4 D4.
Tel (215) 627-3775.

Tower Records
100 S Broad St.
Map 3 C2.
Tel (215) 568-8001.

SPORTING GOODS

Eastern Mountain Sports
King of Prussia Mall.
Tel (610) 337-4210.

Modell's Sporting Goods
934 Market St. **Map** 3 C2.
Tel (215) 629-0900.
King of Prussia Mall.
Tel (610) 337-4522.

ENTERTAINMENT IN PHILADELPHIA

Stretching along the "Avenue of the Arts," Broad Street is home to a plethora of renowned performing arts facilities. Heading the list are the Kimmel Center for the Performing Arts and the Academy of Music, home to the world-class Philly POPS, Philadelphia Orchestra, Opera Company of Philadelphia, and the Pennsylvania Ballet. Numerous other venues feature

Detail of façade at the Forrest Theater

live chamber music, theater productions and musicals, rock, hip hop and jazz-fusion concerts, and varied programs of gospel. Universities also put on several music, theater, and dance shows. Nightclubs hosting live bands abound in Old City and South Street, while a drive or train ride of an hour or so brings you to Atlantic City's glittering casinos on the New Jersey shoreline.

Visitors wait for a show at Kimmel Center for the Performing Arts

INFORMATION

There are several websites and newspapers that carry the latest information on musical concerts, theatrical performances, nightlife, and other entertainment options in and around the city.

The *Weekend* section of the **Philadelphia Inquirer**, published every Friday, details the goings-on in town, from the latest movies to gallery exhibitions to extensive listings of live performances, including ballet, chamber and classical music, opera, theater, and jazz. The art district has its own website, Avenue of the Arts.

The **Philadelphia City Paper** and **Philadelphia Weekly** also showcase arts, music, and cinema listings. They also have extended information on daily nightclub acts and performances. These two publications are weeklies and are available free at many cafés, pubs, and bookstores throughout the city. They also have websites with up-to-date listings.

Philadelphia's most comprehensive news website is **www.phillyfunguide.com**. It has information on all types of activities in the city and also has a number of saver deals.

TICKETS

Seats for most of the major symphony, opera, chamber music, ballet, and pop performances in Philadelphia can be booked through **Ticket Philadelphia**. The main box office is in the **Kimmel Center for the Performing Arts**. Tickets can be bought in person, on the phone or online. Tickets for various events and theatrical performances can also be bought at the box office of each venue, or over the phone, online or in person via **Ticketmaster**. Be aware, however, that ticketing services often add a fee to the total cost. Ticketmaster is one of the world's largest e-commerce sites, in addition to having more than 3,300 retail outlets and 19 worldwide telephone call centers. It acts as the exclusive ticketing service for various performing arts venues and theaters.

Some hotels may also sell show tickets, especially those in Center City or near the theater district. Check with the concierge in your hotel for the best ticketing options.

The Philadelphia Orchestra at Verizon Hall in the Kimmel Center

"Avenue of the Arts" lights up for a night of theater and culture

ENTERTAINMENT DISTRICTS

The hub of Philadelphia's performing arts and theater district extends south of City Hall on South Broad Street, called the **Avenue of the Arts**. This two-block area is anchored by the Kimmel Center for the Performing Arts and the world-renowned **Academy of Music** *(see p76)*. Also located in this area is the Merriam Theater, hosting professional touring productions, as well as the 300-seat Wilma Theater *(see p164)*, whose productions address current political and social issues. Three blocks east of the area is the Forrest Theatre *(see p164)*, while the Prince Music Theater is on Chestnut Street. Inside the Bellevue Building at the corner of South Broad Street and Walnut Street is the city's prominent jazz club, Zanzibar Blue *(see p166)*.

Besides theater and cultural activities, Philadelphia has a thriving nightlife with scores of restaurants, nightclubs, smaller theater venues, and comedy clubs concentrated along South Street. A vibrant nightlife scene also abounds in the Old City area around Chestnut, Market, Front, and 2nd Streets with restaurants, cozy pubs, and martini bars.

Along the Delaware River, Columbus Avenue is home to some of Philadelphia's up-and-coming nightspots north and south of Penn's Landing – some on piers stretching into the river, while others are seasonal outdoor clubs.

Much of the city's lesbian and gay nightlife centers on the neighborhood between Pine and Chestnut Streets north to south and Broad and 11th Streets west to east.

Across the Delaware, meanwhile, the Tweeter Center at the Camden Waterfront *(see p101)* hosts concerts through the year, drawing big-name musical acts, as does the Wachovia Complex in south Philadelphia *(see p166)*.

Going beyond Philadelphia, Atlantic City *(see p127)* is an entertainment destination in itself with more than a dozen sprawling casino hotels and resorts, most of which have popular nightclubs, concert venues, and pulsing and glitzy discos.

South Street – an entertainment hub for the younger crowd

DISABLED ACCESS

Most of the major concert halls and theaters in Philadelphia accommodate disabled patrons and wheelchairs. The Kimmel Center for the Performing Arts and the Academy of Music have accessible wheelchair seating locations for performances, captioning for the hearing impaired, and assisted listening devices available on a first-come, first-served basis. Call ahead for details.

Some smaller venues and clubs may be less than adequate in accommodating disabled patrons. Check with the venue or the **Mayor's Commission on People with Disabilities** for more information. The commission provides a forum for the disabled to express opinions on programs and services in Philadelphia.

DIRECTORY

TICKETING

Ticketmaster
Various Outlets.
Tel (215) 336-2000.
www.ticketmaster.com

Ticket Philadelphia
Tel (215) 893-1999.
www.ticketphiladelphia.org

DISABLED ACCESS

Kimmel Center & Academy of Music
Department of Audience & Visitor Services. **Map** 2 E5.
Tel (215) 670-2327.
www.kimmelcenter.org

Mayor's Commission on People with Disabilities
1401 JFK Blvd. **Map** 2 F4.
Tel (215) 686-2798.
www.phila.gov/aco/index.html

USEFUL WEBSITES

Avenue of the Arts
www.avenueofthearts.org

Philadelphia Citypaper.net
www.citypaper.net

Philadelphia Fun Guide
www.phillyfunguide.com

Philadelphia Weekly Online
www.philadelphiaweekly.com

Philly.com (Philadelphia Inquirer)
www.philly.com

The Arts in Philadelphia

A cultural Mecca for the performing arts, Philadelphia has world-class venues that host excellent chamber and symphony music, and some of the finest performances in opera, ballet, and theater. Topping the list are concerts by the renowned Philadelphia Orchestra and Philly POPS, which are performed in the city's premier venue, the multitheater Kimmel Center for the Performing Arts. Chamber music ensembles play before smaller crowds, while grand opera and ballet productions take the stage in the Victorian-era Academy of Music. Several theaters in and around Center City host performances that range from Broadway productions and musicals to African-American theater. Entertainment is also provided by choral groups and the area's top music schools, which hold classical concerts and dance performances by students.

Forrest Theater, host to touring dance and theater companies

CLASSICAL MUSIC AND SYMPHONY

One of the city's best, the **Philadelphia Orchestra** has shared the stage with some of the world's most influential classical musicians for more than 100 years. The orchestra's home was the **Academy of Music**, but it now performs at the Verizon Hall in the **Kimmel Center for the Performing Arts**.

Also performing at Verizon Hall is one of the nation's most-renowned POPS orchestras playing big band, classics, Broadway hits, and rock'n roll tunes. Grammy Award-winning pianist and band leader Peter Nero has been leading the **Philly POPS** since 1979. In summer, both orchestras perform at an outdoor venue, the **Mann Center for the Performing Arts**, also home to jazz, dance, opera, and musical theater programs.

Chamber music can be enjoyed on Sunday afternoons and Monday evenings at the Kimmel Center's Perelman Theater. The **Chamber Orchestra of Philadelphia** performs here, playing a musical repertoire from the 18th century to the present day. The **Philadelphia Chamber Music Society** presents more than 60 chamber music, piano, vocal, and choral concerts a year, which are performed by internationally-known groups as

Pennsylvania Ballet dancer performing *Swan Lake*

well as emerging artists. Presenting a unique classical experience is the **Philomel Baroque Orchestra** – a small ensemble of accomplished musicians who play early classical and Baroque music on period instruments.

THEATERS AND THEATER COMPANIES

Stage productions run the gamut from national touring shows to politically inspired acts produced locally. The **Philadelphia Theatre Company** is the city's leading producer of contemporary American theater, while the **Arden Theatre Company** brings to life dramatic and theatrical stories by the greatest storytellers of all time.

The **Forrest Theatre** hosts Broadway shows and is the city's premier theatrical arts venue. The **Walnut Street Theatre** – America's oldest – is home to musicals and plays.

The **Wilma Theater** has productions with contemporary themes, while the smaller **Society Hill Playhouse** features offbeat and "off-Broad Street" productions. The **Freedom Theatre**, located on the northern stretch of the Avenue of the Arts, is one of the country's leading venues for African-American performances.

OPERA AND BALLET

Local lovers of grand opera have been enjoying performances by the Opera Company of Philadelphia for more than 30 years. The Pennsylvania Ballet, which has been thrilling audiences for over 40 years, performs at the Academy of Music and the Merriam Theater. Its season has six productions, including the old Yuletide favorite, The Nutcracker *(see p35)*, which has become an annual Philadelphia tradition.

Academy of Music, oldest opera house in the US still used for its original purpose

VOCAL ARTS AND CHOIRS

There are several choral groups in the city such as the renowned **Philadelphia Boys Choir and Chorale**. The 100-member choir performs patriotic music and Broadway show tunes. The group holds more than 40 performances each year, and travels on international tours.

The **Philadelphia Singers**, an ensemble of 24 professional vocalists, performs with leading national and local orchestras and other performing arts organizations such as the Philadelphia Orchestra, the Pennsylvania Ballet, and the Curtis Institute of Music. A 100-voice symphonic chorus, the **Choral Arts Society of Philadelphia** also appears often with the Philadelphia Orchestra. The **Academy of Vocal Arts**, around since 1934, produces operas with the **Chamber Orchestra of Philadelphia**. The academy's resident artists also hold recitals and concerts.

MUSIC SCHOOLS' PERFORMANCES

Often considered one of the most prestigious conservatories, the **Curtis Institute of Music** trains some of the best young musicians from around the world. The students hold free public recitals and concerts in the institute's Field Concert Hall located opposite Rittenhouse Square, and play in various venues around the city when they are not touring.

Local musicians and students training in classical, jazz, dance, and theater arts also hold recitals and concerts at the **University of the Arts**, Temple University's **Esther Boyer College of Music and Dance**, and through **PENN Presents** at the University of Pennsylvania's Annenberg Center for the Performing Arts.

DIRECTORY

CLASSICAL MUSIC AND SYMPHONY

Academy of Music
240 S Broad & Locust Sts.
Map 2 E5.
Tel (215) 790-5800;
box office: (215) 893-
1999.

Chamber Orchestra of Philadelphia
Perelman Theater,
Kimmel Center.
Map 2 E5.
Tel (215) 545-5451;
box office: (215) 893-
1999.

Kimmel Center for the Performing Arts
Broad & Spruce Sts.
Map 2 E5.
Tel (215) 790-5800;
box office: (215) 893-
1999.

Mann Center for the Performing Arts
52nd St & Parkside Ave.
Tel (215) 546-7900; box
office: (215) 893-1999.

Peter Nero & the Philly POPS
Verizon Hall,
Kimmel Center.
Map 2 E5.
Tel (215) 546-6400;
box office: (215) 893-
1999.

Philadelphia Chamber Music Society
Various venues.
Tel (215) 569-8587;
box office: (215) 569-
8080.

Philadelphia Orchestra
Verizon Hall, Kimmel
Center. **Map** 2 E5.
Tel (215) 893-1900; box
office: (215) 893-1999.

Philomel Baroque Orchestra
Various venues.
Tel (215) 487–2344;
box office: (215) 569-
9700.

THEATERS AND THEATER COMPANIES

Arden Theatre Company
40 N 2nd St. **Map** 4 E2.
Tel (215) 922-1122.

Forrest Theatre
1114 Walnut St.
Map 3 B3.
Tel (215) 923-1515.

Freedom Theatre
1346 N Broad St.
Tel (215) 765-2793.

Philadelphia Theatre Company
480 S Broad St.
Map 2 D5.
Tel (215) 985-1400; box
office: (215) 985-0420.

Society Hill Playhouse
507 S 8th St. **Map** 3 C4.
Tel (215) 923-0210.

Walnut Street Theatre
825 Walnut St. **Map** 3
C3. *Tel (215) 574-3550.*

Wilma Theater
265 S Broad St.
Map 2 E5.
Tel box office: (215) 546-
7824.

OPERA AND BALLET

Opera Company of Philadelphia
Academy of Music.
Map 2 E5.
Tel (215) 893-3600; box
office: (215) 732-8400.

Pennsylvania Ballet
Merriam Theater,
Academy of Music.
Map 2 E5.
Tel (215) 551-7000.

VOCAL ARTS AND CHOIRS

Academy of Vocal Arts
Various venues.
Tel (215) 735-1685.

Choral Arts Society of Philadelphia
Various venues.
Tel box office: (215) 545-
8634.

Philadelphia Boys Choir and Chorale
225 N 32nd St.
Map 1 B2.
Tel (215) 222-3500.

Philadelphia Singers
Kimmel Center
& various venues.
Map 2 E5.
Tel (215) 751-9494.

MUSIC SCHOOLS' PERFORMANCES

Curtis Institute of Music
Field Concert Hall
& various venues.
1726 Locust St.
Map 2 E5.
Tel (215) 893-7902; box
office: (215) 893-1999

Esther Boyer College of Music and Dance
Temple University,
1715 N Broad St.
Tel (215) 204-8301.

PENN Presents
Annenberg Center for
the Performing Arts,
University of Pennsylvania.
Tel (215) 898-6701;
box office: (215) 898-
3900.

University of the Arts
Broad & Pine Sts.
Map 2 E5.
Tel (800) 616-2787.

Music and Nightlife

Philadelphia fills its after-dark hours with the latest sounds in rock, folk, pop, jazz-fusion, hip-hop, and salsa. These rhythms can be heard at venues offering live music, sometimes seven days a week. Many are clustered within the prominent entertainment districts of South Street, Old City, Main Street Manayunk, and the areas along the Delaware Avenue waterfront. Philadelphia is often a regular stop for major bands and musical acts on world tours, including top rock, jazz, hip-hop, and country and pop musicians. Those opting for a less energized night out can enjoy conversation and cocktails at friendly neighborhood taverns and bars located throughout the city.

ROCK AND FOLK MUSIC

For the top touring rock bands, check listings in local newspapers *(see p162)* for concerts at the **Wachovia Complex** and other major venues, including the **Tower Theater, Keswick Theatre**, and the **Susquehanna Bank Center**, located on the waterfront. Also check listings for concerts held in Atlantic City.

For a taste of local rock music, **Khyber** in Old City has shows several nights a week and is a mainstay for Philadelphia's rock scene. Live performances by local rock groups also take place at the **Pontiac Grille** on South Street and the **Grape Street Pub** in Manayunk.

Folk musicians and fans frequent the **Tin Angel** in Old City. One of the region's newest venues that attracts folk artists, gospel choirs and alternative rock acts is **World Café Live**, located on the campus in University City.

BLUES, JAZZ, AND WORLD MUSIC

Blues and jazz clubs range from upbeat nightspots and restaurants, where top artists

Alma de Cuba, famous for its Cuban cuisine and live music

perform, to smaller and cozier lounges. **Warmdaddy's** is a popular southern blues club and restaurant offering live jazz. Its 100-seat dining room overlooks the main stage where artists perform nightly; Tuesdays are reserved for open jam sessions made up of local musicians. **Ortlieb's Jazzhaus** is another hot venue that offers world-class jazz music six nights a week. **Chris' Jazz Club**, on Samson Street, has become something of an institution amongst the city's jazz lovers. The line-up includes a good mix of up-and-coming and established talent. Some clubs offer a range of international music,

Performers at the popular Chris' Jazz club

such as salsa, flamenco, and more. For instance, musicians at **Alma de Cuba** belt out live Cuban music performances every week.

NIGHTCLUBS AND DISCOS

Philadelphia offers a wide range of late-night venues to suit all musical persuasions. The city's younger crowd parties late into the night with clubs churning out music until 2am. The cutting-edge dance club **Shampoo** features dance halls and lounges with multiple bars and DJs. Along Delaware Avenue, **Cavanaugh's River Deck** features concerts and DJs in an all-outdoors venue along the Delaware River.

A trendy nightspot for the city's chic elite is the **32° Luxe Lounge** in Old City. It includes two premium bars and a lush VIP lounge with European bottle service. The Polynesian-themed **Tiki Bob's Cantina** has a signature drink, the Tiki Nut. For classic funk to old-school hip-hop and reggae, to the latest DJ mixes, **Bleu Martini** in Old City is the place to be seen in Philadelphia.

BARS AND TAVERNS

Many Center City hotels and restaurants have comfortable bars that are ideal for relaxing and for conversation. Philadelphia also has a number of neighborhood bars and pubs that play live music. **Monk's Café** in south Philadelphia is a bistro with more than 200 beer brands from around the world and 20 Belgian draught ales. If you are not sure what to go for, their *Beer Bible* gives a description of each beer available.

Draught Guinness

Irish pubs with great food and Guinness beer on tap include **Fergie's Pub**, which has live music most evenings and a traditional Irish menu, and the **Irish Pub** that serves Irish-American food in a casual dining ambience.

McEllin's Olde Ale House
is the oldest operating tavern in the city, offering a great selection of beer. The **Bishop's Collar** has a friendly atmosphere with a selection of microbrews, and creative but inexpensive pub fare. It is a great place to unwind after visiting the Museum of Art or Boathouse Row.

GAY CLUBS AND BARS

Several nightclubs and bars are centered in the city's main gay and lesbian district, located between Broad and 11th Streets, and Chestnut to Pine Streets. The **Bump Lounge** is the city's premier gay lounge serving food and cocktails seven days a week. With three floors of energizing house music, disco, and hip-hop, **Pure** has been the city's prominent gay nightspot for

more than 30 years. Nearby is **Sisters**, the city's largest lesbian bar with dining and dancing. For more information, visit the Greater Philadelphia Tourism and Marketing Corporation's website *(see p133)* or look at the Philadelphia Convention and Visitors Bureau's *Gay and Lesbian Travel Guide*, available at the Independence Visitors Center.

COMEDY CLUBS

Many clubs in town and across the river in New Jersey feature stand-up comedy acts. The city's "Original Comedy Club," the **Laff House** on

Pure, a prominent gay nightspot in Philadelphia

South Street, brings in comedians from all over the country, with open mike nights, and main acts on Friday and Saturday nights. The **Helium Comedy Club** draws the nation's top acts to this 250-seat theater. Two lounges inside the club offer food and specialty drinks. Punters buying a drink before 7pm on Wednesdays can see that night's show for free.

DIRECTORY

Outdoor Activities and Sports

Whether you are an active participant or simply a
spectator, there is no shortage of sporting activities in
Philadelphia all year round. In the warmer months, the
region's many recreational areas and parks are packed
with hikers, bicyclists, joggers, and golfers. In
the winter months, outdoor enthusiasts opt
for ice-skating or head for the nearby ski
slopes in the Pocono Mountains. Local
sports fans are passionate about their
many professional home teams that
play throughout the year. They flock to
the city's stadiums and arenas to watch
baseball, football, basketball, and
hockey. The area's colleges and
universities compete in the above
sports and others such as volleyball,
swimming, and gymnastics.

Inline skater

BICYCLING, JOGGING, AND SKATING

Philadelphia has an
extensive greenbelt running
through it with miles of
walking and biking trails,
most of which are found
in Fairmount Park *(see p95)*.
On warmer days of the
year, hundreds of enthusiasts
take to the city's most
popular trail, the 8.4-mile
(13.5-km) paved inline
skating, walking, and biking
path that runs parallel to
Kelly and Martin Luther King
Jr Boulevard *(see p96)* along
both sides of the Schuylkill
River. The **Bicycle Club of**

Philadelphia has information
about the various bike
paths within the area, and
schedules bike rides each
weekend for cyclists of
all experience levels.

Other popular hiking and
biking trails can be found
along Wissahickon Gorge
in Fairmount Park. There
are also 6 miles (9.6 km)
of trails within **Valley Forge
National Historic Park** *(see
p129)*. Valley Forge is a
starting point for the 22-mile
(35-km) bike path ending
in Fairmount Park. The
path runs on a former
railroad track route along
the Schuylkill River.

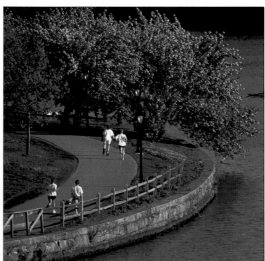

Paved walking and biking path in Fairmount Park *(see p95)*

GOLF AND TENNIS

The Philadelphia area has
numerous 18-hole golf
courses that challenge players
at all levels. Courses situated
in the city include the
Cobbs Creek Golf Club and
the **Walnut Lane Golf Club**,
located within Wissahickon
Valley Park. The professionally
ranked **Tattersall Golf Club**
sits in scenic West Chester
countryside, while **Makefield
Highlands** is the only true
links-style golf course in
the Tri-State area.

Public tennis courts in
many parks are free on a
first-come, first-served basis.
Local tennis clubs that
charge a fee include **Friends
of Chamounix Tennis**
situated in Fairmount Park
and **Aqua Hab** in nearby
Bala Cynwyd.

WINTER ACTIVITIES

As Christmas approaches,
many outdoor enthusiasts
bundle up and trade their
inline blades for ice skates.
Philadelphia and its sur-
rounding areas have several
ice-skating rinks, but the most
popular is the **Blue Cross
RiverRink** at Penn's Landing,
where skaters enjoy an
Olympic-sized rink with views
of the Ben Franklin Bridge
and the Delaware River.

Skiers head to the Pocono
Mountains. This usually
involves a day trip, and
most ski slopes are within
a two-hour drive. The
**Pocono Mountains
Vacation Bureau, Inc.**
has information about ski
slopes and snow conditions.

PROFESSIONAL SPECTATOR SPORTS

South Philadelphia's modern
stadiums are the venue for
most professional sports
competitions held in the city.
The **Philadelphia Phillies** play
throughout the summer
season at the Citizens Bank
Park. The 43,000-seat stadium
is one of the most fan-friendly
ballparks to host major league
baseball games. Rough-and-
tumble football action kicks
off in August as the

Philadelphia Eagles start their season with games at Lincoln Financial Field, a 68,000-seat stadium.

During the cold winter months, sports fans head back indoors to watch basketball played by the **Philadelphia 76ers** at the Wachovia Center, which seats 21,000. Hockey fans flock to the Wachovia Center as well for spirited games on ice with the **Philadelphia Flyers**. The area's minor league baseball team, the **Camden Riversharks**, plays ball at Campbell's Field at the Camden Waterfront. Other popular home teams play soccer and lacrosse.

For horse racing fans, the **Philadelphia Park Casino & Racetrack** has live thorough-bred racing all year round every Saturday through Tuesday. The racetrack is home to the GII Pennsylvania Derby on Labor Day.

Camden Riversharks in baseball action at Campbell's Field

COLLEGE SPORTS

Over a dozen colleges and universities in the Philadelphia area take part in intercollegiate sports programs and competitions, a tradition that dates back more than 200 years. Some of the nation's best college basketball is played by what is called the Big Five – **St. Joseph's University**, **University of Pennsylvania**, **Temple University**, **Villanova University**, and **LaSalle University**. Schools in the area have both men's and women's activities in a full range of other sports, and competitions in football, soccer, field hockey, volley-ball, swimming, gymnastics, and more are held regularly.

DIRECTORY

BICYCLING, JOGGING, AND SKATING

Bicycle Club of Philadelphia
Tel *(215) 735-2453*.
www.phillybikeclub.org

Valley Forge National Historic Park
Rt 23 & N Gulph Rd.
Tel *(610) 783-1077*.
www.nps.gov/vafo

GOLF AND TENNIS

Aqua Hab
600 Righters Ferry Rd, Bala Cynwyd, PA.
Tel *(610) 664-6475*.
www.aquahab.com

Cobbs Creek Golf Club
72nd & Lansdowne Aves.
Tel *(215) 877-8707*.

Friends of Chamounix Tennis
50 Chamounix Dr, Fairmount Park.
Tel *(215) 877-6845*.

Makefield Highlands Golf Club
1418 Woodside Road, Yardly, PA.
Tel *(215) 321-7000*.
www.makefieldhighlands.com

Tattersall Golf Club
1520 Tattersall Way, West Chester, PA.
Tel *(610) 738-4410*.
www.tattersallgolfclub.com

Walnut Lane Golf Club
800 Walnut Lane.
Tel *(215) 482-3370*.
www.golfphilly.com

WINTER ACTIVITIES

Blue Cross RiverRink
Penn's Landing. **Map** 4 F3. Tel *(215) 925-7465*.
www.riverrink.com

Pocono Mountains Vacation Bureau, Inc.
1004 Main St, Stroudsburg, PA 18360.
Tel *(800) 762-6667*.
www.800poconos.com

PROFESSIONAL SPECTATOR SPORTS

Camden Riversharks
Campbell's Field, 401 N Delaware Ave, Camden.
Tel *(856) 963-2600*.
www.riversharks.com

Philadelphia 76ers
Wachovia Center, 3601 S Broad St.
Tel *(215) 339-7600*.
www.nba.com/sixers

Philadelphia Eagles
Lincoln Financial Field, 1020 Pattison Ave.
Tel *(267) 570-4510*.
www.philadelphiaeagles.com

Philadelphia Flyers
Wachovia Center, 3601 S Broad St.
Tel *(215) 465-4500*.
www.philadelphiaflyers.com

Philadelphia Park Casino & Racetrack
3001 Street Rd, Bensalem.
Tel *(215) 639-9000*,
(800) 523-6886. www.philadelphiapark.com

Philadelphia Phillies
Citizens Bank Park, 1 Citizen Bank Way.
Tel *(215) 463-1000*.
www.phillies.com

COLLEGE SPORTS

LaSalle University
1900 W Olney Ave.
Tel *(215) 951-1000*.
www.lasalle.edu

St. Joseph's University
5600 City Ave.
Tel *(610) 660-1712*.
www.sju.edu

Temple University
801 N Broad St.
Map 2 F1.
Tel *(215) 204-8499*.
www.temple.edu

University of Pennsylvania
3451 Walnut St.
Map 1 A4.
Tel *(215) 898-6151*.
www.upenn.edu

Villanova University
Tel *(610) 519-4500*.
www.villanova.edu

CHILDREN'S PHILADELPHIA

Parents will find a plethora of activities that will keep their children amused when in Philadelphia and the surrounding area. Museums, such as The Franklin and the Academy of Natural Sciences, thrill kids with hands-on exhibits and workshops, while the Adventure Aquarium and the Philadelphia Zoo

Actor dressed as George Washington

entertain with an array of sea creatures and animals. Educational tours can be taken at historic buildings, where actors dress up as colonial figures and perform skits. In the Dutch Country, kids can enjoy Amish-style buggy rides and much more at the Dutch Wonderland Family Amusement Park in Lancaster.

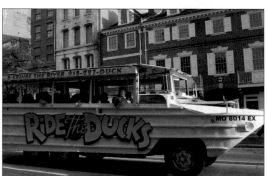

Ride the Ducks pleasure craft going around Philadelphia

HISTORIC SIGHTS AND TOURS

Tour guides at key historic buildings provide informative tours to young and old alike; however, some sights will interest children more than others. The **National Constitution Center** (see pp48–9) features interactive exhibits explaining the US Constitution, where children, for example, might try on a judge's robe at a replica of the Supreme Court bench, or cast their ballot for their all-time favorite president. Many tours

cater to families, such as the popular **Ride the Ducks** (see p175). Using amphibious vehicles, the tour whisks visitors through Old City and Society Hill and Penn's Landing before taking a dip in the Delaware River for an exhilarating cruise. Children and parents show their enthusiasm by raucously blowing colorful "duck whistles."

Kids also enjoy the multimedia **Lights of Liberty Show** (see p175), a brisk walking tour through Old Town at dusk. Participants don headphones and watch images – which tell the story of the American Revolution – projected on historic buildings. For younger children, ask for a special version for ages six to 12.

MUSEUMS

Philadelphia's premier museum for children is the **Please Touch Museum**. Aimed at kids aged under eight, it has several

exhibits that enhance a child's ability to learn discovery and play. For instance, the Alice's Adventures in Wonderland exhibit is based on the popular classic story and includes many settings from the book to encourage problem solving and language skills. The SuperMarket has checkouts, shopping carts, and toy food items, while Barnyard Babies teaches about life on a farm. Other activities include interactive theater performances with musicians, dancers, and storytellers. The museum is located in Memorial Hall in the Fairmount Park District.

The Franklin (see p85) has hands-on exhibits, with some such as Electricity Hall reflecting Benjamin Franklin's inventions. Children learn about the human heart and bioscience at the Giant Walk-Through Heart. Other exhibits include the Train Factory, which has an actual 350-ton (770,000-lb) locomotive, and the Franklin Air Show, which has a flight simulator. The Fels Planetarium features virtual tours through space. At the **Academy of Natural Sciences** (see p85), children can see the fossils of a Tyrannosaurus rex and other species in Dinosaur Hall. Youngsters can also check out the Live Animal Center, which houses over 100 animals, and live butterflies stored in a tropical rainforest habitat that has been replicated at the museum. In addition to

Banner at the Academy of Natural Sciences

Historic Lights of Liberty show at Independence Hall

model boats and deep-sea diving apparatus, kids enjoy squeezing through the small hatches and passageways of the submarine *Becuna* at the **Independence Seaport Museum** *(see pp64–5)*. Boys, in particular, enjoy the old fire engines and pumpers at **Fireman's Hall** *(see p51)*.

At the **Fairmount Water Works** *(see p86)*, interactive exhibits challenge children to learn about city water resources. The center also has a virtual helicopter tour of the watershed.

The **National Liberty Museum** *(see p53)* takes a more serious approach to entertaining children by helping combat violence and bigotry through interactive exhibits, glass artworks, and more. One display is Kids Vote, which asks youngsters to take a stand on such issues as handgun law and the death penalty. Another exhibit, Jellybean People, features two life-sized models made of multicolored jellybeans to show that people are the same inside, regardless of skin color.

For children with an artistic flair, the **Philadelphia Museum of Art** *(see pp88–91)* offers drawing classes and gallery tours on Sundays. The **Pennsylvania Academy of the Fine Arts** *(see pp74–5)* has workshops on most Saturday mornings.

Beyond Philadelphia, in the Pennsylvania Dutch Country, Strasburg offers kids train

Philadelphia Zoo, home to many animal species

displays, a train museum, and rides on the **Strasburg Railroad** *(see p119)*. In Hershey, children will love the simulated chocolate factory at **Chocolate World** *(see p124)*, and the roller coaster rides and attractions at Hershey Park.

GARDENS, ZOOS, AND WATERFRONT ACTIVITIES

An instant hit with children is the **Philadelphia Zoo** *(see p96)*. While close-up views of wild animals such as lions and rare white tigers are a big draw, kids also enjoy the Tastykake Children's Zoo, where they can pet docile sheep, rabbits, and newly hatched chicks.

At the **Philadelphia Insectarium**, youngsters can safely observe the workings of a beehive from behind a glass partition, touch the likes of tarantulas and giant beetles, and see thousands of

Tarantulas at the Insectarium

other live and mounted insects. Kids can also play in a man-made spider web.

The **Adventure Aquarium** at the Camden Waterfront *(see p101)* has a huge tank with hundreds of aquatic species, including sharks, sea turtles, and more than 1,000 kinds of fish. Kids can touch harmless species in the Touch-a-Shark exhibit and see seals frolic in outdoor pools. Also at the waterfront, the **Camden Children's Garden** is an interactive park with different areas, including the Butterfly Garden, Railroad Garden, Dinosaur Garden, and the Storybook Gardens. The latter has themes from classic children's books such as Frances Hodgson Burnett's *The Secret Garden* and Lewis Carroll's *Alice in Wonderland*.

DIRECTORY

MUSEUMS

Please Touch Museum
4231 Avenue of the Republic.
Tel (215) 963-0667.
www.pleasetouchmuseum.
org

GARDENS, ZOOS, AND WATERFRONT ACTIVITIES

Adventure Aquarium
1 Aquarium Dr, Camden, NJ.
Tel (856) 365-3300.
www.adventurequarium.
com

Camden Children's Garden
3 Riverside Drive, Camden, NJ.
Tel (856) 365-8733.
www.camdenchildrensgarden.
org

Philadelphia Insectarium
8046 Frankford Ave.
Tel (215) 335-9500.
www.myinsectarium.com

Interactive exhibits inside Fairmount Waterworks

SURVIVAL
GUIDE

PRACTICAL INFORMATION

Philadelphia thrives on tourism thanks to its rich colonial history and culture, and its world-class museums and restaurants. Efficient infrastructure – such as clearly marked signs, a state-of-the-art visitor center, and a well-planned city transit system – has been created by the city authorities and the National Park Service to give visitors a memorable holiday. Although an abundance of local operators provide tours and sightseeing packages, most of Philadelphia's central neighborhoods can be easily explored on foot. Most areas in the city are safe, but visitors should always take sensible precautions as they would in any major city. The following pages include tips on a wide range of practical matters to help ensure a trouble-free stay in Philadelphia and its surrounding areas.

Independence Visitor Center sign

Tour guide in colonial attire leads tourists in Old City

VISITOR INFORMATION

The modern **Independence Visitor Center** *(see p45)* is located in the heart of Independence National Historical Park and is within walking distance of many sights in Philadelphia's central historic core. Brochure racks are full of information and discount passes for shopping, attractions, restaurants, and hotels in the city and its surrounding areas.

The **Philadelphia Convention & Visitors Bureau** provides information for tour groups, conventions, and international visitors on their website. Staff are always at hand to answer questions and help plan sightseeing itineraries. Most hotels also provide tourism information and help with planning.

OPENING HOURS

Most historic buildings and museums are open from 9am or 10am until 5pm. Some of the smaller colonial houses and attractions in Independence National Historic Park have varying hours and touring schedules. For the most part, businesses and banks maintain standard 9am–5pm hours, with a few banks closing earlier or staying open later. Stores in central Philadelphia open around 10am and stay open till 6pm, with many extending hours on Wednesday evenings. Malls around the city do not close until 9pm or 9:30pm.

ETIQUETTE

Smoking is prohibited in most buildings and stores, except in designated areas. Smoking is now strictly prohibited in all taverns, pubs, and restaurants throughout the city. Waiters and waitresses expect tips of a minimum of 15 percent of the final bill, and up to 20 percent or more for excellent service. At the bar, $1 per drink is usually a good rule of thumb. At hotels, tip $1 per bag and at least that much for the room maid ($2 at upscale properties). Up to $10 or more would be appreciated by a helpful hotel concierge, while airport porters also expect $1 per bag. Tips are commonplace for valet parking attendants and should be $1–$2 while cab drivers should be tipped 10–15 percent of the fare.

No smoking sign

TAXES

The state sales tax levied in Pennsylvania is 6 percent, but the city imposes an additional 1 percent, making it 7 percent in Philadelphia. However, there is no sales tax on clothing and shoes and footwear. Hotel taxes in the city are 14 percent, while car rental taxes and fees can add up to 20 percent or more.

FOREIGN VISITORS AND CUSTOMS

Security measures in the US now require that visitors who plan to stay in the US for up to 90 days, under the Visa Waiver Program, must comply with new US customs regulations. This includes registering with the online Electronic System for Travel Authorisation (ESTA) before departure. Visit www.esta.cbp.dhs.gov. It is advised that this is done in advance and will be valid for two years when issued. All foreign visitors are advised to check with their national passport-issuing agency for more information.

LIQUOR LAWS

The legal drinking age in Pennsylvania is 21. Young people need to show photo identification as proof of age when ordering alcohol in pubs and restaurants. Liquor and wine can be bought only at state-run stores, while beer is sold at special distribution centers or by the six-pack over-the-counter in bars.

The ISIC card provides a range of student discounts

STUDENTS AND SENIORS

The Philadelphia area has numerous colleges and universities, so an International Student Identification Card (ISIC) or Student Advantage Card for American students are recommended and are widely accepted to receive discounts. Senior citizens also receive wide-ranging discounts, including reduced movie prices and admission to many events and attractions.

DISABLED TRAVELERS

Most city buildings and side-walks accommodate disabled persons as required by US law, but some historic colonial structures do not have the required provisions. Two companies, **SEPTA CCT** and **ADA Paratransit**, offer transportation for the disabled with lift-equipped vehicles. The **Mayor's Commission on People with Disabilities** provides information for disabled visitors to Philadelphia.

ELECTRICITY

Electricity in the US is discharged at 110–120 volts using a standard two flat-pronged plug. Adapters may be needed for 220-volt appliances with different plugs, but keep in mind that most hotel rooms have hair dryers, irons, and dedicated sockets for electric shavers.

GUIDED TOURS

Most city tours, ranging from walking tours to horse-drawn carriage tours, are centered around the Independence National Historical Park district. The **Big Bus Company** offers tours on double-decker, open-roof buses with unlimited hop-ons and hop-offs at the 20 sights included in its loop. The **Constitutional Walking Tour of Philadelphia** provides many options for

Historic Lights of Liberty Show at Independence Hall

walking through the city's historic district including MP3 player tours. The popular **Ride the Ducks** is a driving tour in an amphibious vehicle that finally takes a dip in the Delaware River for a cruise near Penn's Landing, with passengers blowing loud "duck whistles". **Ghost Tours of Philadelphia** includes a candlelit walk with haunting tales through Old City and Society Hill. The **Lights of Liberty Show** is a nighttime tour through Old City, with participants watching projections on buildings while narrators tell the story of America's struggle for independence.

DIRECTORY

VISITOR INFORMATION

Independence Visitor Center
6th & Market Sts.
Map 4 D2.
Tel (215) 965-7676.
www.independence visitor-center.com

Philadelphia Convention & Visitors Bureau
1700 Market St.
Map 2 E4.
Tel (215) 636-3300.
www.philadelphiausa. travel

DISABLED TRAVELERS

ADA Paratransit
Tel (215) 580-7145.

Mayor's Commission on People with Disabilities
9th Floor, 1401 JFK Blvd.
Map 2 F4.
Tel (215) 686-2798.
www.phila.gov/aco/ index.html

SEPTA CCT
1234 Market St.
Map 2 F4.
Tel (215) 580-7145.

GUIDED TOURS

Big Bus Company
111 S Independence Mall East. **Map** 4 D3.
Tel (215) 923-5008.
www.bigbustours.com

Constitutional Walking Tour of Philadelphia
Tel (215) 525-1776.
www.theconstitutional. com

Ghost Tours of Philadelphia
Tel (215) 413-1997.
www.ghosttour.com

Lights of Liberty Show
6th & Chestnut Sts. **Map** 4 D3. **Tel** (877) 462-1776.
www.lightsofliberty.org

Ride the Ducks
6th & Chestnut Sts. **Map** 4 D3. **Tel** (215) 227-3825.
www.phillyducks.com

USEFUL INFORMATION

Travelers Aid Society
1201 Chestnut St. **Map** 3 B3. **Tel** (215) 523-7580.
www.taphilly.org

Personal Security and Health

Philadelphia police insignia

For the most part, central Philadelphia is generally safe and the majority of visitors touring the sights do not have any problems with crime. Nonetheless, like in any big American city, taking common sense precautions will ensure a trouble-free visit. Although major crime is rare in high-density tourist areas, it is advisable to always be aware of your surroundings. Public transportation and walking much of the central area is usually safe during the day, but visitors should opt for a taxi at night or for staying in prominent nightlife areas such as those in Old City, Center City, and Society Hill and Penn's Landing.

Philadelphia police officers on bicycles

LAW ENFORCEMENT

With increased security in recent years, there is often a heavy, 24-hour presence of police and National Park Service rangers around key sights at Independence Mall. The Philadelphia Police Department provides round-the-clock car patrols as well as bicycle, horseback, and foot patrols. Traffic and parking enforcement officers also make rounds on foot. Most are friendly when approached, but visitors should not take them to be tour guides. Instead, park rangers are usually helpful with answering questions about city sights and attractions.

PERSONAL SAFETY GUIDELINES

Most major crimes in Philadelphia occur in particular neighborhoods to the north and west of Center City, so plan on avoiding those areas unless you are familiar with them or visiting friends and family. In safe areas, it is still wise to watch out for petty criminals such as purse-snatchers and pick-pockets. When possible, stay in heavily frequented tourist spots that have park rangers and regular police patrols, and avoid wandering into deserted streets and dark alleys. Parks are best avoided at night.

Do not leave personal items such as purses or hand-bags unattended, and do not carry lots of cash or wear excessive jewelry. A good idea is to carry only one credit card and enough cash for the day's activities. Other credit cards, traveler's checks, cash, and your passport should be securely locked in the hotel room safe or a safe deposit box. Passports should be carried only when exchanging currency or traveler's checks. Remember to keep the passport separate from your money or wallet. Another option is to carry valuables in a money belt or in a secure inside pocket. In addition, it is wise to make copies of your passport and keep a record of your credit card numbers in case of theft.

Visitors should try and avoid looking like tourists as they are often targets of petty crime. Carry cameras and camcorders securely and close to your body, obscuring them when possible, and study maps and itineraries beforehand to avoid being approached by criminals looking for an opportunity. Avoid making eye contact with the homeless, as some may be aggressive and will insist on a cash handout.

MEDICAL CONCERNS AND PHARMACIES

Philadelphia has excellent medical facilities should you become ill during your visit. As in any metropolis in the world, there are a number of walk-in clinics that will treat minor ailments, while all main hospitals in the city offer accident and emergency care.

Hospital sign

Visitors should be advised, however, that medical care can be expensive. Even if carrying medical insurance, you may still have to pay upfront and claim reimbursement from your insurance company later, so do not forget to ask for all necessary forms and receipts. Most medical facilities in the city accept credit cards.

A 24-hour CVS pharmacy in a Philadelphia neighborhood

Police car

Police SUV

Fire engine

Pack enough prescription drugs, and it is advisable to keep two sets of the same medicines in different travel bags, in the unlikely event that one is lost or stolen.

Central Philadelphia as well as areas in the outer reaches of the city have several 24-hour pharmacies, if needed. Visitors can ask hotel personnel to pinpoint the one nearest to them.

EMERGENCIES

As in other parts of the United States, call 911 to report life-or-death emergency situations or matters requiring an immediate response from medical, police or fire department personnel. Most hospital emergency rooms in and around the city are open 24 hours a day, seven days a week and take walk-in patients or those delivered by ambulance. Hotel personnel can help you locate the nearest one, or arrange a doctor's appointment for non-life threatening medical conditions. The city also has a number of separate agencies assisting in dental emergencies and accidental poisonings. It is best to ask your hotel staff for assistance.

TRAVEL INSURANCE

Purchasing travel insurance is strongly urged when visiting the US, mostly because of the high cost of medical care. Packages should include medical and dental coverage, along with other options such as trip cancellation, flight delay, lost or stolen baggage, and even death and dismemberment insurance. Visitors should check the details with a travel agency or travel insurance provider in their home countries.

LOST PROPERTY

If your property is lost or stolen, bear in mind that chances of recovery are slim. Nonetheless, contact local police through the non-emergency line to file a report and keep a copy of the same for insurance purposes. At times, it is helpful to contact the Lost and Found Department in department stores or airports. Similarly, visitors can try contacting a taxi company or public transit system in the event missing items turn up when in transit.

Call your credit card company to report a lost or stolen credit card, and contact your currency exchange provider for lost traveler's checks. If your passport is lost or stolen, contact your country's consulate or embassy immediately.

DIRECTORY

CRISIS PHONE NUMBERS

All Emergencies
Tel 911 for police, fire, and emergency medical attention.

Accidental Poisoning
Tel (215) 386-2100, (800) 222-1222 (outside Philadelphia).

Airport Medical Emergencies
Tel (215) 937-3111.

Dental Emergencies
Tel (215) 925-6050.

Finding a Doctor (Non-emergency)
Tel (215) 563-5343.

Philadelphia Police (Non-emergency)
Tel (215) 686-1776.

Special Assistance (Relay Services)
Tel (800) 654-5984.

US Customs
Tel (215) 597-4605.

24-HOUR PHARMACIES

CVS
1826 Chestnut St.
Map 2 D4.
Tel (215) 972-0909.

Rite Aid
2301 Walnut St.
Map 1 C4.
Tel (215) 636-9634.
5040 City Line Ave.
Tel (215) 877-2116.

LOST OR STOLEN CREDIT CARDS

American Express
Tel (800) 528-4800.

MasterCard
Tel (800) 307-7309.

Visa
Tel (800) 847-2911.

Banking and Currency

There is no shortage of prominent banks in Philadelphia, and most banks' headquarters and some branches are located in Center City. Cash can be easily withdrawn through the numerous automated teller machines (ATMs) placed throughout the city. Foreign notes can be exchanged for American dollars in hotels and at currency exchange offices. However, be advised that most currency exchange offices and banks are closed on Sundays, and it is prudent not to carry all your money and credit cards on you at the same time.

Express, Discover Card, and Diners Club are the most prominent and are accepted in restaurants, stores, kiosks at malls, and even some fast food restaurants. It is essential to have a credit card to rent a car, and most hotels ask for a credit card number to make a room reservation.

Besides being safer than carrying lots of cash, some credit cards also offer insurance benefits on retail goods while providing reward points or airline miles. For travelers, credit cards are essential in the event of a medical emergency, as they are honored as payment at most US hospitals.

Façade of PNC Bank in Philadelphia

BANKS

Most Philadelphia banks are open on weekdays from 9am until 5pm. However, some bank branches have varying hours – a few close earlier than 5pm, while others remain open later on Fridays. Most banks also open on Saturdays from 9am until noon. An exception is the New Jersey-based **Commerce Bank**, with branches in Philadelphia, that has lobby hours seven days a week, and extended hours on some days. Other prominent area banks include **PNC Bank** and **Wachovia Bank**.

ATMS

Cash is easily accessible through the numerous ATMs in the Philadelphia area. They are found at bank entrances, in office complexes, at shopping malls, grocery stores and restaurants, and even in convenience stores. Cash is distributed in $10 and $20 bills, and can be withdrawn with an ATM card or credit card, including VISA or **MasterCard**.

ATMs often charge a fee for withdrawals by non-bank members, while the user's bank might also charge a fee. Check with your bank which transaction fees apply. Use ATMs during the day when more people are nearby to avoid being robbed.

CREDIT CARDS

Major credit cards are accepted at most locations throughout the area. Visa, MasterCard, American

Automated Teller Machines (ATM) dispense cash and accept deposits

CURRENCY EXCHANGE

Unlike european countries, there are few currency exchange stands in America and they are not always easily accessible. Also, the commissions charged can be high. Banks and hotels do accept foreign currency, but it is advisable to first check the fees, which are often higher at hotels. Currency exchanges in Philadelphia are located in Center City, and are usually open from 9am to 5pm. They include the **American Express Travel Services Office** and Thomas Cook Currency Services, which also has kiosks at the airport. It is a good idea to bring in $100 when entering the US in case exchange services are not readily available.

CASHING TRAVELER'S CHECKS

Most restaurants, shops, and hotels accept traveler's checks in US dollars as payment without charging a fee. These can also be cashed at local banks, though proper identification is required in the form of a passport, driver's license or student identification card to do so.

Checks in foreign currency can be cashed at a bank branch offering foreign currency exchange, usually at the bank's main locations. Personal checks in foreign currency are rarely accepted in the US.

Coins

American coins (actual size shown) come in 1-, 5-, 10- and 25-cent, as well as $1 denominations; 50-cent pieces are minted but rarely used. Each coin has its own name: 1-cent coins are known as pennies; 5-cent coins as nickels; 10-cent coins as dimes; and 1-dollar coins (and bills) are sometimes called "bucks."

**25-cent coin
(a quarter)**

**10-cent coin
(a dime)**

**5-cent coin
(a nickel)**

**1-cent coin
(a penny)**

Bank Notes

The units of currency in the US are dollars and cents, with 100-cents to the dollar. Notes, or "bills," come in $1, $5, $10, $20, $50, and $100 denominations. There is also a $2 bill, but it is rarely used and is more of a collector's item. In recent years, new versions of the $5, $10, and $20 bills have been produced to thwart counterfeiters. The new bills have slight variations of color, and portraits of the presidents and other notable figures in US history are larger and positioned off center.

1-dollar bill ($1)
5-dollar bill ($5)
10-dollar bill ($10)
20-dollar bill ($20)
50-dollar bill ($50)
100-dollar bill ($100)

Communications and Media

A colorful US postage stamp

Philadelphia has a wide spectrum of the latest communications systems. Card- or coin-operated pay phones abound in hotels, malls, restaurants, and on many street corners. The US Postal Service is reliable and efficient, with regular pickups at mailboxes placed throughout the city. Media outlets include numerous local television and radio stations, as well as two major daily newspapers. Internet, e-mail, fax services, and cell phone signals are readily available, and wireless hotspots are located throughout the city.

among others. Signals are strong throughout the region, but can drop off in heavily wooded areas and in valleys that run through some of the densely-forested suburbs. American cell services are often not compatible with those in other countries other than Canada and Mexico, so check with your own carrier if you plan on using one. Cell phones can be rented locally through **AllCell Rental** in Center City.

PAY TELEPHONES

The main local telephone companies providing phone services throughout the greater Philadelphia area are Verizon and AT&T. Numerous coin-operated and credit card pay phones are located in hotel and office lobbies, shopping areas and malls, restaurants, gas stations, bars, and along city streets.

Local calls usually require only a few coins, but prices can vary for calls outside the local area and abroad as different telephone companies set their own rates. It is best to check with an operator first, but note that operator-assisted calls are usually more costly than calling direct. Make sure you have lots of dimes, nickels, and quarters when using a coin-operated phone.

For more information about calling in Philadelphia, check the local *Yellow Pages* directory, which also lists country codes for international calls.

CELL PHONES

Several companies provide cell phone services in Philadelphia, such as Sprint, Verizon, AT&T, and Nextel,

USING A COIN-OPERATED PHONE

1 Lift the receiver and listen for the dial tone.

3 Dial or press the number.

Coins
Make sure you have the correct coins before you dial.

5 cents

10 cents

25 cents

2 Insert the necessary coin or coins. The coin drops as soon as you insert it.

4 If you do not want to complete your call or it does not get through, retrieve the coin(s) by pressing the coin return.

5 If the call is answered and you talk longer than the allotted three minutes, the operator will interrupt and ask you to deposit more coins. Pay phones do not give change.

USEFUL DIALING CODES

- Area code for central Philadelphia is **215**, which is also used in areas north of the city along with **267** and **445**. Western suburbs and surrounding areas use **610**, **484**, and **835**. The area code for the Pennsylvania Dutch Country and Gettysburg is **717**.
- For calls outside the local area but within the US and Canada, dial **1** followed by the area code and phone number.
- For local operator assistance, dial **0**.
- For local directory inquiries, dial **411**. Directory assistance for toll-free numbers is **1–800–555–1212**, and **411** for other numbers.
- For emergency police, fire, or ambulance services, dial **911**.
- **1–800** indicates a toll-free number, as do numbers with the area codes **888**, **877**, and **866**.
- For international direct-dial calls, dial **011** followed by the country code, city or area code, and number.
- To make an international call via the operator, dial **01** and then follow the same procedure as detailed above.
- For international directory inquiries, dial **00**.

INTERNET, E-MAIL AND FAXES

Internet access is available to visitors throughout the city at Internet cafés, public libraries, and at some office-supply and photocopy centers such as FedEx Kinko's, which may also have fax services. Philadelphia is a destination for a large number of business travelers, and many of the larger hotels have business centers for guests to check their e-mails or to send and receive faxes. These business center services are usually charged by the minute or by 15-minute blocks, which can add up quickly. It is therefore a good idea to check the business facilities offered by a hotel before making reservations. Library Internet services are often free but may have time limits.

POSTAL SERVICES

Post offices are located throughout the city, catering to separate neighborhoods. Philadelphia's **Main Post Office** is at Market and 30th Streets, directly across from the 30th Street Station, and has window service 18 hours a day, seven days a week. All other area post offices, including those outside the city, are open from 9am to 5pm Monday through Friday, with most also open on Saturday from 9am to noon. Post offices in the US are closed on Sundays and on all federal holidays.

Letters and parcels that weigh under 16 ounces require only stamps and can be mailed in standard blue mailboxes on street corners, or in letter slots in all hotels and office buildings. Many hotels sell stamps and will mail letters for their guests. Larger packages often require a trip to a post office to ensure proper postage and prompt delivery. The US

Standard blue mailbox, found on most streets

Postal Service offers different delivery services including standard first-class mail for most letters, Priority Mail for guaranteed delivery in two to three days, and Express Mail for overnight deliveries on business days. Courier companies offer both domestic and international delivery services. **FedEx** and **DHL** offer a variety of overnight letter and parcel services, while **UPS** delivers large boxes and packages. Letters or packages must be inserted into proper courier envelops or boxes and the paperwork should be filled out accurately. Smaller parcels can be deposited in the many courier mailboxes scattered around town for pickup at the end of the business day. Alternatively, the courier can be asked to pick up the parcel.

TV AND RADIO

Philadelphia's television stations represent the major US broadcast networks. They include CBS on channel 3, ABC on channel 6, NBC on channel 10, PBS on channel 12, FOX on channel 29, and CW on channel 57. Cable companies carry a host of popular sports, news, and entertainment and movie networks, such as ESPN, HBO, and CNN. Radio

Selection of local Philadelphia newspapers at a newsstand

stations, on both the AM and FM frequencies, include a variety of music, talk, and news shows. The city's most popular 24-hour news and talk radio programming can be heard on KYW 1060(Hz) AM.

NEWSPAPERS

The city has two major daily newspapers, the *Philadelphia Inquirer* (see p162) and the *Philadelphia Daily News*, both of which provide a gamut of information. Other news and current affairs publications include the *Philadelphia Tribune* that caters to and targets the African-American community, and the *Philadelphia Business Journal* that covers financial stories. For those interested in entertainment and political news, refer to the *Philadelphia City Paper* and the *Philadelphia Weekly*.

GETTING TO PHILADELPHIA

Whether traveling from within or outside the country, Philadelphia is easily accessible by air, train, bus, and car. The city is served by Philadelphia International Airport. Amtrak's 30th Street Station is a busy rail hub on the Northeast Corridor line that runs between Washington DC and Boston. The station is also a stop for trains arriving from other regions of the country. A number of interstate highways, which crisscross most of the Philadelphia metropolitan area, cater to motorists and long-distance bus services. The city also has a cruise ship terminal along the Delaware River, which serves as a stop on some liners' itineraries.

US Airways plane

View of Terminal A at Philadelphia International Airport

ARRIVING BY AIR

While driving may be the most comfortable mode of transportation, the easiest way to get to Philadelphia is by air. The city is about five hours flying time from US destinations on the West Coast, between one to three hours from the Midwest, three to five hours from the Caribbean, and seven to ten hours from Europe. Philadelphia is a hub for **US Airways** and **Southwest Airlines**, and is also served by airlines such as **Air Canada**, **Air France**, **British Airways**, **American Airlines**, **Continental Airlines**, and **Delta Airlines**.

PHILADELPHIA INTERNATIONAL AIRPORT

Philadelphia's only major airport, this modern facility is located 8 miles (5 km) south of Center City. Its six terminals accommodate more than 1,400 arrival and departure flights daily to and from more than 122 cities, including 30 international destinations. Services include non-stop flights to Europe, Canada, and the Caribbean, and also connecting flights to Asia.

Opened in May 2003, the International Terminal (with concourses A-West and A-East) is a four-level facility with 13 gates and 60 ticket counters for international flights. The spacious terminal also has two-dozen retail shops and restaurants. Its Arrivals Hall welcomes foreign visitors with large inscriptions and signatures from the Declaration of Independence emblazoned on the walls. The terminal is served by US Airways' international flights as well as British Airways, **Lufthansa**, Air France, American Airlines, and others.

Terminals B and C are dominated by departures and arrivals for US Airways' and **America West Airlines** domestic flights. Terminal D has Air Canada, AirTran Airways, Continental Airlines, and **United Airlines**. Terminal E includes **Northwest Airlines** and Southwest Airlines, while Terminal F serves US Airways Express commuter flights.

The airport also features more than 100 shops, restaurants, eateries, and fast food stands scattered throughout the terminals, with more than 30 contained in the Philadelphia Market-Place located between

Arrivals Hall at Philadelphia International Airport features words from the Declaration of Independence

terminals B and C. Shops sell items ranging from sunglasses to office supplies and souvenirs. Businesses also provide other services and specialty carts that function as currency exchanges, newsstands, and airport information desks.

AIR FARES

When searching for reasonable airfares, it is worth taking the time to look around. It is best to book departing flights at least 14 to 21 days in advance to get the lowest fares, and at least seven days in advance to secure a reasonably-priced ticket. However, be aware that these tickets carry penalties if you change your reservation, so ask about those before purchasing the ticket.

Checking directly with airlines and with travel agents can often land you a good fare, but it is certainly worth examining popular travel Internet sites as well, such as **Expedia Travels**, **Priceline**, and **Lowestfare.com** to name a few. These websites often sell consolidated tickets, which are also available through travel agents.

SEPTA bus, ferrying passengers to Philadelphia

Other options include ticket bookings with smaller airline carriers and flying during the off-season. Philadelphia's high season peaks in the summer months, around Thanksgiving (late November), and in the week before Christmas until after New Year. Also, keep in mind that airline tickets are priced lower when flying on Tuesdays, Wednesdays, and Thursdays.

TRANSPORT INTO THE CITY

Septa's Airport Rail Line, the R1 train, operates every half hour and connects all terminals with Center City and Amtrak's 30th Street Station, which has rail connections to other points in the city and beyond. The train stations for each terminal lie between the ticketing areas and the baggage claim areas, and visitors should look for the relevant signs. SEPTA buses 37 and 108 also ferry passengers into the city.

For shuttle van services, search for **Centralized Ground Transportation** counters in all baggage claim areas. Taxis are plentiful at each terminal, and they charge about $20 for a trip into the city. Rental car companies also operate at airports and most have information phones at all baggage claim areas.

DIRECTORY

AIRPORTS

Philadelphia International Airport
*Tel (215) 937-6937,
(800) 745-4283.*
www.phl.org

AIRLINE NUMBERS

Air Canada
Tel (888) 247-2262.

Air France
Tel (800) 237-2747.

American Airlines
Tel (800) 433-7300.

British Airways
Tel (800) 247-9297.

Continental Airlines
Tel (800) 525-0280.

Delta Airlines
Tel (800) 221-1212.

Lufthansa
Tel (800) 645-3880.

Northwest Airlines
Tel (800) 225-2525.

Southwest Airlines
Tel (800) 435-9792.

United Airlines
Tel (800) 241-6522.

US Airways
Tel (800) 428-4322.

AIR FARES

Expedia Travels
www.expedia.com

Lowestfare.com
www.lowestfare.com

Priceline
www.priceline.com

AIRPORT SHUTTLES

Centralized Ground Transportation
Tel (215) 937-6958.

Philadelphia Airport Shuttle
Tel (215) 969-1818.

AIRPORT HOTELS

Embassy Suites Philadelphia
9000 Bartram Ave.
Tel (215) 365-4500, (800) 362-2779
www.embassysuites.com

Hilton Philadelphia Airport
4509 Island Ave.
*Tel (215) 365-4150,
(800) 445-8667*
www.hilton.com

Philadelphia Airport Marriott
1 Arrivals Rd.
*Tel (215) 492-9000,
(800) 682-4087.*
www.marriott.com

Sheraton Suites Philadelphia Airport
4101 Island Ave.
Tel (215) 365-6600.
www.sheraton.com

Renaissance Philadelphia Hotel Airport
500 Stevens Dr.
*Tel (610) 521-5900,
(800) 468-3571.*

Philadelphia's 30th Street Station on Amtrak's Northeast Corridor, the second busiest of the Amtrak system

ARRIVING BY TRAIN

Philadelphia is served by **Amtrak**, the country's passenger rail service, which links the city to the entire nation and to Canada. Most trains serving the city operate along the Northeast Corridor from Boston to Washington DC, with stops in Baltimore, New York and a number of locations in New Jersey, Delaware, Connecticut, and Rhode Island. Amtrak's lines also provide express services such as the premium, high-speed Metroliner Service and the Acela Express.

Tickets can be booked online or by calling Amtrak. When booking, it is best to reserve well in advance and be as flexible as possible to ensure good seating and prices. Note that certain discounts may apply, including those for students and senior citizens. If reserved in advance, tickets can be picked up on the day of travel at either the Amtrak service window or through kiosks at stations. Due to increased security measures, passengers from the US, Canada, and Mexico require photo identification, which may be a driver's license or passport, while other foreign visitors need a passport.

Passenger cars are comfortable and have snack bar services as well as dining cars on longer routes. Seats in coach class for most routes are reserved, but they can be unreserved for shorter trips. Quarters for sleeping are considered first class and are available on trains with longer routes, and some of the first class sleeping accommodations have showers and toilets in the compartment.

Philadelphia's main train hub is Amtrak's 30th Street Station – an impressive Beaux-Arts building with a columned front façade and large atrium. Inside are ticket booths to both Amtrak and SEPTA regional rail lines, restaurants, fast food eateries, gift shops, and newsstands. "Red cap" porters are available to help with luggage. Taxis are also plentiful outside, and if you are carrying baggage, they are recommended for the short hop to a central Philadelphia hotel.

ARRIVING BY CAR

Several major roadways and interstate highways lead to Philadelphia from surrounding states and major cities in the northeast. Driving times to Philadelphia from some of these cities are as follows: six hours from Boston, two hours from Baltimore and New York, and three hours from Washington.

The major north-south highway is I-95, which leads into the city center as it parallels the Delaware River. From the east, motorists driving on the New Jersey Turnpike should take Exit 4 and then follow signs to the Ben Franklin Bridge into Philadelphia. An alternative from the New Jersey Turnpike is taking Exit 6 to connect with the Pennsylvania Turnpike that runs north of the city. This turnpike is the major highway leading into Philadelphia from the west. Take the Valley Forge exit and then proceed east on I-76, the Schuylkill Expressway. It is recommended that visitors carry a road atlas map and a city street map for all trips by car.

An Amtrak train – backbone of America's passenger rail system

Greyhound buses, such as these, serve destinations across America

ARRIVING BY BUS

Serving all regions of the United States, **Greyhound Lines** has a bus terminal in Center City, between 10th and 11th Streets on Filbert Street, just one block north of Market Street. The terminal handles arrivals daily, including buses from New England, New York, and points south and southwest of Philadelphia and transcontinental buses on routes through St. Louis and Chicago. Stops in the city include Amtrak's 30th Street Station, and in north and south Philadelphia.

In comparison to other modes of transportation such as taking a train or a flight, Greyhound's fares are the most economical. The company offers wide-ranging fare reductions, including discounts for students, senior citizens, children, military personnel, and veterans, as well as cheaper fares if tickets are purchased online. While advance purchases might save you money, walk-up tickets are available at reasonable costs.

Greyhound's buses are modern and efficient. Much of its fleet is either equipped with lifts or has other equipment to accommodate those passengers that have disabilities or need help. Under certain conditions, personal care attendants may ride with disabled passengers at a reduced rate. For more information, visitors should call the Greyhound Customers with Disabilities Travel Assistance Line at least 48 hours before departure.

CRUISE SHIP TERMINAL

Located in the former Philadelphia Navy Yard, the city's cruise ship berth along the Delaware River is the **Philadelphia Cruise Terminal at Pier 1**. Visitors entering the city this way have access to major tourist sights in central Philadelphia through either their cruise line's shuttle service or public transportation. SEPTA bus 17 from Broad and Flagship Streets, one block north of Pier 1, takes about 30 minutes to reach the Independence Visitor Center and Independence Mall. Among other services, Pier 1 also has ATM machines and cafés nearby. Cruise lines making port calls or departing from the city include Norwegian Cruise Line, Celebrity Cruises, Holland America Line, Radisson Seven Seas Cruises, and Silversea Cruises.

DIRECTORY

TRAIN SERVICES

Amtrak
Tel (800) 872-7245.
www.amtrak.com

LONG-DISTANCE BUS SERVICES

Greyhound Customers with Disabilities Travel Assistance Line
Tel (800) 752-4841.

Greyhound Lines
Tel (800) 231-2222.
www.greyhound.com

Greyhound Lines (Purchase Tickets)
Tel (800) 229-9424.

Greyhound Bus Terminal
1001 Filbert St. **Map** 3 C2.
Tel (215) 931-4000.

STATE INTERSTATES & HIGHWAYS

Pennsylvania Department of Transportation
Travel information & interstate road conditions.
Tel (717) 783-5186.
www.dot.state.pa.us

Pennsylvania Turnpike Commission
Tel (717) 939-9551.
www.paturnpike.com

CRUISE SHIP TERMINAL

Philadelphia Cruise Terminal at Pier 1
5100 S Broad St.
Tel (215) 462-6790.

RiverLink Ferry sets sail across the Delaware River

Getting Around Philadelphia

Taxi sign

Most of Philadelphia's famous sights are on Independence National Historical Park, also known as "America's most historic square mile." These sights, including Independence Hall and the Liberty Bell, are within walking distance of each other in Old City, and just a short walk from attractions in Society Hill and Penn's Landing. A quick ride from the historic area brings visitors to Center City and the Museum District. The Philly Phlash bus service runs through the heart of the city during the warmer months. Buses and subways operated by the Southeastern Pennsylvania Transit Authority (SEPTA) run year-round. Taxis are also an easy and generally affordable option.

WALKING

Without a doubt, the best way to explore Independence National Historical Park and other historic sights in the surrounding areas is on foot. Key sights in and around Independence Park and Society Hill are all contained within several blocks and can take up a whole day or more of sightseeing. When traveling up to ten blocks or more, a taxi or public transportation may be the better alternative.

Although almost all city streets are flanked by sidewalks, be careful while crossing. Pedestrians should use the electronic "Walk" signs, which indicate when it is safe to proceed. These are located at many of the larger intersections. Some even have a button that pedestrians can press to activate them.

Walking around the city is safe, as pedestrian walkways are located in Indepedence Mall, Old City, and Society Hill and Penn's Landing.

STREET GRID

Central Philadelphia's city grid is simple, with a crisscross of streets and five squares, as originally laid out by city founder William Penn and surveyor Thomas Holmes (see p18).

Numbered streets run north and south in an ascending westward order – starting with Front Street near the Delaware River to 30th Street just beyond the Schuylkill

River. Many streets running east and west are named after trees, once again according to Penn's original city plan.

PHILLY PHLASH TOURIST BUS

These colorful purple buses run along Market Street and the Benjamin Franklin Parkway, with round trips from Penn's Landing to the Philadelphia Museum of Art. The buses are in operation seven months a year, from May to November, with a service that runs every 12 minutes from 10am to 6pm. Rides are inexpensive and allow unlimited hop-ons and hop-offs. In most cases, children under five and seniors ride free.

PUBLIC TRANSPORTATION

The main agency for public transportation in the city is **SEPTA** *(see transport map at back)*. Its key subway routes run through districts in central Philadelphia, making connections to regional rail lines at

the Market East, Suburban, and 30th Street Stations.

The Market Frankford Line runs east and west along Market Street with stops at 2nd, 5th, 8th, 11th, 13th, 15th, and 30th Streets. The Broad Street Line runs north and south with stops at Race and Vine Streets, City Hall, Walnut and Locust Streets, and Lombard and South Streets.

SEPTA's bus 38 starts from Independence Mall and runs along Market Street and the Benjamin Franklin Parkway to the Philadelphia Museum of Art and beyond. Bus 21 travels along Chestnut and Walnut Streets from Penn's Landing to the University of Pennsylvania. Bus 42 circles neighborhoods and areas in Society Hill along Spruce Street, and then heads west along Walnut Street to the University of Pennsylvania campus, returning via Chestnut Street.

Most bus fares are $2 and exact change is usually needed. Tokens, discount passes, and day passes can be obtained at SEPTA sales offices or at the Independence Visitor Center *(see p45)*. Visitors should call SEPTA for the locations of these sales offices.

RIVERLINK FERRY

This ferry offers splendid views of the Delaware River as it runs between Penn's Landing and the Camden Waterfront from April through mid-November. **RiverLink Ferry** is the ideal mode of transportation to get to the Adventure Aquarium and the battleship *New Jersey*. The ferry departs

SEPTA bus system, covering the entire city

The RiverLink Ferry at Penn's Landing

every 40 minutes from both Camden and Philadelphia, and visitors can purchase tickets at dockside terminals outside the Independence Seaport Museum for the outbound trip from Philadelphia.

BICYCLES

Only a few streets in central Philadelphia are bicycle-friendly. For example, a designated cycle path runs along the Benjamin Franklin Parkway up to the Philadelphia Museum of Art. This leads to the city's most popular biking route that runs along Kelly Drive and West River Drive. Bicycles can be rented here during the warmer months *(see p168)*. It is advisable to wear a safety helmet when bicycling in the city.

DELAWARE RIVER PORT AUTHORITY
of Pennsylvania & New Jersey

Delaware River Port Authority logo

TAXIS

Taxis roam the streets freely looking for fares, though the best place to find one is at a hotel. Several cab companies serve the city, and if you must reserve a taxi for a specific time, do so at least 30 minutes to an hour in advance. Fares vary for different companies, with at least a $2 base fare and up to another $2 per mile. All taxis accept credit card payments.

DRIVING IN CENTRAL PHILADELPHIA

Except for rush hour traffic, driving in town is not particularly difficult. The main Center City thoroughfares, Broad and Market Streets, have two-way traffic, while most other streets have one-way traffic patterns. Vehicles are driven on the right side in the US, and turns to the right can be made at a red light after a full stop, unless a sign prohibits it. Left turns are also prohibited at some intersections, especially at peak traffic hours. US law dictates you must wear a seatbelt, and violators can incur a fine. With some exceptions, overseas visitors can drive with a valid driver's license issued by their home country. If the license is not in English, an international driving permit is required.

PARKING

Street parking is usually hard to find and costly, though parking meters in some locations around Center City and Independence Mall are in operation seven days a week until 8pm. Most meters provide up to a 2-hour time limit, with the average rate ranging from 15 to 30 minutes

Philadelphia taxi

DIRECTORY

PUBLIC TRANSPORTATION

Philly Phlash
www.phillyphlash.com

RiverLink Ferry
Penn's Landing.
Tel (215) 968-2000.
www.riverlinkferry.org

Southeastern Pennsylvania Transportation Authority (SEPTA)
Tel (215) 580-7800.
www.septa.org

TAXI CAB COMPANIES

City Cab Company
Tel (215) 492-6500.

Olde City Cab Company
Tel (215) 338-0838.

Quaker City Cab
Tel (215) 728-8000.

LIMOUSINES/PRIVATE CARS

Carey International
Tel (800) 336-4646.

King Limousine
Tel (800) 245-5460.

PARKING MATTERS

Philadelphia Parking Authority
Tel (215) 683-9600.

per 25 cents. Make sure you keep the meter fed, as traffic enforcement officers make regular rounds and will write a ticket for an expired meter. Do not park at hydrants or other illegal parking zones. Violators will be ticketed and towed. Retrieving a towed vehicle can cost over $100.

Parking on residential streets is often permitted during the day for non-permit holders, but is restricted at night. Read the signs carefully and abide by them. Parking at the city's many lots is a safe but often expensive alternative, with rates from $15 to $30 and higher charged per day.

Traveling Outside Philadelphia

Philadelphia has an excellent regional rail service with SEPTA trains running from Center City to far western suburbs, parts of nearby New Jersey, and northern Delaware. Amtrak provides a daily train service to Lancaster, Harrisburg, and towns west of Philadelphia. New Jersey Transit takes passengers to Atlantic City and other areas along the Jersey shore. However, it is advisable and more practical to rent a car when traveling to remote sights in the Pennsylvania Dutch Country and Gettysburg.

SEPTA train – an ideal way to go beyond Philadelphia

REGIONAL RAIL SERVICE

Outstanding rail services by **SEPTA** are offered to many of Philadelphia's outermost suburbs to the north, south, and west of the city, with trips to the outermost stops sometimes taking over an hour. Most trains can be boarded at the main train stations in Center City, including **Amtrak**'s 30th Street Station, Market East Station, and Suburban Station.

SEPTA's R1 commuter line provides services to the Philadelphia International Airport *(see p183)*. The R2 travels south with a stop in Wilmington, Delaware. The R5 travels from Center City to points west, including Merion Station for the Barnes Foundation *(see pp98–9)*, and points north with Doylestown *(see p125)* as the last stop. The R6 runs through Manayunk *(see p95)*, while the R7 and R8 end their routes in Chestnut Hill with stops along the way in Germantown *(see pp94–5)*. Train cars are comfortable and air-conditioned, with plenty of seating. However, cars fill up quickly during the morning and afternoon rush hour. Tickets can be purchased at the three Center City stations, on trains, and at suburban stations.

SERVICES TO NEW JERSEY

Several train and bus lines run from Philadelphia to New Jersey locations. The quickest way to Trenton,

Interior of 30th Street Station, one of the biggest in Pennsylvania

the capital of New Jersey, is via SEPTA's R7 commuter train, with services from Center City.

New Jersey's state-wide transportation agency, **New Jersey Transit**, provides bus and rail services to points south and north in the state. Buses 313 and 315 provide daily service from the Greyhound Bus Terminal at 10th and Filbert Streets in Philadelphia to Cape May, with traveling times up to three-and-a-half hours. For commuting to the resort town of Atlantic City, visitors can take the **Atlantic City Rail Line** from Amtrak's 30th Street Station.

The Port Authority Transit Corporation (PATCO) Speedline has a number of stops in Center City. These are at Market and 8th Streets, and Locust and 10th, 12th, and 15th Streets. Speedline takes passengers over the Benjamin Franklin Bridge to the Camden Waterfront.

PENNSYLVANIA DUTCH COUNTRY AND GETTYSBURG

Renting a car is the best way to explore most of the towns and villages that lie beyond Philadelphia. If driving is not possible, then other options include taking organized bus tours and public transportation.

A train service is provided by Amtrak from Philadelphia's bustling 30th Street Station to towns that are located to the west of Philadelphia, including Lancaster and Harrisburg. In Lancaster, the **Red Rose Transit Authority** (RRTA) operates bus services in the city and to surrounding towns in the county, including Pennsylvania Dutch communities. These buses have busy schedules and tend to have limited services to the outlying smaller communities, including Paradise, Lititz, Intercourse, Bird-In-Hand, and Ephrata. Most of the bus services to these areas usually end after the afternoon rush

Traffic on Interstate 76, Philadelphia

hour. On weekends, service to these towns is scaled back, with limited runs on Saturdays and none on Sundays for certain routes.

Renting a car is essential for visitors who plan to travel to Gettysburg, as the town has no public transportation system or bus services catering to it.

INTERSTATES, TURNPIKES, AND TOLL ROADS

Turnpikes are sometimes interstate highways, but they are always toll roads. In particular, the Pennsylvania Turnpike and the New Jersey Turnpike both require motorists to pick up a toll ticket before entering the highway, and then pay the toll when exiting. The Pennsylvania Turnpike (I-76/276) is the fastest route from Philadelphia to Harrisburg, and a one-way toll can cost in the neighborhood of $5. Although not an interstate, the Atlantic City Expressway is also a toll road. Note that some expressways have both numbers and names, such as the Vine Street Expressway (I-676/30) or the Pennsylvania Turnpike.

When passing through toll booths, be aware there are different types. While some booths take cash or exact change, others operate on an electronic system known as "E-ZPass." This system scans participating vehicles, allowing them to go through while deducting the toll amount from their owners' accounts.

CAR RENTALS AND GASOLINE

To rent a car in the United States, US and Canadian residents must have a valid driver's license, while foreign visitors need an international driver's license and valid passport. The minimum rental age is usually 25, and it is necessary to have a major credit card in your name.

While personal auto insurance often covers rental cars, it is best to check the limitations of coverage with your insurance company. If not, it is always a good idea to purchase liability and collision insurance. Most gas stations in Philadelphia have self-service pumps. However, in New Jersey, state law mandates that attendants must pump gas. Rented cars should be returned to the rental agency with a full tank or additional charges will apply.

Hertz Rent a Car

Sign for Hertz Rent a Car

SPEED LIMITS, FINES, AND DRIVING SAFELY

The speed limit on interstates is usually 65 miles per hour (105 km/h), and 55 miles per hour (88 km/h) on highways in and around Philadelphia. City streets usually have 25 to 35 miles per hour (40 to 56 km/h) limits. It is advisable to heed speed limits whenever possible, as a ticket can result in hefty fines.

Drive carefully during bad weather, as 18-wheeler trucks often spew mist during heavy rainstorms, resulting in poor visibility. Also, bridges and overpasses can become ice-slicked during winter. Safe driving tips include wearing seatbelts, which is required by law, keeping all doors locked, staying on main roads, avoiding unfamiliar neighborhoods, and not drinking alcohol. Be aware that offenses for drinking and driving are vigorously prosecuted in the US.

PHILADELPHIA STREET FINDER

Map references given in this guide for sights, hotels, restaurants, shops, and entertainment venues refer to the Street Finder maps on the following pages *(see How the Map References Work)*. Map references are also given for Philadelphia's hotels *(see pp134–41)* and restaurants *(see pp145–53)*. A complete index of the street names and places of interest marked on the maps can be found on the following pages. The map below shows the area of Philadelphia covered by the four Street Finder maps. This includes the sightseeing areas (which are color-coded) as well as the rest of central Philadelphia. The symbols used to represent sights and useful information on the Street Finder maps are listed in the key below.

KEY	
▪	Major sight
▫	Place of interest
▫	Other building
🚇	SEPTA regional rail station
Ⓢ	SEPTA subway stop
🚌	Greyhound bus terminal
🅿	Parking
ℹ	Visitor information
✚	Hospital
🚓	Police station
✝	Church
✡	Synagogue
☪	Mosque
⊠	Post office
═	Railroad line
▬	Expressway
━	Pedestrianized street

SCALE OF MAP PAGES 1-4

0 meters   500

0 yards   500

HOW THE MAP REFERENCES WORK

The first figure tells you which Street Finder map to turn to.

Eakins Oval ⑧

Benjamin Franklin Parkway. **Map** 1 C1. 🚆 *30th St Station.* 🚇 *Spring Garden.* 🚌 *38, Philly Phlash.*

The letters and numbers form the map coordinates. Letters are along the top of the map, while numbers are along the sides.

Street Finder Index

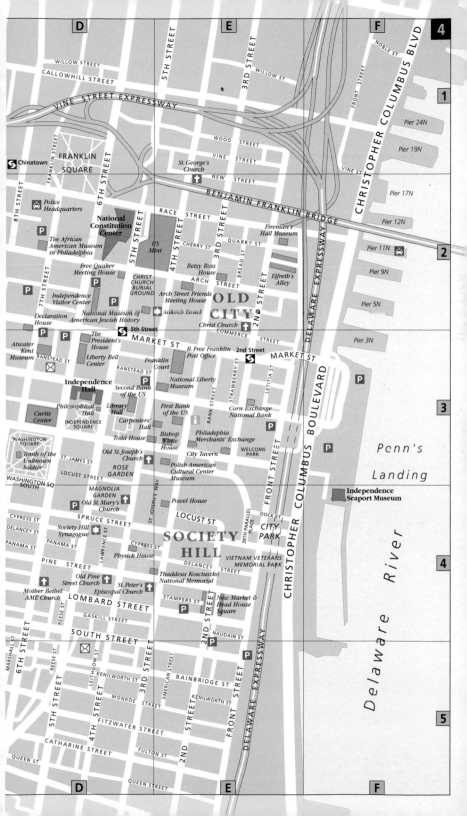

General Index

Acknowledgments

Main Contributor

Richard Varr spent a part of his childhood in Philadelphia and returned to the area in 1999. A former television and newspaper reporter, he now writes for newspapers, magazines, and websites, including Porthole Cruise Magazine and onboard publications of several cruise lines.

Factchecker

Scott Walker

Proofreader

Word-by-Word

Indexer

Jyoti Dhar

DK London

Publisher Douglas Amrine
Publishing Manager Lucinda Cooke
Managing Art Editor Kate Poole
Senior Designer Tessa Bindloss
Senior Cartographic Editor
Casper Morris
Senior DTP Designer Jason Little
Dk Picture Library Martin Copeland,
Romaine Werblow
Production Controller Louise Daly
Beverley Ager, Emma Anacootee, Julie Bond, Anna Freiberger, Rhiannon Furbear, Vinod Harish, Phil Hunt, Marianne Petrou, Jeanette Pierce, Ellen Root, Azeem A. Siddiqui, Jeanette Tallant, Ros Walford.

Additional Photography

Shaen Adey, Paul Bricknell, Geoff Dann, Steve Gorton, Dave King, Andrew Leyerle, Tim Mann, Ray Moller, Stephen Oliver, Ian O'Leary, Tim Ridley, Clive Streeter, Scott Suchman, Matthew Ward, Jerry Young.

Dorling Kindersley would like to thank the following people whose contributions and assistance have made the preparation of this book possible.

Cartography

Back Endpaper reproduced with permission from SEPTA.

Special Assistance

The Barnes Foundation: Henry Butler; Independence National Historical Park: Superintendent; Gettysburg Convention & Visitors Bureau: Stacey Fox; Greater Philadelphia Tourism Marketing Corporation: Paula Butler, Kristen Ciappa, Meryl Levitz, Cara Schneider, Donna Schorr; National Liberty Museum: Amanda Hall; Pennsylvania Convention Center Authority: Patti Spaniak; Pennsylvania Dutch Convention & Visitors Bureau: Cara O'Donnell, Philadelphia Academy of the Fine Arts: Laura Blumenthal, Gene Castellano, Robert Cozzolino, Barbara Katus, Michelle McCaffrey; Philadelphia Convention & Visitors Bureau: Ellen Kornfield, Marissa Phillip; Philadelphia Museum of Art: Holly Frisbee, Rachel Udell; Philadelphia Water Department: Ed Grusheski; Rodin Museum: John Zarobell.

Photography Permissions

Dorling Kindersley would like to thank the following for their assistance and permission to photograph at their establishments:

Academy of Natural Sciences, Atwater Kent Museum, Bishop White House, City Tavern, College of Physicians of Philadelphia/Mütter Museum, Civil War & Underground Railroad Museum of Philadelphia, Eastern State Penitentiary, Ebenezer Maxwell House, Confederate Memorial Hall, New Orleans, Gettysburg National Military Park Visitor Center and Cyclorama Center, Independence Hall, Independence Seaport Museum, Landis Valley Museum, National Constitutional Center, Pennyslvania Academy of the Fine Arts, People's Place Quilt Museum, Reading Terminal Market as well as all the state and national parks, churches, hotels, restaurants, shops, museums, galleries, and other sights too numerous to thank individually.

Picture Credits

t = top; tl = top left; tlc = top left center; tc = top center; tr = top right; trc = top right center; cla = center left above; ca = center above; cra = center right above; cl = center left; c = center; cr = center right; clb = center left below; cb = center below; crb = center right below; bl = bottom left; b = bottom; bc = bottom center; bcl = bottom center left; br = bottom right.

Every effort has been made to trace the copyright holders and we apologize for any unintentional omissions. We would be pleased to insert the appropriate acknowledgments in any subsequent edition of this publication.

Works of art have been reproduced with the permission of the following copyright holders:

© ARS, NY and DACS, London 2005 84b, *Irish Memorial* by Glenna Goodacre 104cr, *Frank Rizzo* by Diane Keller 97br, *Horticulture Mural* by David McShane 87bc, *L'Ouverture* by Ulrick Jean Pierre 51tc, Cover of *The Saturday Evening Post* (June 28, 1958) by Norman Rockwell 27ca.

The publishers would like to thank the following individuals, companies, and picture libraries for their kind permission to reproduce their photographs:

ALAMY: Bernie Epstein 115t; Jeff Greenberg 115bl; Andre Jenny 42tl, 100b; Dennis MacDonald 144cla.

THE BARNES FOUNDATION: 99tl. BRIDGEMAN ART LIBRARY: © The Barnes Foundation, Merion, Pennsylvania, USA *Postman* 1889 (oil on canvas) by Vincent van Gogh (1853–90) 98tr; *Gardanne* 1885–86 (oil on canvas) by Paul Cezanne (1839–1906) 98cl; *After the Concert* 1877 (oil on canvas) by Pierre-Auguste Renoir (1841–1919) 99cra; *Card Players and Girl* 1890–92 (oil on canvas) by Paul Cezanne (1839–1906) 99crb.

CLIVEDEN (A NATIONAL TRUST PROPERTY): 21cra, 107br. CHRIS'S JAZZ CAFÉ: 166bl; CORBIS: 9(inset), 13tl, 18t, 20tr, 21cr, 22crb, 23t, 33bc,

37(inset), 38, 83cra, 111(inset), 173(inset), 185b, 189tl; Dave Bartuff 39t, 40tr; Bettmann 8–9, 17ca, 17bl, 19ca, 19crb, 19bc, 21tl, 21br, 22t, 22bl, 22br, 23bc, 40cla, 53br, 131(inset); Kevin Fleming 92; Rose Hartman 61br; Robert Holmes 36–37; Catherine Karnow 175tr; Kelly-Mooney Photography 127b; Bob Krist 2tr, 80; 68, 172-3, 188bc; Francis G. Mayer 16, 20-21c, 63br, Mary Ann McDonald 115crb; Charles O'Rear 46b; Philadelphia Museum of Art: *Peaceable Kingdom* by Edward Hicks (1780–1849) 18crb, 88tr, *Sunflowers* by Vincent van Gogh (1853–90) 88cl, 89cla, *Dormition of the Virgin* (1427) by Fra Angelico (1387-1455) 90cl, *Jester Vase* (1894) by Marc-Louis-Emmanuel Solon (1835-1913) Joseph E. Temple Fund 90bc, *The Staircase Group* (1795) by Charles Willson Peale (1741-1827) The George W. Elkins Collection 90br; 91tl, *Bird Tree* (1800–1830) Bequest of Lisa Norris Elkins (Mrs. William M. Elkins) 91c, *Gala Ensemble* Italy (late 19th to early 20th century) Bequest of Helen P. McMullen 91b; PictureNet 113 tr; Poodles-Rock 20cl, 20br; Bill Ross 2–3, 127t; Joseph Sohm: Visions of America 21crb, 42bl, 48c; Joseph Sohm- ChromoSohm Inc. 43cla; David H. Wells 83br, 102. CORBIS SABA: Erik Freeland 23crb;

FAIRMOUNT WATERWORKS & INTERPRETIVE CENTER: 171bl FLEISCHMAN GERBER AND ASSOCIATES: Esto/Peter Aaron 77br; FRANKLIN INSTITUTE SCIENCE MUSEUM : 26cb FREE LIBRARY OF PHILADELPHIA: 18bl, 19br, 21bc.

GETTYSBURG CONVENTION & VISITORS BUREAU: Paul Witt 123cl, 123br. GREATER PHILADELPHIA TOURISM MARKETING CORPORATION: 133bl, R.Kennedy 44cra; C. Ridgeway 25ca. GREYHOUND LINES, INC.: 185tl.

LEONARDO MEDIA LTD.: 133tl

MASTERFILE: David Zimmerman 110–111.

NATIONAL CONSTITUTION CENTER: 48tr. NATIONAL MUSEUM OF AMERICAN JEWISH HISTORY: 27cr, 41t.

PENNSYLVANIA ACADEMY OF THE FINE ARTS: 27tl, 74tr, 75cra, 75crb, *The Cello Player* (1896) by Thomas Eakins Oil on canvas. 64 1/4 x 48 1/8 inches. Accession no:1897.3. Joseph E. Temple Fund 74cl, *The Fox Hunt* by Winslow Homer Oil on canvas. 38 x 68 1/2 inches. Accession no: 1894.4. Joseph E. Temple Fund 74br, *Pantocrator* (2002) Oil on linen (triptych) 87 7/8 x 193 3/4 inches. Accession no: 2033.7.a-c by Vincent Desiderio 75tl. PENNYSLAVANIA DUTCH CONVENTION & VISITORS BUREAU: 11br, 34cla, 112b, 118b; K. Baum

113b. PHILADELPHIA CONVENTION & VISITORS BUREAU: ©Alma de Cuba PR 166c; ©Barnes Foundation 25cra, 99bl; ©Bob Krist 14tr; ©Camden Riversharks Baseball/David Brady 169t; ©Cuba Libre Restaurant & Rum Bar/Mimi Janosy 142br; Melvin Epps 58cl; © Independence Seaport Museum/Rusty Kennedy 65cra; ©The Inn at the Union League of Philadelphia 70tr; ©National Constitution Center/Scott Frances Ltd. 25cb, 40cl, 48bl, 49tl, 49cr; Jim McWilliams 32cla, 34br, 168b, 170b, 184t; ©Pennyslavania Academy of the Fine Arts/Rick Echelmeyer 24; ©Pennyslavania Ballet/Steve Belkowitz 164c; ©Pennyslavania Horticultural Society/Rob Ikeler 32br; Jon Perlmutter 30cla; ©Philadelphia International Airport/ Richard McMullin 182b; ©Philadelphia Office of the City Representative 33cra; ©Philadelphia Orchestra/Eric Sellen 162b; ©The Plaza and The Court at King of Prussia 155b; ©PR Le Bec-Fin 143b; ©Ritz Carlton, Philadelphia 132b; Edward Savaria Jr. 10tc, 25bl, 35cla, 35br, 46c, 70cl, 70b, 71crb, 101b, 142cl, 143tl, 158tr, 160cla, 163tl, 170cla; 190tc Anthony Sinagoga 41crb, 44cl, 158bl ©Valley Forge Convention & Visitors Bureau 170t; ©Westin Philadelphia 132t. PHILADELPHIA MUSEUM OF ART, PENNSYLVANIA: Portrait of Dr. Samuel D. Gross (The Gross Clinic) (1875) by Thomas Eakins. Gift of the Alumni Association to Jefferson Medical College in 1878 and purchased by the Pennsylvania Academy of the Fine Arts and The Philadelphia Museum of Art in 2007 with the generous support of some 3,600 donors 89bl; Noah's Ark (1846) by Edward Hicks, Bequest of Lisa Norris Elkins, 1950 89crb; PHILLIES: 32tc PURE: 167tr

RICHARD VARR: 43cr.

WYK HOUSE AND GARDEN: 106t.

Front endpaper: All special photography except CORBIS : cr, Kevin Fleming tr, Bob Krist tl; MASTERFILE: David Zimmerman cl.

JACKET:
Front - ALAMY IMAGES: AM Corporation main image; PHILADELPHIA CONVENTION & VISITORS BUREAU: clb.
Back - ALAMY IMAGES: ImageState/Ethel Davies tl; Andre Jenny cla; CORBIS: Bob Krist clb; DK IMAGES: bl; Demetrio Carrasco bl.
Spine - ALAMY IMAGES: AM Corporation t; courtesy of WWW.HEXSIGNS.COM: design © Jacob Zook b.

All other images © Dorling Kindersley. For more information see www.dkimages.com